TEST SUCCESS

TEST-TAKING TECHNIQUES for the HEALTHCARE STUDENT

TEST SUCCESS

TEST-TAKING TECHNIQUES for the HEALTHCARE STUDENT

Barbara A. Vitale, BS, MA
Instructor
Nassau Community College
Garden City, New York

Patricia M. Nugent, BS, MS, EdM, EdD
Professor
Nassau Community College
Garden City, New York

F. A. DAVIS COMPANY • Philadelphia

F. A. Davis Company
1915 Arch Street
Philadelphia, PA 19103

Printed in the United States of America

Last digit indicates print number 10 9 8 7 6 5 4 3 2 1

Publisher: Robert G. Martone
Developmental Editor: Melanie Freely
Production Editor: Marianne Fithian
Cover Designer: Louis J. Forgione

As new scientific information becomes available through basic and clinical research, recommended treatments and drug therapies undergo changes. The author(s) and publisher have done everything possible to make this book accurate, up to date, and in accord with accepted standards at the time of publication. The authors, editors, and publisher are not responsible for errors or omissions or for consequences from application of the book, and make no warranty, expressed or implied, in regard to the contents of the book. Any practice described in this book should be applied by the reader in accordance with professional standards of care used in regard to the unique circumstances that may apply in each situation. The reader is advised always to check product information (package inserts) for changes and new information regarding dose and contraindications before administering any drug. Caution is especially urged when using new or infrequently ordered drugs.

Library of Congress Cataloging-in-Publication Data
Vitale, Barbara Ann, 1944–
    Test success: test-taking for the healthcare student/Barbara A.
Vitale, Patricia M. Nugent.
        p.   cm.
    Includes bibliographical references and index.
    ISBN 0-8036-0089-5 (alk. paper)
    1. Medicine—Examinations—Study guides.   2. Test-taking skills.
3. Allied health personnel.   I. Nugent, Patricia Mary, 1944–
II. Title.
R834.5.V58   1996
610'.76—dc20   95-31144
                                                CIP

Dedicated to
Joseph Michael, John Andrew, and Christopher Neil Vitale
and
Kelly Marie and Heather Ann Nugent
for all the joy they have brought into our lives

Preface

Government efforts regarding healthcare reform have resulted in renewed interest in the healthcare professions. Because of this renewed interest, applications to these educational programs have increased in number and the programs are highly selective. The increase in knowledge and technology is accelerating at a breathtaking rate. Curricula are stretched to the limit to include all the information students must absorb to successfully complete the requirements to graduate as accountable practitioners. The academic demands on students preparing for a health profession are strenuous. This places greater stress on students to learn what they need to know to provide safe care. For the first time students may be faced with testing formats, particularly multiple-choice questions, that require more than just the regurgitation of information but rather the comprehension, application, or analysis of information. Needless to say, testing situations induce anxiety for these test takers. To succeed in highly selective programs with comprehensive curricula and challenging testing formats, students preparing to become a healthcare professional need supportive textbooks to increase their chances of success.

This book is designed for students who are preparing for a healthcare profession to increase study effectiveness and to improve test performance, particularly on multiple-choice tests. Also, it can be used by faculty members to design a study effectiveness or test-taking workshop for students. Because it takes students 2 to 4 years of study to build a basic body of knowledge on which safe judgments can be made, this book will present only the basic content commonly presented in the supportive and introductory courses associated with the healthcare professions. Sample test items ask questions related to anatomy and physiology, microbiology, medical terminology, pharmacology, and introductory courses to healthcare disciplines. Test items also include topics such as legal/ethical issues, patient rights, pathophysiology, therapeutic interventions, communication and interpersonal relationships, basic behavioral theories, problem solving, and patient safety. The purpose of sample items is for the student to have an opportunity to apply test-taking strategies rather than to learn content associated with a specific healthcare discipline.

The chapters of the book are designed to maximize success by presenting information that can contribute to developing a positive mental attitude, studying and learning more effectively, becoming test wise, identifying the step in the problem solving process being tested by a question, exploring testing formats other than multiple-choice questions, and appreciating computer applications in education and practice. Hundreds of practice questions are provided within the narrative content of Chapters 2 through 7, in content areas in Chapter 8, and two comprehensive tests in Chapter 9. All the test items in the textbook have been reviewed by faculty members representing the various health professions to ensure that the items address basic content commonly presented within their curricula. Questions do not address intermediate or advanced theory or content unique to a specific healthcare discipline. The rationales for the correct and incorrect answers are included for each test item. These rationales should help the learner review some of the basic content in theory and practice and contribute to mastery of the multiple-choice question.

There are some study guides on the shelves that provide learners with practical skills to become more successful learners. However, no book exists that specifically aids students grappling with tests, addressing basic content common to the theory and practice of the healthcare professions. This book was written to fill this void.

We want to thank Alfred J. Smeriglio, EdD, Chairman of Allied Health at Nassau Community College, Garden City, New York, for sharing his expertise regarding curricula for and professional credentialing of healthcare providers. Thanks also go to Bob Martone for guiding and supporting us through the production period; Ruth DeGeorge for providing reliable editorial assistance; and Herbert J. Powell, Jr., Production Manager and Marianne Fithian, Production Editor, for their expertise in producing the final product. Most importantly, we would like to thank our husbands and children: Joe, Joseph, John, and Christopher Vitale—Neil, Kelly, and Heather Nugent for their love and support.

Consultants

Ann Burgess, RN
Director of Nursing
Grossmont College
El Cajon, California

Charles H. Christiansen, EdD, OTR, FAOTA
Dean & Professor
University of Texas Medical—Galveston
School of Allied Health Services
Galveston, Texas

Marcy O. Diehl, CMA-A, CMT
Grossmont College
El Cajon, California

Denise M. Harmening, PhD, MT, CLS
Chairman & Professor
Department of Medical and Research Technology
School of Medicine
University of Maryland at Baltimore
Baltimore, Maryland

Robert R. Harr, MS, MT
Chair
Bowling Green State University
Medical Technology Department
Bowling Green, Ohio

Bonnie J. Lindsey, MA
Department Chair Health Occupations
Idaho State University
School of Applied Technology
Pocatello, Idaho

Stanley M. Pearson, MS, EdD, RRT
Program Coordinator
Respiratory Therapy
Southern Illinois University
College of Technical Careers
Carbonale, Illinois

Darlene Travis, BS, RT(R), RT(T)
Boise State University
Department of Radiologic Sciences
Boise, Idaho

Kristin Von Nieda, MEd, PT
Medical College of Pennsylvania
Hahnemann University
Department of Physical Therapy
Philadelphia, Pennsylvania

Robert L. Wilkins, MA, RRT
Department of Respiratory Therapy
Loma Linda University
School of Allied Health
Loma Linda, California

Contents

CHAPTER 3—THE MULTIPLE-CHOICE QUESTION

CHAPTER 4—THE PROBLEM-SOLVING PROCESS

CHAPTER 5—TEST-TAKING TECHNIQUES FOR MULTIPLE-CHOICE QUESTIONS 63

How To Use This Book To Maximize Success

It is amazing what **you** can achieve when **you** are tenacious, organized, and determined to attain a goal. By purchasing this book **you** have demonstrated a beginning commitment to do what **you** have to do to improve **your** study effectiveness and success in taking examinations. This book is designed to introduce **you** to various techniques that can contribute to a positive mental attitude and help **you** become test-wise. If you are beginning to get the feeling that "you" is an important word, "you" are right! Learning requires you to be an active participant in your own learning. Your ultimate success can be maximized if you progress through this book in a planned and organized fashion and are willing to practice the techniques suggested. Effort is directly correlated with the benefits you will derive from this book. Once you have determined that you are eager and motivated to learn, then you are ready to begin.

Chapter content is organized in a specific order to provide you with information that will contribute to developing a positive mental attitude, studying and learning more effectively, becoming test-wise, identifying the steps in the problem-solving process being tested by a question, exploring testing formats other than multiple-choice questions, and appreciating computer applications in education and practice. Hundreds of multiple-choice questions will afford you the opportunity to practice test-taking techniques. These questions address content that is commonly presented in the supportive and introductory courses associated with the healthcare professions. The purpose of the questions is not to teach or evaluate your knowledge of the information but rather to provide an opportunity to practice test-taking techniques. The two practice tests in Chapter 9 will provide an opportunity to simulate a learning or testing situation.

First read Chapters 1 through 7. Then practice the questions in Chapter 8. It is suggested that you coordinate answering the questions in the specific categories in Chapter 8 after you learn the content in class. When reviewing test items be sure to read and study the rationales for the correct and incorrect answers because this information will review and reinforce the material you are learning or have learned in school. Finally, take the integrated test in Chapter 9.

It is hard work to take responsibility for your own learning. The magnitude of your learning will be in direct proportion to the amount of energy you are willing to expend in the effort to improve your skills. As you function from a position of strength, study more effectively, become test-wise, and are able to apply the problem-solving process to determine what the question is asking, you should become a more successful test-taker. Good luck on your examinations!

Empowerment

DEVELOP A POSITIVE MENTAL ATTITUDE

A positive mental attitude can help you control test anxiety by limiting anxious responses so that you can be a more successful test-taker. A positive mental attitude requires you to function from a position of strength. This does not imply that you have to be powerful, manipulative, or dominant. What it does require is for you to develop techniques that put you in control of your own thoughts and behavior. To be in control of yourself you need to operate from a position of positive self-worth with a feeling of empowerment.

To develop self-worth you must be willing to look within yourself and recognize that you are valuable. Acting from a position of strength requires you to start saying and believing that you are worthwhile. Self-worth increases when you believe down to your very bones that you are important.

A feeling of empowerment arises when you are able to use all your available resources and learned strategies to achieve your goals. To achieve empowerment you need to develop techniques and skills that not only make you feel in control but actually position you in control. When you are in control you function from a position of strength.

To achieve a sense of self-worth and a feeling of empowerment that will help you succeed in test-taking you must learn various techniques that must be practiced prior to taking the test. These learned techniques will help you to control stressful situations, reduce anxious responses, and enhance concentration, thereby improving your analytical and problem-solving ability and strengthening your test performance. By learning and practicing the following techniques, you will have a foundation on which to operate from a position of strength.

1

ESTABLISH A POSITIVE INTERNAL LOCUS OF CONTROL

The term **internal locus of control** refers to how a person's thoughts and actions are stimulated from within the individual. You must recognize that your thoughts and actions can positively or negatively directly influence your success in learning information and achieving success on tests. Therefore, the way you talk to yourself influences the way you think about yourself, and the way you think about yourself influences your performance.

The content of what you say indicates how you feel about the control of your behavior and your life. "I was lucky to pass that test." "I couldn't help failing because the teacher is hard." "I got test anxiety and I just became paralyzed during the test." Each of these internal dialogues indicate that you see yourself as powerless. When you say these things you fail to take responsibility.

To be successful in learning and test taking you must establish a positive internal locus of control. Start by identifying your pattern of talking to yourself. Do you blame others, attribute failure to external causes, and use the words I couldn't, I should, I need, or I have to? If you do, then you are using language that places you in a position of impotence, dependence, defenselessness, and hopelessness. **You must establish a positive internal locus of control.** You do this by replacing impotent language with language that reflects control and strength. You must say, "I can, I want, and I will." When you use these words you imply that you are committed to a task until you succeed. Place index cards around your environment with, **I can**, **I will**, and **I want** on them to cue you into a positive pattern of talking to yourself.

CHALLENGE NEGATIVE THOUGHTS

Your value as an individual should not be coupled with how well you do on an examination. Your self-worth and your test score are distinctly isolated entities. If you believe that you are good when you do well on a test and are bad when you do poorly, then you must alter this logic. You need to work at recognizing that this is illogical thinking. Illogical thinking or negative thinking is self-destructive. Negative thinking must be changed into positive thoughts to build confidence and self-worth. As confidence and self-worth rise, anxiety can be controlled and minimized.

Positive thinking focuses your attention on your desired outcomes. If you think you can do well on a test, you are more likely to fulfill this prophecy. It is critical that you control negative thoughts by developing a positive mental attitude. When you say to yourself, "This is a hard test and I'll never pass" **challenge this statement**. Instead say to yourself, "This is a ridiculous statement, of course I can pass the test. All I have to do is study hard to pass!" It is crucial that you challenge negative thoughts with optimistic thoughts. Optimistic thoughts are valuable because they can be converted into positive actions and feelings, which place you in a position of control.

For this technique to work, a person must first be able to stop one's thoughts. Use the words **arrest negative thoughts**. This symbolizes that you will stop these thoughts in their tracks. To do this you must first identify the pattern of negative thinking that you use as a defense to distract yourself. Envision a police car with flashing lights that signifies **arrest negative thoughts**. You could even place pictures of police cars around your environment to cue you to **arrest negative thoughts**. Once you identify negative thoughts, handcuff them and lock them away so they will no longer be a threat. Actually envision negative thoughts locked up in a cell with bars and throw away the key.

Once you stop a negative thought, replace it with a **positive thought**. If you have difficulty identifying a positive thought, praise yourself or give yourself a compliment. Tell yourself, "Wow! I am really working hard to pass this test." "Congratulations! I was able to arrest that negative thought and be in control." To increase your control make an inventory of the things you can do, the things you want to achieve, and the feelings you want to feel that contribute to a positive mental attitude. Throughout the day take an **attitude inventory**. Identify the status of your mental attitude. If it is not consistent with your list of the feelings you want to feel or the positive image you have of yourself, **challenge this attitude**. Compose statements that support the feelings that you want to feel and read them over and over. "I can pass this test!", or "I am in control of my attitudes and my attitudes are positive!" Make sure that you end the day with a positive thought and even identify an expectation that you want to accomplish the next day. When you forecast positive events it establishes a positive direction in which you can focus your attention.

USE CONTROLLED BREATHING (DIAPHRAGMATIC BREATHING)

An excellent way to reduce feelings of anxiety is to use the technique of controlled breathing. When you control your breathing you can break the pattern of shallow short breaths associated with anxious feelings. Deep abdominal or diaphragmatic breathing enhances the relaxation response. When a person exhales, tense muscles tend to relax. Diaphragmatic breathing causes the diaphragm to flatten and the abdomen to enlarge on inspiration. On exhalation the abdominal muscles contract. As you slowly let out this deep breath, the other muscles of the body will tend to let go and relax. This technique enables you to breath more deeply than if you just expand your chest on inspiration. Controlled breathing can be helpful to reduce anxious responses that occur at the beginning of a test, when stumped with a tough question, or when you are nearing the end of the test. During these critical times you can use controlled breathing to induce the relaxation response.

When practicing diaphragmatic breathing, place your hands lightly over the front of the lower ribs and upper abdomen so you can monitor the movement you are trying to achieve. As you become accomplished in this technique, you will no longer need to position your hands on the body. Practice the following steps:

1. Gently position your hands over the front of the lower ribs and upper abdomen.
2. Exhale gently and fully. Feel your ribs and abdomen sink inward toward the middle of the body.
3. Slowly inhale a deep breath through your nose allowing the abdomen to expand first and then the chest. Do this as you slowly count to four.
4. Hold your breath at the height of inhalation as you count to four.
5. Exhale fully by contracting the abdominal muscles and then the chest. Let out all the air slowly and smoothly through the mouth as you count to eight.

Monitor the pace of your breathing. Notice how your muscles relax each time you exhale. You may feel warm, tingly, and relaxed. Enjoy the feeling as you breathe deeply and evenly. You should practice this technique so that controlled breathing automatically induces the relaxation response after several breaths. Once you are able to induce the relaxation response with controlled breathing, you can effectively draw upon this strategy when you need to be in control.

It is important not to do this exercise too forcefully or too rapidly because it can cause you to hyperventilate. Hyperventilation precipitates dizziness and lightheadedness. If either of these occur, cup your hands over your nose and mouth and slowly rebreathe your exhaled air. These symptoms should subside. Then, you can continue the exercise less vigorously. Always monitor your responses throughout the exercise.

DESENSITIZE YOURSELF TO THE FEAR RESPONSE

Individuals generally connect a certain feeling with a specific situation. Controlling feelings requires you to recognize how you consider and visualize events. It is not uncommon to connect a feeling of fear with an event. In a testing situation the examination is the event and the response of fear is the feeling. If that happens to you, then you need to interrupt this fear response. You have the ability to control how you respond to fear. When you are able to sever the event from the feeling, then you will establish control and become empowered. However, establishing control does not automatically happen. You need to desensitize yourself to the event to control the fear response.

FIRST, you must practice a relaxation response. Controlled breathing is an excellent relaxation technique and has already been described. Once you are comfortable with the technique of controlled breathing, you can use it in the desensitization routine.

SECOND, you should make a list of five events associated with a testing situation that cause fear and rank them starting with the one that causes the most anxiety progressing to the one that causes the least anxiety. The following is an example:
1. Taking an important examination on difficult material
2. Taking an important examination on material you know well
3. Taking a small quiz on difficult material
4. Taking a small quiz on material you know well
5. Taking a practice test that does not count

Event number five should invoke the least amount of fear.

THIRD, you should practice the following routine:
- Practice controlled breathing and become relaxed.
- Now imagine event number five. If you feel fearful then turn off the scene and go back to controlled breathing for about 30 seconds.
- Once you are relaxed, again imagine scene number five. Try to visualize the event for 30 seconds without becoming uncomfortable.
- Once you have accomplished the previous step, move up the list of events until you are able to imagine event number one without feeling uncomfortable.

When you are successful in controlling the fear response in an imagined situation, you can attempt to accomplish the same success in simulated tests at home. Once you are successful in controlling the fear response in simulated tests at home, you can take some simulated tests in a classroom setting. Continue practicing desensitization until you have a feeling of control in an actual test situation.

Another way you can use the concept of desensitization is to practice positive dialogue with yourself. For example, imagine the following internal dialogue with yourself:

"How are you feeling about the examination today?"   "A little uncomfortable and fearful."

"Do you want to feel this way?"

"How do you want to feel?"

"What are you going to do to achieve that feeling?"

"Absolutely not!"

"I want to feel calm, in control, and effective."

"I am going to practice relaxation and controlled breathing."

You might be saying to yourself. "I don't see myself doing this." "This is silly." The resilient and tenacious individual who is flexible and willing to try new techniques is in a position of control. If your goal is to be empowered, you only have to be open and willing to learn.

PERFORM MUSCLE RELAXATION

This technique involves learning how to tense and relax each muscle group of your body until all muscle groups are relaxed. This technique requires practice. The basic technique involves assuming a comfortable position and then sequentially contracting and relaxing each muscle group in your body from the head to the toes. When a muscle group is tensed and then released the muscle smooths out and relaxes. It is not a technique that can be quickly described in a short paragraph. However, the following brief exercise is included as an example:

EXAMPLE
Find a comfortable chair in a quiet place. Close your eyes, and use diaphragmatic breathing, taking several deep breaths to relax. You are now ready to begin progressive muscle relaxation. Sequentially move from one muscle group in the body to another, contracting and relaxing each in an even manner. Contract and relax each muscle group for 10 seconds. After each muscle group is tensed and then relaxed, take a deep, slow breath using diaphragmatic breathing. As you are relaxing, observe how you feel. Experience the sensation. You may want to reinforce the feeling of relaxation by saying, "My muscles are relaxing. I can feel the tension flowing out of my muscles." Remember not to breathe too forcefully to avoid hyperventilation. The following is a sample of muscle groups that should be included in a progressive muscle relaxation routine:

- Bend your head and try to rest you right ear as close as you can to your right shoulder. Count to 10. Assume normal alignment, relax, and take a deep breath.
- Bend your head and try to rest your left ear as close as you can to your left shoulder. Count to 10. Assume normal alignment, relax, and take a deep breath.
- Flex your head and try to touch your chin to your chest. Count to 10. Assume normal alignment, relax, and take a deep breath.
- Hyperextend your head as far back as it can comfortably hyperextend. Count to 10. Assume normal alignment, relax, and take a deep breath.
- Make a fist and tense the right forearm. Count to 10. Relax and take a deep breath.
- Make a fist and tense the left forearm. Count to 10. Relax and take a deep breath.
- Tense the right biceps by tightly bending (flexing) the right arm at the elbow. Count to 10. Relax and take a deep breath.

Continue moving from the head to the arms, trunk, and legs by contracting and relaxing each of the muscle groups within these areas of the body. You can understand and master this technique by obtaining an audio or videotape that is designed to direct and instruct you through the entire routine of tensing and relaxing each muscle group. This technique should be practiced every day over a period of time so that the technique becomes natural. Once you have mastered this technique, you can use a shortened version of progressive relaxation along with controlled breathing at critical times during a test.

USE IMAGERY

Images can establish a state of relaxation. When we remember a fearful event, our heart and respiratory rates increase just as they did when the event occurred. Comparably, when we recall a happy, relaxing period we can regenerate and recreate the atmosphere and feeling that we had during that pleasant event. This is not a difficult technique to master. Just let go and enjoy the experience.

EXAMPLE

Position yourself in a comfortable chair, close your eyes, and construct an image in your mind of a place that makes you feel calm, happy, and relaxed. It may be at the seashore or in a field of wild flowers. Let your mind picture what is happening. Observe the colors of the landscape. Notice the soothing sounds of the environment. Notice the smells in the air, the shapes of objects, and movement around you. Recall the positive feelings that flow over you when you are in that scene and relax. You can now open your eyes relaxed, refreshed, and calm.

At critical times during a test, you can take a few minutes to use imagery to induce the relaxation response. To successfully reduce stress you must position yourself in control. When you are in control your test performance generally improves.

OVERPREPARE FOR A TEST

One of the best ways to reduce test anxiety is to be overprepared. The more prepared you are to take the test the more confident you will be. The more confident you are the more able you are to challenge the fear of being unprepared. Study the textbook, read your notes, take practice tests, and prepare with fellow students in a study group. Even when you think that you know the information, study the same information again to reinforce your learning. For this technique to be successful, you need to plan a significant amount of time for studying. Although studying is time consuming, it does build confidence and reduce anxiety. No one said learning would be easy. Any worthwhile goal deserves the necessary effort to achieve success. Being overprepared is the **best** way to place yourself in a position of strength.

Consider the following scenario: a student was not doing well in school and asked what she could do to improve her performance. The concept of being overprepared was discussed and she worked out a study schedule to follow prior to the test. After the test, the student said she thought she did well because the test was an easy test. It had to be pointed out that the test was perceived as easy because she had attained the knowledge that enabled her to correctly answer the questions. Her eyes lit up as if someone turned on a light bulb in her head. When you recognize that you have the opportunity to be in control and take responsibility for your own learning, then you become all that you can be.

ENGAGE IN REGULAR EXERCISE

Regular exercise assists you to expend nervous energy. Walking, aerobics, swimming, bike riding, or running at least three times a week for 20 minutes is an effective way to maintain or improve your physical and mental status. The most important thing to remember about regular exercise is that you want to slowly increase the degree and duration of the exercise. Your exercise program should not be so rigorous that it leaves you exhausted. It should serve to clear your mind, to make you mentally alert, and better able to cope with the challenge of a test. Regular exercise should become a routine activity in your weekly schedule, not just a response to the tension of an upcoming test. Once you establish a regular exercise program you should experience physical and psychological benefits.

ESTABLISH CONTROL BEFORE AND DURING THE TEST

When you challenge negative thoughts, use language that reflects control, be over-prepared, rely on desensitization, and use controlled breathing and imagery to induce the relaxation response, and you will be functioning from a position of empowerment. It is important to maximize opportunities to feel in control in the testing situation. Additional techniques you can use to establish a tranquil and composed atmosphere require you to take control of your testing equipment, activities before and during a test, and your immediate physical space. Techniques to help create this atmosphere are reinforced in Chapter 5, Test-Taking Techniques for Multiple-Choice Questions. However, they are also discussed here because they can be used to reduce anxiety and promote empowerment.

MANAGE YOUR DAILY ROUTINE BEFORE THE TEST

It is important to maintain your usual daily routine the day before the test. Eat normally but avoid beverages with caffeine. Caffeine can lessen attention span and reduce concentration by overstimulating your metabolism. Go to bed at your regular time and avoid the urge to stay up late. Implementing usual routines can be relaxing and can contribute to a feeling of control.

MANAGE YOUR STUDY HABITS BEFORE THE TEST

Do not stay up late cramming the night before the big test. Squeezing in last minute studying may increase anxiety and contribute to feelings of powerlessness and helplessness. If you have implemented a study routine in preparation for the test you should have confidence in what you have learned. Establish control by saying to yourself, "I have studied hard for this test and I am well prepared. I can relax tonight because I know the material for the test tomorrow and I will do well." Avoid giving in to the desire to cram. Instead, use the various techniques discussed previously in this chapter to maintain a positive mental attitude.

MANAGE YOUR TRAVEL THE DAY OF THE TEST

Plan to arrive early the day of the test. It is important to plan for potential events that could delay you, such as traffic jams or a flat tire. The more important the test, the more time you should schedule for transit. If you live a substantial distance from the testing site, you might ask a fellow student who lives closer to allow you to sleep over the night before the test. The midterm or final examination for a course may be held in a different location than the regularly scheduled classroom used for the lecture. If you are unfamiliar with the examination room, make a practice run to locate where it is and note how long it takes to get there. Nothing produces more anxiety than rushing to a test or arriving after the start of a test. A feeling of control reduces tension and the fear response. You can be in control if you manage your travel time with time to spare.

MANAGE THE SUPPLIES YOU NEED FOR THE TEST

The more variables you have control over, the more calm and relaxed you will feel. Compose a list of the items you want to bring with you to the test. It may include pencils, pens, scrap paper, erasers, a ruler, something to snack on, or even a lucky charm. It is suggested that you collect the items the day before the test. This eliminates a task that you do not have to worry about on the day of the test and contributes to your sense of control.

MANAGE THE TEST ENVIRONMENT

When you arrive early you generally have the choice of where to sit in the room. This contributes to a feeling of control because you are able to sit where you are most comfortable. It helps to sit near the administrator of the test. Directions may be heard more clearly and the administrator's attention may be gained more easily if you need to ask a question. Measures that help you feel in control contribute to a positive mental attitude.

MAINTAIN A POSITIVE MENTAL ATTITUDE

Remind yourself of how hard you worked and how well prepared you are to take this test. Establish control by arresting negative thoughts and focusing on the positive. Say to yourself, "I am ready for this test!" "I will do well on this test!" "I can get an A on this test!" These statements support a positive mental attitude and enhance a feeling of control.

MANAGE YOUR PHYSICAL AND EMOTIONAL RESPONSES

At critical times during the test, you may feel nervous, your breathing may become rapid and shallow, or you may draw a blank on a question. Stop and take a minibreak. Use controlled breathing to induce the relaxation response. You may also use a shortened version of progressive relaxation exercises to induce the relaxation response. Daily practice of breathing and relaxation exercises will enable you to quickly induce the relaxation response during times of stress. Once these techniques are implemented, you should again feel empowered.

SUMMARY

The techniques in this chapter are designed to increase your mastery over the stress of the testing situation. When you feel good about yourself, have a strong self-image, and have a feeling of self-worth, you will develop a sense of control. Challenging negative thoughts, using controlled breathing, desensitizing yourself to the fear response, performing muscle relaxation, using imagery, overpreparing for a test, engaging in regular exercise, and establishing control before and during a test are techniques that empower you to respond to the testing situation with a sense of calmness. Use these techniques to support your self-worth, provide you with a feeling of control and increase your effectiveness in the testing situation.

2

Study Techniques

Learning is the activity by which knowledge, attitudes, and skills are acquired. Learning is an exceedingly complex activity that is influenced by various factors such as genetic endowment, level of maturation, experiential background, effectiveness of formal instruction, self-image, readiness to learn, level of motivation, and extent of self-study. Although some of these factors are unchangeable, others are within your ability to control.

Learning is an active process that takes place within the learner. Therefore, the role of the learner is to participate in or initiate activities that promote learning. Like test-taking skills, the ability to effectively learn is not an innate skill. One way of learning occurs by studying, and studying is a skill that can be perfected through practice. This chapter presents both general and specific study techniques that should increase your ability to learn. The general study techniques to be presented include skills that facilitate learning regardless of the topic being studied. The specific study techniques are presented in relation to levels of thinking processes that are required to answer multiple-choice questions: knowledge, comprehension, application, and analysis. Use of these techniques when studying will help you to comprehend more of what you have studied and retain the information for a longer period of time. This foundation of information should increase your success in answering test questions.

GENERAL STUDY TECHNIQUES

ESTABLISH A ROUTINE

Set aside a regular time to study. Learning requires consistency, repetition, and practice. Deciding to sit down to study is the most difficult part of studying. We generally tend

11

to procrastinate and think of a variety of things we must do instead of studying. By committing yourself to a regular routine, you eliminate the repetitive need to make the decision to study. If you decide that every night from 7:00 PM to 8:30 PM you are going to study, you are using your internal locus of control and establishing an internal readiness to learn. You must be motivated in order to learn.

The study schedule must be reasonable and realistic. Shorter, frequent study periods are more effective than long study periods. For most people, 1- to 3-hour study periods with a 10-minute break each hour are most effective. Periods of learning must be balanced with adequate rest periods because energy and endurance decrease over time and limit learning efficiency. Physical and emotional rest make you more alert and receptive to new information.

When planning a schedule, involve significant family members in the decision making. A family is an open system. An open system consists of parts that are constantly interacting and make up a whole. Therefore, the action of one family member will influence the other family members. If they are involved in the decision making, they will have a vested interest and probably be more supportive of your adherence to the schedule.

SET SHORT- AND LONG-TERM GOALS

A goal is an outcome that a person attempts to attain and may be long term or short term. A long-term goal is the eventual desired outcome. A short-term goal is a desired outcome that can be achieved along the path leading to the long-term goal. In other words, a long-term goal is your destination whereas the short-term goal is the objective that must be attained to help you eventually reach your destination. Each long-term goal may have one or more short-term goals. Goals should be formulated to promote learning that is purposeful, serve as guides for planning action, and establish standards so that learning can be evaluated. Goals must be specific, measurable, realistic, and have a time frame.

- A specific goal states exactly what is to be accomplished.
- A measurable goal sets a minimum acceptable level of performance.
- A realistic goal must be potentially achievable.
- A goal with a time frame states the time parameters in which the goal will be achieved.

A typical long-term goal would be to correctly answer 90% of the study questions at the end of a chapter you are studying within 7 hours. Typical short-term goals might be: to read and highlight important information in Chapter 1 within 2 hours; to list the major principles presented in Chapter 1 within 1 hour; and to compare and contrast information in class notes with information in the textbook within 2 hours. Each of these short-term goals can be achieved as a step toward attaining the long-term goal. It is wise to break a big task into small, manageable tasks because it is easier to learn small bits of information than large blocks of information. The most effective learning is goal-directed learning because it is planned learning with a purpose. In addition, when goals are attained they increase self-esteem and escalate motivation.

SIMULATE A SCHOOL ENVIRONMENT

The familiar is generally less stressful than the unfamiliar. Therefore, your posture, surroundings, and equipment should mimic the school or testing environment. Study at a desk or table and chair. Avoid the temptation to study in a reclining chair, on the couch, or in bed. If you are too comfortable you may become complacent or even fall asleep. Gather all the necessary equipment for studying such as your textbook, class notes, paper, pens, a highlighter, a dictionary, and so on. Use the same tools you plan to use when you take your examinations. Control other factors that reflect the testing environment, such as ensuring adequate light or avoiding eating while you are studying. The study environment should be comfortable enough to promote learning while stringent enough to prevent apathy, indifference, or nonchalance.

CONTROL INTERNAL AND EXTERNAL DISTRACTORS

Stimuli, both internal and external, must be controlled to eliminate distractions. External stimuli are environmental happenings that interrupt your thinking and should be limited. Select a place to study where you will not be interrupted by family members, phone calls, the door bell, or family pets. Do not study while watching television or listening to the radio. These stimuli compete for your attention when you need to be focusing on your work. Internal stimuli are your inner thoughts, feelings, or concerns that interfere with your ability to study. Internal stimuli are often more difficult to control than external stimuli because they involve attitudes. Review the techniques in Chapter 1 that promote a positive mental attitude. By limiting or eliminating internal and external distractors, you should improve your ability to concentrate.

IDENTIFY LEARNING DOMAINS

Learning is the process by which you attain new information (cognitive domain), acquire new skills (psychomotor domain), or formulate new attitudes (affective domain). The characteristics of learning related to a specific domain are unique to that domain and will influence the selection of the most effective study techniques appropriate for that domain.

Cognitive Domain

New information is usually learned through words or pictures. We read them, see them, or hear them. Use all your senses to maximize your acquisition and comprehension of new information. The more routes that information can travel to reach your brain the greater the chances are that you will learn the information. For example, when reading information about the anatomy of the human body, learning is reinforced by viewing pictures of the various systems of the human anatomy.

Psychomotor Domain

New skills involve the physical application of information. It is possible for a person to understand all the goals and steps of a procedure and yet not be able to perform the procedure. For information to get from the head to the hands, the learner must do more than read a book, look at pictures, view a video, or watch other people. The learner must become physically involved. Skills are not learned by osmosis; skills are learned by doing. For example, when learning how to perform cardiopulmonary resuscitation (CPR), the learner can read a book and look at pictures, but the learner must actually practice administering CPR on a mannequin.

Affective Domain

Learning new attitudes represents an increasing internalization or commitment to a feeling, belief, or value. Affective-domain learning is the most difficult type of learning because attitudes result from lifelong learning and tend to be well entrenched. For example, a student may know and understand the theory concerning why a person should be nonjudgmental and yet in clinical situations be judgmental toward their patient. The development of new attitudes is best learned within an atmosphere of acceptance and by exploring feelings, becoming involved in group discussions, and observing appropriate role models. For example, prior to providing hands-on care to a patient for the first time, it is beneficial to explore feelings about invading a patient's personal space.

How we learn is never identical for two different people, nor is it identical for one person in different situations. Over the years you have developed a learning style with which you feel comfortable and which has proven successful. However, be open to a variety of learning approaches.

CAPTURE MOMENTS OF TIME

Using spare moments is a method of maximizing your time for constructive study. You probably have periods of time during the day that are less productive than others, such as waiting at a red light or standing in line at a store. Also there are times that you engage in repetitive tasks, such as vacuuming a rug or raking the leaves. Capture these moments of time and exploit them. Carry flash cards, a vocabulary list, or categories of information that you can contemplate when you have unexpected time. These captured moments should be an adjunct to, rather than replace, your regularly scheduled study periods. There is an old adage that states, "**time is on your side**." Capture spare moments of time and use them to your advantage.

USE APPROPRIATE RESOURCES

The theories and principles of the various healthcare specialties are complex. These theories and principles draw from a variety of disciplines (psychology, sociology, anatomy and physiology, microbiology, and so on), use new terminology, and require unique applications to clinical practice. When studying, learning does not occur on a straight line aimed forward and upward. You may experience plateaus, regressions, and periods of confusion when dealing with complex material. When your forward progress is stymied, identify your needs and immediately seek help. Your professor, another student, a study group, or a tutor may be beneficial. When studying with another student, ensure that the person is a reliable source of correct information. When studying in groups, three to five students is ideal because a group of more than five people becomes a party. The group should be heterogenous; that is, there should be a variety of academic abilities, attitudes, skills, and perspectives among the participants. This variety should enrich the learning experience and provide checks and balances for the sharing of correct information. To use appropriate resources, you must be willing to be open to yourself and others. Have the courage to acknowledge to yourself and others that you need assistance and then be receptive to the sharing process. You learn not only from the professor but also from yourself and your classmates.

BALANCE SACRIFICE AND REWARDS

Learning is like a rose. Learning something new or obtaining a degree represents the growth of a small bud to a beautiful full blossom such as a rose. However, a rose also has thorns. Your commitment to a program of study often requires thorny sacrifices. Your time and energy are being diverted away from your usual activities related to a job, family members, friends, or pleasurable pastimes. To manage your time and responsibilities efficiently and fairly you may have to make difficult decisions. Reducing work hours, sharing household chores, hiring a baby-sitter, or limiting your social life may be necessary strategies to help you attain your goal. Sacrifices in and of themselves should not be viewed from a negative standpoint. Oftentimes these sacrifices are growth promoting for the student and family members.

The reality is that your course of study is rigorous and it will command your time and energy. Rigorous activity, whether it be physical or mental, requires concentration and endurance. However, too much work hinders productivity. Avoid overextending yourself. You must establish a balance between the sacrifices and rewards for your efforts. Rewards can be internal or external. Internal rewards are stimulated from within the learner and relate to feelings associated with meaningful achievement. Learning something new, achieving a goal, or increasing self-respect are examples of internal rewards. External rewards arise from outside the learner. A grade of 100%, respect and appreciation from others, or a present for achieving a goal are examples of external rewards. Unfortunately, the rewards for studying are usually not immediate but rather in the extended future. Graduating from school, passing a certification examination, earning a paycheck, and enjoying the prestige of being a member of a health profession are future-oriented rewards. Therefore, you should be the one to provide immediate rewards for yourself for studying. During study breaks or at the completion of studying, reward yourself by thinking about how much you have learned, reflecting on the good feelings you have about your accomplishments, relaxing with a significant other, having a cup of coffee, watching a favorite television show, calling a friend on the telephone, or taking a weekend off. Short-term rewards promote a positive mental attitude, reinforce motivation, and provide a respite from studying.

SPECIFIC STUDY TECHNIQUES

COGNITIVE LEVELS OF QUESTIONS

Health professionals use a variety of thinking processes. Therefore, examinations must reflect these thinking processes to effectively evaluate safe practice. There are four types of thinking processes that are incorporated into multiple choice questions concerning the delivery of direct or indirect patient care: **knowledge**, **comprehension**, **application**, and **analysis**. These thinking processes are within the cognitive domain and are ordered on the concept of complexity of behavior. That is, a knowledge question requires the lowest level of thinking (recalling information) whereas an analysis question requires the highest level of thinking (comparing and contrasting information).

In this section of the book each cognitive level (knowledge, comprehension, application, and analysis) is discussed, and sample items are presented to illustrate the thinking processes involved in answering the item. In addition, specific study techniques are presented to help you to strengthen your thinking abilities and reinforce learning. Sample items are presented in this chapter for you to have an opportunity to apply test-taking techniques rather than to learn content associated with a specific healthcare discipline. For your information the correct answers for the sample items in this chapter and the rationales for all the options are at the end of this chapter.

KNOWLEDGE QUESTIONS

Knowledge questions require you to **recall** or **remember** information. To answer a knowledge question you need to commit facts to memory. Knowledge questions expect you to know terminology, specific facts, trends, sequences, classifications, categories, criteria, structures, principles, generalizations, or theories.

SAMPLE ITEM 2–1	When implementing a procedure, b.i.d. means:

(1) Once a day
(2) Twice a day
(3) Three times a day
(4) Four times a day

To correctly answer this question you have to know the meaning of the abbreviation b.i.d.

SAMPLE ITEM 2–2	Which of the following ranges of adult radial pulse rates per minute can be considered within the normal range?

(1) 50 to 65
(2) 70 to 85
(3) 90 to 105
(4) 110 to 125

To answer this question correctly you have to know the facts related to the normal range of a radial pulse in an adult.

Memorization/Repetition

Knowledge questions require you to remember information that forms the foundation of your practice. Initially, information can be learned by memorization. Memorization is committing information to the brain through repetition for recall at a later time. Repeatedly studying information by reciting it aloud, reviewing it in your mind, or writing it down increases your chances of remembering the information because a variety of senses is employed. Memorization can be facilitated by the use of lists of related facts, flash cards, or learning wheels. For example:

- On an index card you can list the steps of a procedure. This can be carried with you to study when you capture moments of time.

- On the front of an index card you can write a word and on the back define the word. Develop an entire deck of cards that relates to the terminology within a unit of study. Again, use the flash cards when you have unexpected time to study.
- To make a learning wheel, cut a piece of cardboard into a circle and draw pie-shaped wedges on the front and back. On a front wedge write a unit of measure, such as 30 cc, and on the corresponding back wedge write its conversion to another unit of measure, such as 1 ounce. Then on individual spring clothespins, write each of the units of measure that appear on the back side of the wheel. When you want to study approximate equivalents, mix up the clothespins and attempt to match each one to its corresponding unit of measure. You can turn the wheel over and evaluate your success by determining if the clothespin you attached to the wheel matches the unit of measure on the back of the wheel.

These memorization techniques reinforce learning by the use of repetition, but the information is learned by rote memorization without any in-depth understanding of the information learned. Information learned by repetition uses short-term memory and is generally **quickly forgotten unless reinforced** through additional study techniques or application in your practice.

Alphabet Cues

The memorization of information can be facilitated if the information is associated with letters of the alphabet. Each letter serves as a cue that stimulates the recall of associated information. The most effective alphabet cues are those you formulate yourself. They meet a self-identified need and you must review the information before you can design the alphabet cue. You can use any combination of letters as long as they have significance for you and your learning. Examples of alphabet cues include:

- The **ABCs** of cardiopulmonary resuscitation are: **Airway**—clear the airway; **Breathing**—initiate artificial breathing; **Circulation**—initiate cardiac compression.
- Identify patients at high risk for injury through the letters **A**, **B**, **C**, **D**, **E**, **F**, **G**: **Age**—the young and old; **Blindness**—lack of visual perception; **Consciousness**—decreased level of consciousness; **Deafness**—lack of auditory perception; **Emotional state**—reduced perceptual awareness; **Frequency of accidents**—previous history of accidents; and **Gait**—impaired mobility.
- The three **Ps** for the cardinal signs of diabetes mellitus are: **Polyuria**, **Polydipsia**, and **Polyphagia**.

Acronyms

An acronym is a word formed from the first letters of a series of statements or facts. The acronym itself dynamically relates to the information it represents. It is useful to learning because each letter of the word jostles the memory to recall significant information. An acronym is an effective technique to retrieve previously learned information. Examples of acronyms include:

- The American Cancer Society teaches the early warning signs of cancer through the acronym of **CAUTION**.
  Change in bowel and bladder habits
  A sore that does not heal
  Unusual bleeding or discharge

Thickening or a lump
Indigestion or difficulty in swallowing
Obvious change in a wart or mole
Nagging cough or hoarseness

- When assessing a patient for adaptations indicating the presence of infection remember the acronym, **INFECT**.

Increased pulse and respirations
Nodes are enlarged
Function is impaired
Erythema, edema, exudate
Complaints of discomfort or pain
Temperature—local, systemic, or both

Acrostics

An acrostic is a phrase, motto, or verse in which a letter of each word (usually the first letter) prompts the memory to retrieve important information. A variation of an acrostic is a sentence with content that jogs the memory. Memorizing information can be difficult and boring. This technique is a creative approach to make learning more effective and fun. Examples of acrostics include:

- When studying the fat soluble vitamins recall this motto, "**All Dieters Eat Kilocalories**." This should help you remember that **A**, **D**, **E**, and **K** are the fat soluble vitamins.
- When studying apothecary and metric equivalents remember this verse, "There are **15 grains** of sugar in **1 gram** cracker." This sentence should help you remember that **15 grains** are equivalent to **1 gram**.

COMPREHENSION QUESTIONS

Comprehension questions require you to **understand** information. To answer a comprehension question, not only must you commit facts to memory but it is essential that you can translate, interpret, and determine the implications of the information. You demonstrate understanding when you: translate or paraphrase information; interpret or summarize information; or determine the implications, consequences, corollaries, or effects of information. Comprehension questions expect you to not only know, but understand information being tested without necessarily relating it to other material or seeing its fullest implications.

SAMPLE ITEM 2–3

Which of the following statements is accurate?

(1) The stomach is a system.
(2) Connective tissue supports and protects.
(3) Nerve cells are designed for contraction.
(4) Epithelial tissue transmits electrical impulses.

To answer this question the facts presented in each option had to be reviewed for accuracy. The two parts within the correct option (2) are related whereas the parts in the incorrect options are inaccurate and therefore unrelated.

SAMPLE ITEM 2–4

To understand human circulation one must recognize that blood moves from the:

(1) Right ventricle of the heart into the pulmonary artery
(2) Superior vena cava into the left atrium of the heart
(3) Left atrium of the heart through the tricuspid valve
(4) Four pulmonary veins into the lungs

To answer this question you must understand the anatomy and physiology of the cardiovascular and respiratory systems of the human body.

Explore *Whys* and *Hows*

The difference between knowledge questions and comprehension questions is—to answer knowledge questions you must know facts, and to answer comprehension questions you must understand the significance of facts. Facts can be understood and retained longer if they are relevant and meaningful to the learner. When studying information ask yourself "why" or "how" is this information important. For example, when learning that immobility causes decubitus ulcers explore why they occur. Pressure compresses the capillary beds, which interferes with the transport of oxygen and nutrients to tissues, resulting in ischemia and necroses. When studying a skill such as washing the hands, explore how soap cleans the skin. Soap reduces the surface tension of water and helps remove accumulated oils, perspiration, dead cells, and microorganisms. If you interpret information and identify **how** or **why** the information gained is relevant and useful, then the information has value. Valued information has greater significance and is less readily forgotten.

Study in Small Groups

Once you have studied by yourself, it is usually valuable to study the same information with another person or in a small group. The sharing process promotes comprehension of information because you listen to the impressions and opinions of others, learn new information from a peer tutor, and reinforce your own learning by teaching others. In addition, the members of the group reinforce your interpretation of information and correct your misunderstanding of information. The value of group work is in the exchange process. Group members must listen, share, evaluate, help, support, reinforce, discuss, and debate to promote learning. There is truth in the adage "**One hand washes the other**." Not only do you help another person but you help yourself.

APPLICATION QUESTIONS

Application questions require you to use information. To answer an application question you must take remembered and comprehended abstractions and apply them to concrete situations. The abstractions may be theories, technical principles, rules of procedures, generalizations, or ideas that have to be applied in a presented scenario. Application questions test your ability to use information in a new situation.

SAMPLE ITEM 2–5

When walking, a patient becomes weak and the patient's knees begin to buckle. The best intervention should be to:

(1) Lower the patient to the floor gently
(2) Walk the patient to the closest chair
(3) Call for extra help quickly
(4) Hold the patient up

To answer this question you need to understand the principles related to body mechanics and maintenance of patient safety. It requires the application of this information in a patient situation. Lowering the patient to the floor protects both the caregiver and the patient.

SAMPLE ITEM 2–6

When transporting a fire extinguisher to a fire scene on a level of the building different from the one on which the employee is working, the employee should:

(1) Use the stairs
(2) Pull the safety pin
(3) Run as quickly as possible
(4) Keep it from touching the floor

To answer this question you need to understand the principles related to fire safety and be able to apply the information in a practical situation. Selection of the correct option demonstrates an understanding of a principle of fire safety, always use the stairs not the elevator. To eliminate the distractors you need to understand what is safe and unsafe practice.

Relate New Information to Prior Learning

Learning is easier when information to be learned is associated with what you already know. Therefore, relate new information to your foundation of knowledge, experience, attitudes, and feelings. For example, when studying the principles of body mechanics review which principles are used when you carry a heavy package, move from a lying down to a standing position, or assist an elderly person to walk up a flight of stairs. When studying the principles of surgical asepsis recall and review the various situations when you performed sterile technique and identify the principles that were the foundation of your actions. Visualizing abstractions, such as principles and theories, being applied in concrete situations reinforces the ability to use them in future circumstances.

Recognize Commonalities

The application of information demonstrates a higher level of understanding than just knowing or comprehending information because it requires the learner to **show**, **solve**,

modify, **change**, **use**, or **manipulate** information in a real situation or a presented scenario. To learn to apply information, identify commonalities when studying principles and theories that can be used in a variety of situations. A commonality exists when two different situations require the application of the same or similar principle. For example, when studying the principle of gravity you must understand that it is the force that draws all mass in the earth's sphere toward the center of the earth. Now attempt to identify situations that employ this principle. You apply this principle when you place a urine collection bag below the level of the bladder, hang an intravenous bag higher than the needle insertion site, raise the head of the bed for a patient with dyspnea, and raise the foot of the bed for a patient with dependent edema. This study technique is particularly effective when working in small groups because it involves brainstorming. Others in the group, because of their different perspectives, may identify situations that you would not consider. Recognizing commonalities reinforces information and maximizes the application of information in patient care situations.

ANALYSIS QUESTIONS

Analysis questions require you to **interpret a variety of data** and **recognize the commonalities**, **differences**, and **interrelationships among presented ideas**. Analysis questions make the assumptions that you know, understand, and can apply information. Now you must identify, examine, dissect, evaluate, or investigate the organization, systematic arrangement, or structure of the information presented in the question. This type of question tests your analytical ability.

SAMPLE ITEM 2–7	A patient who is undergoing cancer chemotherapy says, "This is no way to live." Which of the following responses uses reflective technique?

(1) Tell me more about what you are thinking.
(2) You sound discouraged today.
(3) Life is not worth living?
(4) What are you saying?

> To answer this question you must understand the communication techniques of reflection, clarification, and paraphrasing. You also must analyze statements and identify the use of these techniques in presented conversations. This question requires you to understand, interpret, and differentiate information.

SAMPLE ITEM 2–8	A patient moves rapidly from a sitting to a standing position. What should be said to determine the patient's adaptation to standing?

(1) Would you like to stand here for a minute?
(2) Do you feel light-headed or dizzy?

(3) Would you like to sit down again?

(4) Do you normally get up so fast?

To answer this question you are required to recognize the information that will be elicited from each statement. You must differentiate from among these responses and decide which one is most significant in determining the patient's response to standing.

Recognize Differences

Analysis questions require an ability to analyze information, which is a higher thought process than knowing, understanding, or applying information. For example, when studying blood pressure, you first memorize the parameters of a normal blood pressure (knowledge). Then you develop an understanding of what factors produce and influence a normal blood pressure (comprehension). Then you identify a particular patient situation that would necessitate obtaining a blood pressure measurement (application). Finally, you must differentiate among a variety of situations and determine which has the highest priority for assessing the blood pressure (analysis). Analysis questions are difficult because they require a scrutiny of a variety of complex data presented in the stem and options. Because these questions often require you to use differentiation to determine the significance of information, the recognition of differences among learned information is an effective study technique.

To study for complex questions you cannot just memorize and understand facts or recognize the commonalities among facts, you must learn to differentiate. When studying the causes of an elevated blood pressure measurement, identify the different causes and why they would result in an increased blood pressure. For example, a blood pressure can rise for a variety of reasons: infection causes an increased metabolic rate; fluid retention causes hypervolemia; and anxiety causes an autonomic nervous system response that constricts blood vessels. In each situation the blood pressure increases but for a different reason. Recognizing differences is an effective study technique to broaden the interrelationship and significance of learned information.

Practice Test Taking

When taking practice tests and reviewing the rationales for the right and wrong answers you can achieve several objectives. Test taking can help you learn new information (learning mode), identify areas that need further study (self-assessment mode), and promote test-taking abilities (testing mode). The learning and self-assessment modes will be discussed here and the testing mode will be discussed in Chapter 5, Test-Taking Techniques for Multiple-Choice Questions.

When taking practice tests in the **learning mode** you should answer the question and then immediately review the rationales for the answer selected and the other options. Through this activity you can acquire new knowledge, enhance comprehension, apply theories and principles, analyze information, identify commonalities and differences in situations, and reinforce previously learned information. This can be an enjoyable way to learn because it requires you to be an active participant in your own learning.

When taking practice tests in the **self-assessment mode** you can either answer one question at a time and immediately review the rationales or answer all the questions and review all the rationales at the completion of the test. You should assess your performance and determine which questions you answered correctly and which you answered incorrectly. Identify the content areas covered in the questions that you answered incorrectly. This self-assessment should help direct your study so that you can spend your time more efficiently in those areas that require additional study. You should also identify the content areas covered in the questions that you answered correctly. By identifying your strengths you will contribute to a positive mental attitude and promote feelings of empowerment and control.

ANSWERS AND RATIONALES FOR SAMPLE ITEMS

An asterisk (*) is in front of the rationale that explains the correct answer.

2–1   (1) The abbreviation for once a day is q.d. (*quaque die*).
  * (2) The abbreviation for twice a day is b.i.d. (*bis in die*).
   (3) The abbreviation for three times a day is t.i.d. (*ter in die*).
   (4) The abbreviation for four times a day is q.i.d. (*quater in die*).

2–2   (1) This is below the normal range for the pulse rate in an adult.
  * (2) This is within the normal range of 60 to 100 beats per minute for the pulse rate of an adult.
   (3) Although 90 is within the high end of the normal range for the pulse rate of an adult, the 110 is above the normal range.
   (4) This is above the normal range for the pulse rate of an adult.

2–3   (1) The stomach is an organ, not a system.
  * (2) Connective tissue is a fibrous type of body tissue that contains a protein called collagen. It has various functions, including supporting and connecting internal organs, forming the walls of blood vessels, and attaching muscles to bones.
   (3) Nerve cells transmit electrical impulses and are not designed for contraction.
   (4) Nerve tissue, not epithelial tissue, transmits electrical impulses.

2–4 * (1) This accurately describes blood flow.
   (2) Blood moves from the superior vena cava into the right atrium, not the left atrium, of the heart.
   (3) Blood moves from the left atrium of the heart through the bicuspid, not the tricuspid, valve. The bicuspid valve is between the left atrium and left ventricle. The tricuspid valve is between the right atrium and right ventricle.
   (4) Blood moves from the pulmonary veins to the left atrium of the heart, not the lungs.

2–5 * (1) This is the safest action; guiding the patient to the floor helps to break the fall and minimize injury.
   (2) The patient is already falling; this is not safe.
   (3) By the time help arrives, the patient may already be on the floor; calling out can scare the patient and others.
   (4) This could injure the caregiver and cause both the caregiver and the patient to fall.

2–6   * (1) This is safe; elevators must be avoided because they could break down and trap a person.

(2) The safety pin is pulled only when the extinguisher is going to be used, not when *en route* to a fire.

(3) Running should be avoided; it can cause injury and panic.

(4) Often extinguishers are dragged along the floor *en route* to a fire because they are heavy; this is an acceptable practice.

2–7   (1) This response is using the technique of clarification and asks the patient to expand on the message so that it becomes more understandable.

* (2) This response is using reflective technique because it attempts to identify feelings within the patient's message.

(3) This response is using the technique of paraphrasing because it restates the patient's basic message in similar words.

(4) Same as answer number one.

2–8   (1) This is unsafe because in the presence of orthostatic hypotension the patient could fall. This distractor suggests an action rather than obtains information about the patient's response to standing.

* (2) This directly assesses the patient's response to standing; it seeks subjective information about orthostatic hypotension directly from the patient who is the primary source.

(3) This distractor suggests an action rather than obtains information about the patient's response to standing. If the patient prefers to sit down the caregiver may infer that the client is dizzy, but this would be an assumption not based on fact.

(4) This information is irrelevant for the safety of the patient at this point in time. This information may be helpful when teaching the patient how to avoid orthostatic hypotension.

The Multiple-Choice
Question

In our society success is generally measured in relation with levels of achievement. Prior to entering formal institutions of learning, your achievement was subjectively appraised by your family and friends. Success was rewarded by smiles, positive statements, and perhaps favors or gifts. Lack of achievement or failure was acknowledged by omission of recognition, verbal corrections, and possibly punishment or scorn. When you entered school, your performance was directly measured against acceptable standards. In an effort to eliminate subjectivity, you were exposed to objective testing. These tests included true-false questions, matching columns, and multiple-choice questions. Achievement was reflected by numerical grades or letter grades. These grades indicated your level of achievement and by themselves provided rewards and punishments.

In the provision of health care, achievement can be assessed in a variety of ways: a patient's physiological response (Did the patient's condition improve?), a patient's verbal response (Did the patient state improvement?), healthcare students' clinical performance (Did the students do what they were supposed to do?), and healthcare students' levels of cognitive competency (Did the students know what they were supposed to know?). In higher levels of education, multiple-choice questions are frequently used to evaluate student progress throughout the curriculum and determine if minimum standards are met for professional certification or licensure. Multiple-choice questions are used because they are objective, time efficient, and can comprehensively assess curriculum content that has depth and breadth. Therefore, it is important for you to understand the components and dynamics of multiple-choice questions early in your education.

A multiple-choice question is an objective test item. It is objective because the perceptions or opinions of another person do not influence the grade. In a multiple-choice question, a question is asked, three or more potential answers are presented, and only one of the potential answers is correct. Either the student answers the question correctly or not.

Sample items have been included in this chapter so that you can apply test-taking strategies rather than learn content associated with a specific healthcare discipline. The content covered in the questions reflect information generally taught in supportive and introductory courses associated with the healthcare professions. For your information the correct answers for the sample items and the rationales for all the options are at the end of this chapter.

COMPONENTS OF A MULTIPLE-CHOICE QUESTION

The entire multiple-choice question is called an **item**. Each item consists of two parts. The first part is known as the **stem**. The stem is the statement that asks the question. The second part contains the possible responses offered by the item, which are called **options**. One of the options answers the question posed in the stem and is the **correct answer**. The remaining options are the incorrect answers and are called **distractors** because they are designed to distract you from the correct answer.

The correct answers and the rationales for all the options of the sample items in this chapter are at the end of this chapter. Test yourself and see if you can correctly answer the following sample items.

SAMPLE ITEM 3–1	When providing care to a patient with a naso-gastric tube it is important to recognize that the tube goes into the:	S T E M	
	(1) Stomach — CORRECT ANSWER (2) Bronchi — DISTRACTOR (3) Trachea — DISTRACTOR (4) Duodenum — DISTRACTOR	O P T I O N S	I T E M

THE STEM

The stem is the initial part of a multiple-choice item. The purpose of the stem is to present a problem in a clear and concise manner. The stem should contain all the details necessary to answer the question. The stem of an item can be a **complete sentence** that asks a question. It can also be presented as an **incomplete sentence** that becomes a complete sentence when it is combined with one of the options in the item. In addition to sentence structure, a characteristic of a stem that must be considered is its polarity. The polarity of the stem can be formulated in either a positive or negative context. A stem with **positive polarity** asks the question in relation to what is true whereas a stem with **negative polarity** asks the question in relation to what is false.

THE STEM THAT IS A COMPLETE SENTENCE

A complete sentence is a group of words that is capable of standing independently. When a stem is a complete sentence, it will pose a question and end with a question mark. The question should clearly and concisely formulate a problem that could be answered by you before actually reading the options.

SAMPLE ITEM 3–2	What should be the first action when a fire alarm rings in a healthcare facility? (1) Close all doors on the unit. (2) Take an extinguisher to the fire scene. (3) Check the code chart to locate the fire. (4) Move patients laterally toward the stairs.

THE STEM THAT IS AN INCOMPLETE SENTENCE

When a stem is an incomplete sentence it is a group of words that forms the beginning portion of a sentence. The sentence becomes complete when it is combined with one of the options in the item. Some tests will have a period at the completion of each option and others will not. Whether there is a period or not, each option should complete the sentence with grammatical accuracy. However, the answer is the only option that correctly completes the sentence in relation to the informational content. When reading a stem that is an incomplete sentence, it is usually necessary to read the options before the question can be answered.

SAMPLE ITEM 3–3	People should be encouraged not to smoke in bed because it could: (1) Result in a fire (2) Upset a family member (3) Precipitate lung cancer (4) Trigger a smoke alarm

THE STEM WITH POSITIVE POLARITY

The stem with positive polarity is concerned with truth. It asks the question with a positive statement. The correct answer is accurately related to the statement. It is in accord with a fact or principle, or it is an action that should be implemented. A positively worded stem attempts to determine if you are able to understand, apply, or differentiate correct information.

SAMPLE ITEM 3–4	Which of the following actions most accurately supports the concept of informed consent? (1) Involving the family in decisions (2) Obtaining the patient's signature (3) Exploring the patient's preferences (4) Explaining what is being done and why

THE STEM WITH NEGATIVE POLARITY

The stem with negative polarity is concerned with what is false. It asks the question with a negative statement. The stem usually incorporates words such as "except," "not," or "never." These words are obvious. However, sometimes the words that are used are more obscure, for example, "contraindicated," "unacceptable," "least," and "avoid." When a negative term is used it may be emphasized by an underline (except), italics (*least*), bold type (**not**), or capitals (NEVER). A negatively worded stem strives to ascertain if you can specify exceptions, detect errors, or identify interventions that are unacceptable or contraindicated. Some examinations do not emphasize the negative word when used in a stem, and many examinations do not have questions with negative polarity. However, this information has been included in the event that you may be challenged by questions with negative polarity.

SAMPLE ITEM 3–5	What position would be **contraindicated** for the patient who has dyspnea? (1) Supine (2) Contour (3) Fowler's (4) Orthopneic

THE OPTIONS

All of the possible answers offered within an item are called options. One of the options is the best response and is therefore the correct answer. The other options are incorrect and distract you from selecting the correct answer. These options are called distractors. An item must have a minimum of three options to be considered a multiple-choice item, but the actual number varies among tests. The typical number of options is four or five responses, which reduces the probability of guessing the correct answer while limiting the amount of reading to a sensible level. Options are usually listed by number (1, 2, 3, and 4), lower case letters (a, b, c, and d), or upper case letters (A, B, C, and D). The grammatical presentation of options can appear in four different formats. An option can be a sentence, complete the sentence begun in the stem, be an incomplete sentence, or be a single word.

THE OPTION THAT IS A SENTENCE

A sentence is a unit of language that contains a stated or implied subject and verb. It is a statement that contains an entire thought and is autonomous. Options can appear as complete sentences. Some tests will have a period at the end of these options and others will not. Whether there is a period or not, each option should be grammatically correct. When the option is a verbal response, it should be grammatically correct and incorporate the appropriate punctuation such as quotation marks, commas, exclamation point, question mark, or period.

SAMPLE ITEM 3–6	Before performing a procedure for a hospitalized patient, what should be done first? (1) Raise the patient's bed to its highest position. (2) Collect equipment necessary for the procedure. (3) Position the patient for the procedure. (4) Explain the procedure to the patient.

THE OPTION THAT COMPLETES THE SENTENCE BEGUN IN THE STEM

When the option completes the sentence begun in the stem, the stem and the option together should form a sentence. Some tests will have correct punctuation at the end of these options and others will not. Whether there is a period or not, each option should complete the stem in a manner that is grammatically accurate.

SAMPLE ITEM 3–7	The primary cause of obesity is a: (1) Lack of balance in foods from the food guide pyramid (2) Glandular disorder that prevents weight loss (3) Psychological problem that results in overeating (4) Caloric intake that exceeds metabolic needs

THE OPTION THAT IS AN INCOMPLETE SENTENCE

When an option is an incomplete sentence, it will be a group of words that do not contain all the parts of speech (e.g., nouns, verbs, and adjectives) necessary to construct a complete sentence. The option that is an incomplete sentence is usually a phrase or group of related words. Although not a complete sentence, it conveys a unit of thought, an idea, or a concept.

SAMPLE ITEM 3–8	Which of the following precautions is associated with all types of isolation (standard- and transmission-based precautions)?
	(1) Donning a mask
	(2) Wearing a gown
	(3) Washing the hands
	(4) Keeping visitors out

THE OPTION THAT IS A WORD

A word is the most basic unit of language. It is capable of communicating a message. The option that is a single word can be almost any part of speech (e.g., noun, pronoun, verb, adverb) as long as it conveys information.

SAMPLE ITEM 3–9	Which of the following is a primary source for obtaining information?
	(1) Chart
	(2) Patient
	(3) Physician
	(4) Supervisor

ANSWERS AND RATIONALES FOR SAMPLE ITEMS

An asterisk (*) is in front of the rationale that explains the correct answer.

3–1   * (1) The tube enters the nose, passes through the posterior nasopharynx and esophagus, and enters the stomach through the cardiac sphincter.

(2) These are passages between the trachea and bronchioles and are part of the respiratory system.

(3) This is a passage between the posterior nasopharynx and bronchi and is part of the respiratory system.

(4) This is distal to the stomach and is the first portion of the small intestine; a nasogastric tube is designed to be advanced into the stomach, not the duodenum.

3–2   (1) The location of the fire must be identified first to determine if the unit is in danger.

(2) To do this, the location of the fire must be identified first.

* (3) The location of the fire will influence the next action. If a healthcare provider is the first to see the fire then the **RACE** procedure should be followed: **R—Remove** all patients from danger; **A**—activate the **alarm** procedure to report the location of the fire; **C—Confine** the fire by closing the doors; **E—Extinguish** the fire.

(4) This is unsafe; patients only need to be moved if they are in danger.

3–3   * (1) Confused, weak, or lethargic individuals may drop lighted cigarettes or ashes, which can ignite bed linens.

(2) Although smoking can physically and emotionally disturb a family member, safety is the priority.

(3) Although smoking may precipitate lung cancer, safety is the priority.

(4) Smoking will not trigger a smoke alarm; considerable smoke is needed to set off a smoke alarm.

3–4   (1) Although this may be done, it is the patient who must sign the informed consent.

(2) Although obtaining the patient's signature is part of consent, the signature by itself does not imply that the patient understands.

(3) Exploring patient preferences supports a concept related to the Patient's Bill of Rights, not informed consent.

* (4) The patient's knowledge and understanding of what is going to be done, why it is being done, and what the outcomes will be is what constitutes being informed prior to giving consent.

3–5   * (1) In this position the abdominal contents press against the diaphragm, impeding expansion of the lungs.

(2) This position is desirable because the abdominal contents drop by gravity permitting efficient contraction of the diaphragm and expansion of the thoracic cavity.

(3) Same as answer number two.

(4) Same as answer number two.

3–6   (1) This could be frightening if the patient does not know why the procedure is being done.

(2) This would be done after the patient agrees to the procedure.

(3) Same as answer number one.

* (4) This meets the patient's right to know why and how care will be provided.

3–7   (1) This would result in malnutrition, not necessarily obesity; it could also result in weight loss.

(2) Although glandular disorders such as hypothyroidism may result in obesity, they are not the primary causes of obesity.

(3) This is only one of many factors that influence overeating; it is not the primary cause of obesity.

* (4) If more calories are ingested than the body requires for energy, then they will be converted to adipose tissue, which causes weight gain.

3–8   (1) A mask is worn for respiratory (droplet, airborne) and strict (contact) isolation; it is also worn with universal (standard) precautions if splashing of body secretions is a possibility.

(2) A gown is worn for strict (contact) isolation or if there is a potential for exposure to contaminated material.

* (3) This is required prior to and following care and is associated with all types of isolation.

(4) People who have been taught how to maintain medical asepsis may visit patients who have transmittable infections. Visitors with infections or immunosuppressive disorders are the exceptions.

3–9   (1) This is generally considered a secondary source.

* (2) The primary and most important source for obtaining information referring to the patient is the patient; patient responses are identified by direct contact with the patient.

(3) This is a secondary source.

(4) Same as answer number three.

4

The Problem-Solving Process

The problem-solving process is a scientific process that provides a framework for identifying solutions to complex problems. It is a step-by-step process that uses a systematic approach. One might say that scientific problem solving is a blueprint that can be followed to identify and solve problems. The concept of problem solving is used by all healthcare providers within the context of their own job responsibilities. When applying the problem-solving process to the healthcare professions the process contains five basic steps: **assessment and data collection; analysis; planning; implementation; and evaluation**.

Because the problem-solving process is the method of critical thinking used by healthcare providers to meet job responsibilities and patients' needs, examinations may be designed to test content as it is used within this process. Well written test items are not haphazard. They are carefully designed to test your knowledge of a specific concept, skill, theory, and so on, from the perspective of one of the five steps of the problem-solving process. When reading an item if you are able to identify its place within the problem-solving process, it should contribute to your ability to recognize what the test item is asking. To do this you must focus on the critical words within the item.

This chapter explores the five steps of the problem-solving process. Sample items are presented to demonstrate item construction as they relate to each step. Critical words associated with each step of the process are illustrated within the sample items. Attempt to identify variations of critical words within the sample items, indicating activities associated with each step of the process. The more understanding you have about the focus of the item you are reading, the better you will be at identifying what is being asked and the greater your chances of selecting the correct answer. The questions reflect information that generally is included in the curricula of a variety of healthcare disciplines. Practice answering the questions. The correct answers and the rationales for all the options of the sample items in this chapter are at the end of this chapter.

ASSESSMENT AND DATA COLLECTION

With assessment and data collection, information must be accurately collected, verified, and communicated. Assessment and data collection items are related to the assessment of the patient and healthcare situation. These items are designed to test your knowledge of information, theories, principles, and skills related to the assessment of the patient and healthcare situation. It establishes the foundation on which healthcare providers base the subsequent steps of the problem-solving process. Assessment and data collection questions may ask a healthcare professional to:

- Obtain vital statistics
- Perform a physical assessment
- Collect specimens
- Identify patient adaptations that are objective and subjective
- Identify patient adaptations that are verbal and nonverbal
- Identify adaptations that are normal and abnormal
- Use various data collection methods
- Identify sources of data
- Verify critical findings
- Identify commonalities and differences in response to disease
- Communicate information about assessments and data collected to appropriate members of the health team

Critical words used within a test item that generally indicate that the item is focused on assessment and data collection include "inspect, identify, verify, observe, notify, inform, question, communicate, verbal, nonverbal, signs, symptoms, sources, perceptions, check, and assess." Most testing errors occur in the assessment and data collection phase of the problem-solving process when options are selected that:

- Collect insufficient data
- Have data that are inaccurately collected
- Use unsystematic methods of data collection
- Rely on a secondary source rather than the primary source, that is, the patient
- Contain irrelevant data
- Fail to verify data
- Reflect bias or prejudice
- Fail to accurately communicate data

COLLECTING DATA

Healthcare providers collect data through specific **methods of data collection** such as performing a physical examination, interviewing, and reviewing records. Physical examinations performed may include the assessment techniques of inspection, palpation, auscultation, and percussion. It may also include obtaining the vital signs and recognizing normal and abnormal parameters of obtained values. Interviewing is used to collect data using a formal approach (e.g., obtaining specific information) or by an informal approach (e.g., exploring concerns or seeking feedback while providing care). Review of records includes reports such as the results of laboratory tests, diagnostic procedures, and assessments or consultations by other members of the health team.

SAMPLE ITEM 4–1

The rate of the radial pulse reflects the function of the:

(1) Arteries
(2) Veins
(3) Blood
(4) Heart

This item tests your ability to recognize that a pulse reflects the contractions of the heart. Note that the question specifically referred to *rate* of the radial pulse, not the regularity or volume of the pulse nor the status of the artery. This item demonstrates how a basic physiological concept is related to collection of data and assessment.

SAMPLE ITEM 4–2

Which of the following would **most** likely indicate that a patient is having difficulty breathing?

(1) 16 breaths per minute and deep
(2) 18 breaths per minute and through the mouth
(3) 20 breaths per minute and shallow
(4) 28 breaths per minute and labored

This item tests your ability to identify the option that reflects a respiratory rate and characteristic that is outside normal parameters. To successfully answer this question you need to know the rate and characteristics of normal, as well as abnormal, respirations.

SAMPLE ITEM 4–3

When determining if a person's body weight is appropriate it is important to assess the person's:

(1) Body height
(2) Daily intake
(3) Clothing size
(4) Food preferences

This item tests your ability to recognize that to calculate the patient's ideal body weight you must also know the patient's height. The ideal body weight is the measurement that reflects the range of weight that would be considered appropriate in relation to the patient's height. The ideal body weight is the measurement against which the patient's present weight is compared to determine if the patient is underweight or obese. Although the question does not address these concepts, you must also know the patient's age and extent of bone structure.

Data can be objective or subjective. **Objective data** are measureable assessments collected when a person uses sight, touch, smell or hearing to acquire information. Examples of objective data include, diaphoresis (excessive perspiration), rhonchi (a type of abnormal breath sounds), and vital signs. **Subjective data** can be collected only when the patient shares feelings, perceptions, thoughts and sensations about a health problem or concern. Examples of subjective data include patient statements about pain, shortness of breath, or feeling depressed.

SAMPLE ITEM 4–4	A patient with painful terminal cancer says, "Life is not worth living. I'm going to kill myself." This patient's statement is: (1) Primary data (2) Objective data (3) Secondary data (4) Subjective data This item tests your ability to differentiate the types of information collected during the assessment and data collection phase of the problem-solving process. You should know the type of data for the purpose of determining its significance. Any information that a patient shares regarding feelings, thoughts, and concerns are subjective.

Data can be gathered not only by different methods but also from different sources. **Sources of data** are primary, secondary, or tertiary. There is only one **primary source**, the patient. Each healthcare provider must be able to recognize significant signs and symptoms exhibited or verbalized by the patient that relates to one's area of practice. The patient is the most valuable source because the data that are collected are most current and specific to the patient. A **secondary source** produces information from someplace other than the patient. A family member is a secondary source who can contribute information about the patient's preferences, similarities and differences in behavior, and functioning before and during the health problem. The patient's medical record (chart) is another example of a secondary source. It is a legal document and comprises information that concerns the patient's physical, psychosocial, religious and economic history; documents the patient's physical and emotional adaptations; and reflects the result of diagnostic tests. Controversy surrounds the labeling of diagnostic test results in a chart as being either primary or secondary sources. Although the chart itself is a secondary source, diagnostic test results are direct objective measurements of the patient's status and therefore are considered by some healthcare providers to be a primary source. You must remember that the information in a chart is history and does not reflect the current status of the patient because the patient is dynamic and constantly changing. The patient's immediate environment should also be considered a secondary source of data. The immediate environment must be assessed to establish a data base on which to base decisions regarding the need for planning interventions to protect a patient's safety. Secondary sources are valuable for gathering supplementary information about a patient. A **tertiary source** provides information from outside the specific patient's frame of reference. Examples of tertiary sources include textbooks, the caregiver's experience, and accepted commonalities among patients with similar adaptations. Included under tertiary sources are the caregiver's own responses or other health team members' responses to the patient.

SAMPLE ITEM 4–5

When asking a patient's wife specific questions about the patient's health complaints, information is being collected from a:

(1) Primary source
(2) Tertiary source
(3) Secondary source
(4) Subjective source

This item tests your ability to recognize that a family member is a secondary source of information. Secondary sources provide information that is supplemental to the primary information collected from the patient.

Collected data can be verbal or nonverbal. **Verbal data** are collected via the spoken or written word. For example, statements made by the patient are verbal data. **Nonverbal data** are collected via transmission of messages without words. Crying, a fearful facial expression, the appearance of the patient, and gestures are all examples of nonverbal data.

SAMPLE ITEM 4–6

An example of nonverbal communication is:

(1) A letter
(2) Holding hands
(3) Noise in the room
(4) A telephone message

This item tests your ability to recognize that holding hands is a form of nonverbal communication. Nonverbal communication does not use words. Touch, gestures, posture, and facial expressions are examples of nonverbal communication.

When assessing and collecting data both deductive and inductive reasoning should be used. **Deductive reasoning** moves from the general to the specific. For example, you use deductive reasoning when collecting data about a patient who has a local infection. If it is accepted that patients develop an inflammatory response to an infection, then you should recognize that a patient with a local infection will respond with swelling (edema), redness (erythema), heat, discomfort, a loss of function in the affected body part, and an increase in the white blood cell count. **Inductive reasoning** moves from the specific to the general. For example, you use inductive reasoning when collecting data related to a patient's specific complaint of local swelling. From this specific piece of data you should recognize the need to further assess for additional signs of infection such as redness, heat, discomfort, loss of function, and an increase in the white blood cell count. Inductive and deductive reasoning are based on a strong theoretical foundation of knowledge that is drawn on when collecting data.

SAMPLE ITEM 4–7	Which of the following types of wounds would heal by primary intention?

(1) Surgical incisions
(2) Lacerations
(3) Deep burns
(4) Abrasions

This item requires you to use deductive reasoning. You must move from the general (concept of healing by primary intention) to the specific (identifying an example of a wound that heals by primary intention).

VERIFYING DATA

Once data are collected the information must be verified. **Verifying data** is the confirming of information by collecting additional data, obtaining judgments and conclusions from other team members when appropriate, and by collecting data oneself rather than relying on technology. Verifying data ensures its authenticity and accuracy. For example, when a vital statistic is outside the normal range or is a measurement that is unexpected, the results must be substantiated by collecting the data again, collecting additional data to supplement the original information, or both.

SAMPLE ITEM 4–8	When taking the patient's blood pressure a diastolic pressure of 120 is obtained. The first action should be to:

(1) Take the other vital signs
(2) Retake the blood pressure
(3) Notify the nurse
(4) Notify the physician

This item tests your ability to recognize that you need to verify data when they are unexpected or outside normal parameters. The first action should be to retake the blood pressure after waiting a minute. An error may have been made when taking the blood pressure. Once the blood pressure is verified as being outside normal parameters, then the other vital signs should be taken and the appropriate health team members notified.

COMMUNICATING INFORMATION ABOUT ASSESSMENT AND DATA COLLECTED

The last component of assessment and data collection includes the ability to communicate information obtained from assessment and data collection activities. Sharing vital information about a patient is essential if members of the health team are to be alerted to the most current status of the patient. Communication methods vary (e.g., progress notes, verbal notification, flow sheets); however, they all share the need to be accurate, concise, thorough, current, organized, and confidential.

| SAMPLE ITEM 4–9 | When providing care to an elderly hospitalized woman, a caregiver identifies a change in pulse from 88 to 56 beats per minute. After reassessing the pulse and obtaining the same result, the caregiver should: |

(1) Wait 15 minutes and retake the pulse
(2) Ask the patient about her activity
(3) Call the physician
(4) Alert the nurse

This item tests your ability to recognize that when a patient's vital signs are abnormal the person immediately responsible for the patient must be notified. Communicating data to appropriate health team members is a component of the assessment process.

ANALYSIS

Analysis is the second step of the problem-solving process and is the most difficult component. Analysis requires the interpretation of data, collection of additional data, identification and communication of identified problems, and assurance that the patient's needs are appropriately met. To be interpreted, data must be validated, clustered, and its significance determined before coming to a conclusion that leads to the identification of a problem. To analyze data you will need to have a strong foundation in scientific principles related to the physical sciences, social sciences, the commonalities and differences in patients' response to various stresses, and your specific health discipline. You will need to use deductive and inductive reasoning to apply your knowledge and experience when answering analysis items. Analysis questions will ask you to:

- Cluster data
- Identify clustered data as meaningful
- Validate data
- Identify when additional data are necessary to validate clustered data
- Interpret validated and clustered data
- Communicate information to others
- Identify patients' needs associated with your healthcare discipline
- Ensure that the patient's healthcare needs can be appropriately met

Critical words used within a test item that generally indicate that the item is focused on analysis include "valid, organize, categorize, cluster, reexamine, pattern, formulate, reflect, relate, problem, interpret, contribute, relevant, decision, significant, deduction, statement, and analysis." See if you can identify variations of these critical words indicating analysis activities in the sample items in this chapter. Testing errors occur in the analysis phase of the problem-solving process when options are selected that:

- Omit data
- Cluster data prematurely
- Come to a conclusion before all significant data have been collected and clustered

INTERPRETATION OF DATA

Interpretation of data is a critical step in the process of analysis. It is related to the ability to validate data, cluster data, determine significance of clustered data, and come to a conclusion. In analysis, data are validated to determine significance. Information is more meaningful when its relationship to other data is established. Clustering enables you to organize data; eliminate that which is insignificant, irrelevant, and redundant; and reduce the remaining data into manageable categories. Once organized into general categories, data are clustered specifically based on the healthcare needs of the patient or healthcare situation. To do this effectively, you must refer to theoretical knowledge and scientific principles, the data base that identifies the patient's specific adaptation to stress, and the practice of clinical judgment. This process depends on a combination of intellectual skills. Deductive and inductive reasoning draws from the knowledge of commonalities and differences. These same intellectual skills also are used to determine significance of clustered data.

Significance in this context refers to some consequence, importance, implication or gravity connected to the cluster as it relates to the patient's health problem or healthcare situation. Data can be overt and easy to cluster or covert and difficult to cluster. Some data are easily clustered because the information collected is clearly related to only one system of the body. Other data are more difficult to cluster because the patient's adaptations may involve a variety of systems of the body. At first the facts collected may not appear to be related. However, with a thorough analysis you should recognize that the data are interrelated.

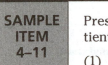

SAMPLE ITEM 4–10

A patient has anemia that has compromised the ability to meet the body's oxygen needs. This oxygen problem is related to the inability to:

(1) Transport oxygen
(2) Exchange oxygen
(3) Perfuse oxygen
(4) Diffuse oxygen

This item tests your ability to interpret collected data. It relies on a knowledge of the pathophysiology related to oxygen problems and specifically to anemia. Basic anatomy, physiology, and pathophysiology must be understood before the significance of patient adaptations can be identified.

SAMPLE ITEM 4–11

Pressure ulcers (decubiti) are most often associated with patients who:

(1) Are immobilized
(2) Have psychiatric diagnoses
(3) Experience respiratory distress
(4) Need close supervision for safety

This item tests your ability to recognize the relationship between immobility and the formation of pressure ulcers. It is designed to test your knowledge of the fact that prolonged pressure interferes with cellular oxygenation, which causes cell death resulting in a pressure ulcer.

Once significance is determined a conclusion is made regarding the clustered data. **Conclusions** are opinions, decisions, or inferences made after careful deliberation of data. Conclusions are inferred from scientific theory, collected data unique to the patient, generally accepted commonalities, and the physical and social sciences.

SAMPLE ITEM 4–12

A patient has loss of appetite (anorexia) and difficulty sleeping (insomnia) and has lost interest in the activities of daily living. This behavior is reflective of feelings associated with:

(1) Anger
(2) Denial
(3) Depression
(4) Acceptance

> This item tests your ability to come to a conclusion based on a cluster of data. The word "reflective" in the stem cues you to the fact that this is an analysis question. You need to draw from your knowledge of commonalities of human behavior and theories of grieving and use reasoning to arrive at the conclusion that the patient is probably depressed.

COLLECTION OF ADDITIONAL DATA

Once significance is determined, but prior to arriving at a final conclusion, additional data collection might be indicated to provide more information to support the conclusion. This is done to establish and ensure the relationship among the original data. The healthcare provider continually reassesses the condition of the patient and the presence of needs, recognizing that the patient is dynamic and ever changing throughout all phases of the problem-solving process.

SAMPLE ITEM 4–13

The victim of a motor vehicle accident is brought into the emergency room. The patient is pale, has a decreased blood pressure, and weak thready pulse. The patient should be assessed for additional signs of:

(1) Hemorrhage
(2) Infection
(3) Anxiety
(4) Pain

This item is designed to test your ability to recognize that additional data are needed to reinforce the proposed conclusion. Pallor, hypotension, and a weak thready pulse are related to a decreased blood volume, which is associated with hemorrhage and shock.

IDENTIFYING AND COMMUNICATING PATIENT PROBLEMS AND OUTCOMES

Taking a conclusion and converting it into a diagnostic problem statement or patient need statement moves from the general to the specific. A statement of a specific health problem as it relates to your discipline should meet the standards of the discipline and those things that you are legally permitted or certified to engage in or treat. The diagnostic statement includes the problem and may also include factors that contributed to the development of the problem. The plan of care communicates the problem/need statement, expected outcomes, and planned interventions. The section of this chapter on planning will discuss outcomes and planned interventions in more detail.

SAMPLE ITEM 4–14	The patient had a stroke that resulted in a residual paralysis of the left side, drooling of saliva, slurred speech, difficulty swallowing, and urinary retention. A problem/need statement that has the highest priority for this patient is, The patient:

(1) Has expressive aphasia
(2) Is at risk for aspiration
(3) Is unable to provide self care
(4) Has urinary incontinence

This item tests your ability to recognize a cluster of data that indicate a patient is at risk for aspiration. Oxygenation is a basic physiological need and therefore adaptations that may place a patient at risk for aspiration must be identified by all healthcare providers.

ENSURING THAT PATIENTS' HEALTHCARE NEEDS ARE APPROPRIATELY MET

The health team has a responsibility to ensure the public that healthcare needs will be appropriately met. During the analysis phase of the problem-solving process you may identify that the patient's healthcare needs cannot be met by the individual providing the care because the person's expertise is in a discipline unrelated to the patient's needs, the person is inexperienced in caring for a patient with a particular problem, or there is inadequate staffing. If you perceive a risk to patient safety you are obligated to take an action that will ensure that appropriate care will be provided. This might necessitate rearranging the assignment with another caregiver or it may require intervention by a supervisor. Once you embark on a duty of care you are obligated to provide a standard of care defined by your profession or the law in the state in which you work.

SAMPLE ITEM 4–15	A healthcare provider arrives on duty and discovers that several staff members have just called in sick. The most appropriate response would be to:

(1) Inform the supervisor and ask for additional staff
(2) Identify which patients need the most care and assign staff accordingly
(3) Stay, but refuse to accept responsibility for the standard of care delivered
(4) Explain to patients that when staffing is short only essential care can be provided

This item tests your ability to recognize your responsibility to ensure that patients' needs are appropriately met.

> When you perceive a risk to patient safety you are obligated to take action that will ensure that appropriate care will be provided.

PLANNING

Planning is the third step of the problem-solving process. It involves setting goals, establishing priorities, identifying expected outcomes, identifying interventions designed to achieve goals and outcomes, modifying the plan as necessary, and collaborating with other health team members to ensure that care is coordinated. Goals, outcomes, and identified interventions are formulated in response to the problem/need statements that were identified in the previous step (analysis) of the problem-solving process. The problem/need statement, goals, outcomes, and identified interventions make up the plan of care. To plan care you need to have a strong foundation of scientific theory, understand the commonalities and differences in response to interventions, and be able to establish priority of needs. Test-takers need to use reasoning to apply knowledge and clinical experience when answering planning questions. Planning items will ask you to:

- Set goals
- Establish priorities
- Plan appropriate interventions
- Involve the patient in the planning process when appropriate
- Anticipate patient needs
- Recognize the need to collaborate with others
- Recognize that plans must be flexible and modified based on changing patient needs
- Recognize the need to coordinate planned care with other disciplines
- Establish expected outcomes against which results of care can be compared for the purpose of evaluation

Critical words used within a test item that generally indicate that the item is focused on planning include "achieve, desired, plan, effective, desired result, goal, priority, develop, formulate, establish, design, prevent, strategy, select, determine, anticipate, modify, collaborate, arrange, coordinate, expect, and outcome." See if you can identify variations of these critical words indicating planning activities in the sample items in this chapter. Testing errors occur during the planning phase when options are selected that:

- Do not include the patient in setting goals and priorities when appropriate
- Are inappropriate goals
- Misidentify priorities
- Reflect outcomes that are unrealistic and unmeasurable
- Reflect planned interventions that are inappropriate or incomplete
- Fail to include family members and significant others when appropriate
- Fail to coordinate and collaborate with other health team members

The planning component of the problem-solving process generates a statement of goals, expected outcomes, and interventions that are planned to meet these goals and outcomes. This plan may be written or "understood" by the caregiver based on standards of practice. This plan becomes the blueprint for interventions and is dictated by the patient's individual needs and preferences.

IDENTIFYING GOALS

Goals are general statements that direct interventions, provide broad parameters for determining results, and stimulate motivation. Goals can be long-term goals or short-term goals. A **long-term goal** is one that will take time to achieve (weeks to months). A **short-term goal** is one that can be achieved relatively quickly (usually within 1 to 2 weeks). Eventually the goal is further developed to formulate the expected outcome. Projecting expected outcomes will be discussed in more detail later in this chapter.

SAMPLE ITEM 4–16	A patient is placed on a drug regimen. An appropriate goal related to compliance would be:

(1) The patient will take prescribed drugs
(2) Tolerance to the drug will be achieved
(3) The patient's symptoms have subsided
(4) A cumulative effect will result

This item tests your ability to recognize a short-term goal in relation to the concept of compliance. It also requires you to understand the pharmacological concepts of tolerance and cumulative effects to eliminate distractors two and four.

SETTING PRIORITIES

Setting priorities is an important step in the planning process. Once problem/need statements and goals are identified, they must be ranked in order of importance. Maslow's Hierarchy of Needs is helpful in establishing priorities. Basic physiological needs are ranked first, with the need for safety and security, belonging and love, self-esteem, and self actualization following in rank order. It is important, however, to recognize that at any one point in time any one of Maslow's Needs may take priority depending on the needs of the individual patient. Obviously if someone is having a cardiac arrest, cardiopulmonary resuscitation would be the priority. However, there are times when the emergency or immediate need of the patient is in the psychological dimension. You must be aware of the patient's perceptions and perspective when setting priorities because patients are the center of the healthcare team. When possible, the patient should always be involved in setting priorities.

SAMPLE ITEM 4–17	When a conscious adult patient chokes on food and a total obstruction is identified, the caregiver should first:

(1) Clap between the scapulae three times
(2) Initiate the abdominal thrust maneuver
(3) Instruct the patient to swallow forcefully
(4) Begin rescue breathing within 4 minutes

> This item tests your ability to prioritize care. Oxygenation is essential to sustain life and therefore maintaining a patent airway is the priority.

IDENTIFYING INTERVENTIONS

After priorities are established a plan of action must be formulated. To appropriately plan you must rely on scientific knowledge, clinical judgment, and knowledge about the patient, and you must use the reasoning process. Relying on this background, you determine what measures would be most effective in assisting the patient to achieve a goal or outcome. When planning care, you must know the rationales for interventions so that the interventions selected are the most appropriate for the patient care situation. It is not enough to just know **how**. You must know **why**!

SAMPLE ITEM 4–18

The most effective way to prevent the spread of the flu in a hospital is by:

(1) Using strict isolation/contact precautions
(2) Limiting the spread of microorganisms
(3) Administering antibiotics to sick patients
(4) Keeping the patient's windows closed during the winter

This item tests your ability to recognize that planning to limit the spread of microorganisms can prevent the spread of infection. This is a question that focuses on a general concept applicable to all patients because it involves planning a variety of interventions that can protect many patients.

SAMPLE ITEM 4–19

When planning interventions to prevent falls in the elderly, caregivers should recognize that the frequency of falls increase:

(1) At night
(2) After meals
(3) During visiting hours
(4) When getting up in the morning

This item tests your ability to recognize the needs of the hospitalized elderly. The word "planning" used in the stem is an obvious clue that this is a planning question.

PROJECTING EXPECTED OUTCOMES

Expected outcomes are the changes in the patient's condition that are expected in response to care given. Expected outcomes are derived from goal statements, but they are more specific because they describe the behavior or data that should be demonstrated once the goal is achieved. Expected outcomes are the bench marks against which the actual outcomes are compared to determine the effectiveness of the interventions provided. To be meaningful they must be patient-centered, specific, realistic, measurable, and must have a time frame. The process of comparing actual outcomes with expected outcomes occurs in the evaluation phase, which is the next step in the problem-solving process. Examples of outcomes are, "The patient states a reduction in anxiety in 1 week," and "The patient's diastolic blood pressure is below 90 mm Hg by discharge." Sometimes the goal and outcomes are stated together. For example, "The patient will continuously maintain an effective airway clearance as evidenced by expectoration of sputum, clear lung fields, and noiseless breathing." The first part of the statement is the goal and what follows "as evidenced by" are the expected outcomes. The first part of the statement is more general and the second part is more specific.

SAMPLE ITEM 4–20	A therapeutic outcome related to the use of a vest restraint would be, The patient will:

(1) Be immobilized
(2) Have less agitation
(3) Not fall out of bed
(4) Have limited movement

This item tests your ability to recognize a statement that reflects a desirable expected outcome. To answer this question you need to know that the only appropriate reason for the use of a vest restraint is to protect the patient from injury. Although distractors one and four may be additional outcomes, they are not desirable outcomes by themselves but may occur when a vest restraint is inappropriately applied. A goal related to the use of a vest restraint would be, "the patient will be free from injury." This was a particularly difficult question because it required you to identify the most significant therapeutic outcome.

MODIFYING THE PLAN OF CARE AS NEEDED

Planning generally takes place prior to care being given. However, patient needs sometimes change while you are in the process of providing care and the plan must be immediately modified. It is important to recognize that plans of care are not set in stone but are modified in response to the changing needs of the patient. Because a patient's needs are dynamic, the plan of care is also dynamic. It must be continually changed to be kept current, substituting new problem/need statements, goals, and planned interventions as indicated by the patient's changing needs.

| SAMPLE ITEM 4–21 | During the middle of a procedure the patient complains of being short of breath. The initial action should be to: |

(1) Obtain vital signs
(2) Raise the head of the bed
(3) Administer emergency oxygen
(4) Encourage pursed-lip breathing

This item tests your ability to recognize that the priority of care may be altered in response to the changing needs of the patient. Facilitating breathing takes precedence over the procedure. The plan of care had to be modified.

COLLABORATING WITH OTHER HEALTHCARE TEAM MEMBERS

Another component of planning is consultation and collaboration with other health team members to brainstorm, seek additional input, and delegate and coordinate the delivery of health services. Each health team member provides a unique service, and these services should be provided through collaboration. For example:

- The physical therapist, in collaboration with the nurse, may arrange for a patient to go to physical therapy in the morning before the patient tires.
- The medical technologist, in collaboration with the dietitian, may obtain a blood sample for a fasting blood glucose test prior to the patient being fed breakfast.
- Interdisciplinary conferences (patient care conferences) are routinely conducted for each resident in all nursing homes nationwide.

Effective planning contributes to the delivery of patient care that has continuity and is patient-centered, coordinated, and individualized.

| SAMPLE ITEM 4–22 | A patient with dementia is often confused, argumentative, and demanding. When planning care a health team member should: |

(1) Plan for a team conference
(2) Bring another staff member as a witness
(3) Explain that you would appreciate some cooperation
(4) Accept the behavior as probably a lifelong pattern

The correct answer provides input from multiple disciplines, individualizes care, and promotes continuity of care. It provides for collaboration among health team members and places the patient at the center of the health team.

IMPLEMENTATION

Implementation is the step of the problem-solving process whereby planned actions are initiated and completed. It includes tasks such as organizing and managing planned care; providing total or partial assistance with activities required during the delivery of care; teaching the patient and significant others; providing planned care; supervising, coordinating, and evaluating the process of the delivery of care by members of your specific discipline (this does not include the actual delegation of care that occurs in planning or the evaluation of the patient's response to care, which occurs in evaluation); and recording and sharing data related to care implemented.

To implement safe care designed to achieve goals and expected outcomes, you must understand and follow the implementation process. In addition, you must have knowledge of scientific rationales for procedures related to your discipline, psychomotor skills to implement procedures safely, and the ability to use different strategies to effectively implement planned care. Implementation items will ask you to:

- Recognize steps in the implementation process
- Identify independent, dependent, and interdependent actions of the healthcare provider
- Implement a procedure or treatment
- Identify and respond to common or uncommon outcomes related to interventions
- Identify or respond to life-threatening or adverse events
- Prepare a patient for a procedure, treatment, or surgery
- Choose an approach that is most appropriate when implementing care
- Identify safe or unsafe practice
- Rationalize a step in a procedure
- Identify or use concepts related to teaching
- Identify or use principles related to motivation and therapeutic communication
- Recognize the relationship between a procedure and an expected outcome
- Identify when an intervention must be modified in response to a change in the patient's condition
- Identify when additional assistance is required to provide safe care
- Recognize your responsibility associated with supervising and evaluating care delivered by those to whom interventions have been delegated
- Recognize how and when to document or report care given along with the patient's response

Critical words used within a test item that generally indicate that the item is focused on implementation include "dependent, independent, interdependent, change, assist, counsel, teach, give, supervise, perform, method, procedure, treatment, instruct, strategy, facilitate, provide, inform, refer, technique, motivate, delegate, implement, and continually assess." See if you can identify variations of these critical words indicating implementation activities in the sample items in this section. Testing errors occur during the implementation phase of the nursing process when options are selected that:

- Implement actions outside a person's scope of practice
- Fail to identify or appropriately respond to an adverse or life-threatening situation
- Fail to continually assess the patient
- Fail to modify interventions in response to the changing needs of the patient

- Fail to identify when additional assistance is required for the delivery of safe care
- Reflect a lack of knowledge to safely implement interventions
- Do not accurately document the patient's response to care given
- Fail to supervise and evaluate the delivery of delegated interventions

THE PROCESS OF IMPLEMENTATION

Effective implementation of care is based on:

- Continually assessing the patient
- Reviewing and modifying the plan of care when indicated
- Identifying when additional help in either staff or resources is needed to safely implement the plan
- Implementing types of interventions
- Using methods of intervention
- Communicating strategies verbally or in writing

The first three actions in this list have been discussed in detail in previous steps from the perspective of assessment, analysis, and planning. When considered from the perspective of intervention you must remember that the principles described in the prior sections apply here as well. The concept to be internalized is that these actions are ongoing throughout the problem-solving process. The last three actions listed above are discussed next in more detail.

TYPES OF INTERVENTIONS

Interventions can be dependent, independent, or interdependent in nature. **Dependent interventions** are interventions that require a physician's order. Administering a medication, drawing blood, taking a radiograph, and administering a radiation treatment are examples of dependent interventions because they all require a physician's order. When implementing a dependent intervention you must not blindly follow the order but determine whether the order is correct or appropriate. A caregiver who does not question and carries out an incorrect or inappropriate order is contributing to the initial error and will be held accountable. **Independent interventions** are those actions that a healthcare provider is permitted to implement with no direction or supervision from a member of another discipline. Independent interventions do not require a physician's order. Tasks related to collecting data, providing a safe environment, and teaching health care, are in the realm of independent practice. Encouraging coughing and deep breathing, promoting verbalization of concerns, and teaching a patient about a procedure are examples of specific independent interventions. **Interdependent interventions** are actions implemented in collaboration with other appropriate healthcare providers. An example of an interdependent intervention is implementing actions identified in standing orders or a protocol. These situations delineate the parameters within which the caregiver is permitted to administer to the patient. Protocols and standing orders are commonly found in emergency and critical care areas, physicians' offices, and situations where certain care is commonly and routinely administered.

SAMPLE ITEM 4–23	A supervisor directs a healthcare provider to perform a non-protocol (no standing physician orders) procedure without the required physician's order. The healthcare provider should:

(1) Notify a higher administrator immediately
(2) Complete the task and grieve later
(3) Decline to do the assigned task
(4) Inform the union representative

This question is designed to test your ability to recognize that caregivers must work within their scope of practice. Caregivers have a responsibility and a right to refuse to follow illegal or unreasonable orders.

METHODS OF IMPLEMENTATION

Care is delivered by using various implementation methods such as assisting with activities during a procedure or treatment, teaching, implementing strategies to achieve outcomes such as preparing a patient for a procedure or performing a procedure, implementing preventive measures, responding to adverse reactions, or implementing lifesaving actions, supervising and evaluating the effectiveness of delegated interventions, and sharing results of actions verbally and in writing.

Providing assistance with positioning or moving, before, during, or after a procedure or treatment is an integral part of most interactions with patients. Because the need for assistance is so common in the delivery of patient care, it may be addressed in test items.

Teaching enables a caregiver to assist a patient to adapt to actual or evolving changes that are caused by loss, illness, disability, or stress. To effectively teach in the cognitive (learning new information), psychomotor (learning new skills), and affective (developing new attitudes, values and beliefs) domains you must apply teaching-learning principles to motivate patients to learn and grow. People are complex and care must comprehensively address the physical, emotional, and mental realms.

Preparing patients physically and emotionally for a diagnostic test, procedure (treatment), or surgery or actually performing a procedure are components of implementing the plan of care. You must know how and when to implement a procedure and the expected outcomes of the procedure. For example, positioning an extremity, ambulating the patient, or instructing the patient to take a deep breath may be a component of a procedure. Because care often involves the "laying on of hands," concepts related to procedures and psychomotor skills may be tested.

Providing an environment that supports the achievement of healthcare goals and outcomes is also an important component of implementation. Providing for privacy, promoting a motivating climate, accepting feelings, and providing for environmental safety all contribute to a supportive environment. Supportive environments influence both the physical and emotional status of patients. Concepts related to maintaining a therapeutic environment are commonly tested principles because they are second level needs identified by Maslow in his theory concerning hierarchy of needs.

As part of assisting patients to achieve therapeutic goals you must also implement preventive measures and identify and respond to adverse reactions or life-threatening situations. Preventive actions are those activities that help the patient avoid a health problem. Administering immunizations and verifying a patient's name via the identification bracelet are examples of preventive measures. To provide safe care you must identify when a patient has an adverse or life-threatening response and intervene appropriately. An example of identifying and responding to adverse reactions would be stopping a procedure when the patient complains of pain or feeling dizzy. Initiating cardiopulmonary resuscitation, implementing the abdominal thrust (Heimlich maneuver), or maintaining an airway after a tonic-clonic seizure are examples of interventions related to life-threatening situations. Most of these interventions address basic physiological needs required for survival and may therefore be tested.

Occasionally the caregiver who formulates the plan of care delegates all or part of the implementation of that care to another member of the discipline. Uncomplicated and basic interventions are often delegated to a technician, assistant, or aide. The person who delegates is responsible for the plan of care and is accountable for ensuring that the plan of care is delivered according to standards of the profession.

SAMPLE ITEM 4–24

When positioning a patient the **most** important principle of body mechanics is:

(1) Elevating the arms on pillows
(2) Making the patient comfortable
(3) Maintaining functional alignment
(4) Keeping the head higher than the heart

This item tests your ability to identify a basic concept inherent in body mechanics. This intervention will help the patient achieve the therapeutic goal of maintaining musculoskeletal integrity.

SAMPLE ITEM 4–25

When a patient vomits while in the supine position the caregiver should:

(1) Raise the patient's head
(2) Turn the patient on the side
(3) Transfer the patient to the bathroom
(4) Position the patient's head between their knees

This item is designed to test your ability to appropriately respond to an event. To answer this question you need to recognize that it is important to quickly assist the patient to expectorate the vomitus to avoid aspiration. In addition, you need to know that turning the patient on the side is the best position to facilitate drainage of matter from the mouth. Responding to an event by implementing an action is an implementation question.

SAMPLE ITEM 4–26

The safest way to identify a hospitalized patient before giving care is to:

(1) Ask the patient his or her name
(2) Look at the name on the bed
(3) Check the identification bracelet
(4) Call the patient's name and observe the response

This test item is designed to see if you can correctly provide a safe environment for a patient by verifying the patient's identity. In this set of options checking the identification bracelet is the most reliable and safest method to verify a patient's identity.

DOCUMENTING AND REPORTING PATIENT CARE AND RESPONSES

Once care is delivered, it is often recorded along with an assessment of the patient's response to care. Instead of or in addition to documenting care given you may verbally share results with other health team members. Verbal reports are usually given when changing shifts, responding to an emergency, and reporting responses to care.

SAMPLE ITEM 4–27

Which of the following facts about ambulation is most important to document in the patient's medical record?

(1) When the patient is ambulated
(2) Where the patient is ambulated
(3) The patient's response to ambulation
(4) The length of time it took to ambulate the patient

This question is based on the concept that documenting care is a component of the implementation step. It is also patient centered because it focuses on the patient's response.

EVALUATION

Evaluation is the fifth and final step of the problem-solving process. Evaluation is a process that consists of four steps that must be implemented after care is delivered if effectiveness of the plan of care is to be determined. The evaluation process includes identifying patient responses to care, comparing a patient's actual responses to the expected outcomes, analyzing factors that affected the actual outcomes for the purpose of drawing conclusions about the success or failure of specific interventions, and modifying the plan of care when necessary. Evaluation items will ask you to:

- Identify the steps in the evaluation process
- Identify actual outcomes as being desirable or undesirable
- Identify whether an outcome in a situation is met or not met
- Identify progress or lack of progress toward an expected outcome
- Recognize the need to modify the plan of care in response to a change in the status of the patient or a plan that is ineffective
- Recognize that the process of evaluation is continuous
- Recognize that the problem-solving process is dynamic and cyclical

Critical words used within a test item that generally indicate that the item is focused on evaluation include "expected, met, desired, compared, succeeded, failed, achieved, modified, reassess, ineffective, effective, response, compliance, noncompliance, evaluate." See if you can identify variations of these critical words indicating evaluation activities in the sample items. Most testing errors occur during the evaluation phase of the problem-solving process when options are selected that:

- Do not thoroughly and accurately reassess the patient after care is implemented
- Fail to appropriately cluster new data
- Fail to determine significance of new data
- Come to inappropriate or inaccurate conclusions
- Fail to modify the plan of care in response to the changing needs of the patient or in response to an ineffective plan

IDENTIFYING PATIENT RESPONSES

The process of evaluation begins with a reassessment that collects new information. Once care is implemented, the patient is reassessed and new clusters of data are identified and significance determined. In the literature the term "evaluation" has often been used interchangeably with the term "assessment," which causes confusion. It is important to remember that assessment is only one component in the process of evaluation. You need to first reassess to identify actual patient outcomes. Actual patient outcomes are the patient's responses to care. These data are then clustered and their significance determined before these actual patient outcomes can be compared with expected outcomes.

SAMPLE ITEM 4–28	To ensure that a patient understands the content of a teaching session, the caregiver should:

(1) Ask the patient what was learned
(2) Speak distinctly when giving directions
(3) Speak slowly when talking with the patient
(4) Use simple vocabulary and sentence structure

This item tests your ability to recognize an action that reassesses the patient after care has been given. A conclusion about the effectiveness of care can be determined from the data collected. In distractors two, three, and four the focus is on transmission of the message to the patient rather than on what was learned.

COMPARING ACTUAL OUTCOMES WITH EXPECTED OUTCOMES

Goals and outcomes are the criteria that are established for evaluation of care. A comparison is made between the actual outcomes and the expected outcomes to determine the effectiveness of the intervention. The new data when compared with expected outcomes determine which outcomes have been achieved and those that have not been achieved. The closer the patient's actual outcomes are to expected outcomes the more positive the evaluation. Negative evaluations are based on the fact that actual outcomes did not achieve expected outcomes. Negative evaluations indicate that an error occurred in the implementation of the problem-solving process or care was ineffective. A caregiver raises a patient to a sitting position before a standing position, expecting that the patient will not become dizzy once standing. After performing this activity, the caregiver determines that this intervention was effective and the evaluation of care is positive because the patient did not experience dizziness. If the patient experiences dizziness the intervention was ineffective and the evaluation of care is negative.

SAMPLE ITEM 4–29

The caregiver would know that the abdominal thrusts used in the Heimlich maneuver is effective when:

(1) The patient vomits
(2) Air is forced out of the patient's lungs
(3) The patient's systemic circulation is increased
(4) Pressure is placed on the apex of the patient's heart

This item tests your knowledge of the expected outcome of the abdominal thrust procedure. Forcing air out of the lungs should propel a mechanical obstruction out of the respiratory passages. If air is able to pass out of the lungs then the obstruction is relieved and the airway is patent. A comparison of the patient's response to the desired response allows the caregiver to determine the effectiveness of the intervention.

ANALYZING FACTORS THAT AFFECT ACTUAL OUTCOMES OF CARE

Once a determination of whether care is effective or not is made, then you must come to some conclusions about the potential factors that contributed to the success or failure of the plan of care. If a plan of care is ineffective you must examine what contributed to its failure. This requires you to start at step one of the problem-solving process with assessment and work through the entire process again in an attempt to identify why the plan was ineffective. Questions you must ask include: "Was the original assessment accurate?" "Was the problem/need statement accurate?" "Was the goal realistic?" "Were the outcomes measurable?" "Were the interventions consistently implemented?" These questions should be answered before formulating a new plan of care.

SAMPLE ITEM 4–30

When providing two-person cardiopulmonary resuscitation (CPR) to an adult patient who is in cardiac arrest, it is determined that the patient is not responding as expected. One of the rescuers identifies that the CPR protocol is not being appropriately implemented when the:

(1) Compression-ventilation ratio is 5:1
(2) Patient is positioned on a firm surface
(3) Sternum is being compressed 0.5 to 1 inch
(4) Compressions are on the lower half of the sternum

This item is designed to test your ability to recognize that a caregiver must analyze the factors that influence outcomes of care. It also requires you to know the acceptable protocol for administering two-person CPR to an adult and recognize which action does not adhere to the protocol.

MODIFYING THE PLAN OF CARE

Once it is determined that a plan of care is ineffective the plan must be modified. The changes in the plan of care are based on new patient assessments and revision of the problem/need statement, goals, and strategies that are designed to address the specific needs of the patient. The modified plan of care must then be implemented and the whole evaluation process begins again. As you can see, the process of evaluation is continuous.

SAMPLE ITEM 4–31

During a session an elderly female patient consistently becomes short of breath and tired. When planning to meet this patient's needs in the future, the caregiver should:

(1) Cancel her sessions for a few days
(2) Provide more frequent rest periods
(3) Provide care as quickly as possible
(4) Care for her immediately when she arrives

This item is designed to test your ability to recognize that the plan of care must be modified when care is inappropriate because of the changing needs of the patient. Patients are dynamic and their needs are constantly changing. When care is inappropriate, ineffective, or insufficient the plan of care must be revised.

ANSWERS AND RATIONALES FOR SAMPLE ITEMS IN CHAPTER FOUR

An asterisk is in front of the rationale that explains the correct answer.

Assessment

4–1
  (1) Elasticity and rigidity of the vessel walls and the quality and equality of pulses provide data about the status of the arteries.
  (2) A pulse is palpated in an artery, not a vein.
  (3) This is assessed through laboratory tests performed on blood specimens.
* (4) The heart is a pulsatile pump that ejects blood into the arterial system with each ventricular contraction; the pulse is the vibration transmitted with each contraction.

4–2
  (1) These are within the normal range.
  (2) Same as answer number one.
  (3) Same as answer number one.
* (4) These are outside the normal range. Normal respirations are 12 to 20, effortless and noiseless. This patient may be having respiratory distress.

4–3
* (1) To calculate ideal body weight a person needs to know the patient's height, age, and extent of bone structure.
  (2) This reflects the amount of food the patient is ingesting. This information does not contribute to the calculation of ideal body weight.
  (3) This is determined by weight and inches, reflecting circumference of the chest and waist. This information does not contribute to the calculation of ideal body weight.
  (4) This supports the patient's right to make choices about care. This information does not contribute to the calculation of ideal body weight.

4–4
  (1) Data are classified as objective or subjective not primary; primary refers to a source of data. A patient is the primary source of data.
  (2) Objective data can be measured or assessed by one of the senses.
  (3) Types of data are classified as objective or subjective not secondary. Secondary refers to sources of data. A secondary source of data produces information from a source other than the patient.
* (4) Subjective data are collected when the patient shares feelings, perceptions, sensations, and thoughts.

4–5
  (1) The wife is a secondary source, not a primary source.
  (2) The wife is a secondary source, not a tertiary source.
* (3) Family members are secondary sources; secondary sources produce information from someplace other than the patient; secondary sources provide supplemental information about the patient.
  (4) The wife is not a subjective source; subjective refers to types of data; subjective data are collected when the patient shares feelings, perceptions, sensation, and thoughts about a health problem.

4–6
  (1) This is considered verbal; words are written.
* (2) This is nonverbal; a message is transmitted without using words; crying,

facial expressions, and the patient's appearance are further examples of nonverbal communication.

(3) Sounds may or may not communicate meaning; a sound that communicates a meaning is considered verbal communication.

(4) This is verbal communication; words are generally spoken in a telephone message.

4–7   * (1) Primary intention is the normal healing process that consists of the stages of defensive, reconstructive, and maturative healing; it involves a clean wound with edges that are closely approximated.

(2) A laceration results from trauma; the wound probably contains microorganisms, and the tissue is torn with irregular wound edges.

(3) The wound edges are not approximated, and the wound is usually wide and open.

(4) An abrasion is an open wound resulting from friction; the wound edges are not approximated.

4–8   (1) This is done once the initial blood pressure is verified; once one vital sign is identified and verified as abnormal all the vital signs should be assessed.

* (2) The reading should be verified by retaking the blood pressure because a mistake may have been made when originally taking the blood pressure.

(3) This may be done after the blood pressure is verified and all the vital signs are taken.

(4) Same as answer number three.

4–9   (1) This is unsafe; intervention may be necessary.

(2) Activity would increase, not decrease, the heart rate.

(3) Corroboration with other appropriate health team members should occur first; eventually the physician may be called.

* (4) Corroboration with the nurse should occur first; nurses are at the bedside 24 hours a day and are appropriate secondary sources. Also, the physician may have left orders that can be implemented in this situation.

Analysis

4–10   * (1) The hemoglobin portion of red blood cells carries oxygen from the alveolar capillaries to distant tissue sites.

(2) This occurs in the capillary beds of the alveoli via the process of diffusion; this is unrelated to anemia.

(3) This relates to the extent of inflow and outflow of air between the alveoli and pulmonary capillaries, integrity of pulmonary blood vessels, or extent of blood flow to the pulmonary capillary bed; perfusion is not related to red blood cell levels.

(4) A problem with diffusion occurs at the alveolar capillary beds and is not related to anemia.

4–11   * (1) Patients who are immobilized are subject to increased pressure over bony prominences with a subsequent decrease in circulation to tissues.

(2) This is unrelated to the development of pressure ulcers.

(3) Same as answer number two.

(4) Same as answer number two.

4–12 (1) Acting out behaviors commonly reflect anger.

(2) Refusing to believe or accept a situation, not depressive behaviors, are reflective of denial.

* (3) Depression is commonly exhibited by patients with behaviors such as avoiding contact with others, withdrawing, not eating, and not sleeping.

(4) Acceptance is related to the final step of grieving; a patient reconciles and accepts the situation and is at peace within the self.

4–13 * (1) These patient adaptations are related to a decreased blood volume associated with hemorrhage and shock.

(2) With this problem the patient would more likely be hypertensive with a rapid pulse.

(3) Same as answer number two.

(4) Same as answer number two.

4–14 (1) Expressive aphasia, the inability to communicate thoughts verbally or in writing, is not supported by the data presented; although communication is important, it is not the priority when the airway may be compromised.

* (2) Drooling, slurred speech, and difficulty swallowing all contribute to the inability to manage oral secretions and food or fluid intake, contributing to a potential for aspiration.

(3) There are not enough data to support this statement.

(4) Same as answer number three.

4–15 * (1) The health team member has an obligation to ensure that all patients' needs will be appropriately met; this is the only option that addresses this concept.

(2) This is inappropriate; all patients must have their needs met.

(3) This is inappropriate; once a health team member assumes a course of duty this individual is responsible for the care that is delivered.

(4) This action does not ensure that appropriate care will be provided; this action will increase anxiety and cause patients to doubt the quality of care being provided.

Planning

4–16 * (1) Compliance is when the patient fulfills a prescribed course of treatment.

(2) This is undesirable. Tolerance denotes the need for increasing doses of a drug to maintain a constant response.

(3) This is not necessarily a measure of compliance. A patient may be compliant but not achieve the desired outcome. Another patient may not be compliant and yet the symptoms may subside.

(4) This is undesirable. If a drug is ineffectively metabolized or slowly excreted, the serum concentration increases with each dose; a cumulative effect tends to occur in the elderly and people with decreased functioning of the liver, kidneys, or thyroid gland.

4–17 (1) This could cause aspirated food to lodge deeper in the respiratory passages.

* (2) This maneuver pushes trapped air out of the lungs forcing out the obstructing food.

(3) This will not clear the airway; air needs to be forced out of the lungs; attempting to swallow could cause further aspiration.

(4) This could force the obstruction deeper into the breathing passages; the caregiver first needs to implement the abdominal thrust maneuver (Heimlich maneuver).

4–18   (1) This is unnecessary; respiratory isolation (droplet or airborne precautions) is used for microorganisms transmitted in respiratory secretions.

* (2) Measures such as covering a cough, frequent handwashing, and correct disposal of soiled tissues can limit the spread of microorganisms.

(3) Antibiotics are usually not given to prevent infection, but to treat an infection.

(4) This is unnecessary; fresh air does not spread the flu.

4–19   * (1) Because of a dark, unfamiliar environment at night elderly patients may become confused and disoriented, which contribute to the occurrence of falls.

(2) This is generally unrelated to falls.

(3) Same as answer number two.

(4) The risk of falls on awakening is not as high as it is at night when the lights are dim or off; the light of day and the use of lights promote orientation.

4–20   (1) A vest restraint should be snug yet loose enough for some movement; immobilization is not the purpose of this restraint.

(2) Restraints of any kind can increase agitation; if a vest is used when a patient is severely agitated it can cause injury.

* (3) This is the primary reason for the use of a vest restraint; it is used as a last resort to protect the patient from self-injury.

(4) The purpose of a vest restraint is to prevent injury, not limit movement.

4–21   (1) This action does not facilitate breathing.

* (2) This facilitates breathing; gravity aids the expansion of the diaphragm during inspiration; it also reduces the resistance of body weight on the chest during inspiration.

(3) This can further compromise respiratory compensatory mechanisms if the cause of the shortness of breath is related to chronic obstructive pulmonary disease (COPD); oxygen can precipitate CO_2 narcosis in patients with COPD.

(4) This helps patients with emphysema to exhale; diaphragmatic breathing is most effective for patients who are short of breath.

4–22   * (1) A health team conference focuses on the patient and the patient's needs; collaboration among health team members facilitates this process.

(2) This is a defensive response; all behavior has meaning; the caregiver should initially accept the behavior and identify the reason for the behavior.

(3) This is judgmental and takes away the patient's coping mechanism.

(4) This is an assumption; many people cope with anxiety by being argumentative and demanding; this behavior may be an attempt to gain control in a situation where the individual feels out of control.

Implementation

4–23   (1) The first action should be to respectfully decline to perform the task without a physician's order; a caregiver should notify a higher administrator only if the supervisor continues to insist that the task be performed.

     (2) Caregivers should perform only those tasks that they are licensed, certified, or permitted to perform within their role; in addition, dependent functions require a physician's order.

  * (3) It is unsafe to perform a task that is outside the legal definition of a profession, the professional guidelines related to certification or licensure, or an acceptable role; a caregiver has a responsibility to implement only dependent functions with a physician's order.

     (4) A union representative is usually notified only in the event that the supervisor threatens the caregiver; not all agencies are unionized.

4–24   (1) The arms do not have to be elevated to be in normal alignment.

     (2) What is a comfortable position for the patient may not be correct alignment necessary to prevent complications; although comfort is important, functional alignment takes priority.

  * (3) Anatomical alignment maintains physical functioning, minimizes strain and stress on muscles and joints, and prevents contractures.

     (4) The head can be at the same level as the heart, it does not have to be higher.

4–25   (1) This position does not facilitate the exit of vomitus from the mouth.

  * (2) This drains the mouth via gravity and reduces the risk of aspiration.

     (3) This is unsafe; vomiting takes energy and could cause the patient to become weak during the transfer.

     (4) This does not support or protect the vomiting patient; this position is often used to increase cerebral profusion when a person feels dizzy, not to facilitate vomiting.

4–26   (1) This is unsafe; the patient could be cognitively impaired.

     (2) This is unsafe; the patient could be in the wrong bed.

  * (3) This is the safest method to identify a patient; it is the most reliable because each patient on admission receives an identification bracelet with their name and an identification number.

     (4) Same as answer number one.

4–27   (1) Although this would be documented, the patient's response to care is the most important fact.

     (2) Same as answer number one.

  * (3) This is most important because the patient's response will indicate if the care given was appropriate and effective and if future care should be altered.

     (4) Same as answer number one.

Evaluation

4–28 * (1) Seeking feedback enables the caregiver to know whether or not the message was understood as intended.

     (2) This helps to send a clearer message, but it does not inform the sender whether the receiver understood the message.

(3) Same as answer number two.

(4) Same as answer number two.

4–29　(1) The obstruction is in the trachea of the respiratory system, not the esophagus of the gastrointestinal system.

* (2) The rise in intra-abdominal and intrathoracic pressure and the abrupt jolt to the diaphragm use air within the bronchial tree behind the obstruction to force out whatever is causing the obstruction in the trachea.

(3) This occurs during cardiac compression associated with cardiopulmonary resuscitation (CPR). If this occurs during the abdominal thrust procedure compression is being applied over the sternum rather than the epigastric area.

(4) Same as answer number three.

4–30　(1) This action is a component of the CPR protocol for an adult.

(2) Same as answer number one.

* (3) This action is not a component of the correct protocol for adult CPR because the sternum must be compressed 1.5 to 2 inches to be effective. Compression of the sternum to a depth of 0.5 to 1 inch would be appropriate for an infant, not an adult.

(4) Same as answer number one.

4–31　(1) This may be unnecessary if more frequent rest periods are provided.

* (2) Individualizing care to address needs of the patient will maximize outcomes. Modifying the plan of care to include more frequent rest periods addresses this patient's specific needs.

(3) This is contraindicated; the patient is experiencing an activity intolerance and this will place further demands on the patient.

(4) Although this may help conserve the patient's energy, this may not reduce the patient's fatigue or shortness of breath during the therapy session.

5

Test-Taking Techniques for Multiple-Choice Questions

Performing well on multiple-choice questions requires both roots and wings. The previous chapters were concerned with factors that provided you with roots. Each root grounded you through information about formulating a positive mental attitude, exploring a variety of study skills, introducing you to the multiple-choice question, and familiarizing you with the problem-solving process. This chapter attempts to provide you with the wings necessary to accurately fly through multiple-choice questions. Flying through multiple-choice questions has nothing to do with speed; it relates to being test-wise and able to navigate through complex information with ease.

Tests in the various healthcare disciplines involve complex information that has depth and breadth. As well as each healthcare profession having its own body of knowledge, they all draw from a variety of common disciplines, such as medical terminology, anatomy and physiology, pathophysiology, pharmacology, medical therapies, clinical procedures, psychology and sociology. To perform well on an examination, you must understand and integrate the subject matter. Nothing can replace effective study habits or knowledge about the subject being tested. However, being test-wise can maximize the application of the information you possess.

Being test-wise entails specific techniques related to individual question analysis and general techniques related to conquering the challenge of an examination. One rationale for learning how to use these techniques is to provide you with skills that increase your command over the testing situation. If you are in control, you will maintain a positive attitude and increase your chances of selecting the correct answers. When you have knowledge and are test-wise you should fly through a test by gliding and soaring, rather than by flapping and fluttering.

SPECIFIC TEST-TAKING TECHNIQUES

A specific test-taking technique is a strategy that uses skill and forethought to analyze a test item before selecting an answer. A technique is not a gimmick but a method of examining a question with consideration and thoughtfulness. Hopefully, the outcome will be the selection of the correct answer. When an item has four options, the chance of selecting the correct answer is one out of four or 25%. When you eliminate one distractor, the chance of selecting the correct answer is one out of three or 33.3%. If you are able to throw out two distractors, the chance of selecting the correct answer is one out of two or 50%. Each time you successfully eliminate a distractor, you dramatically increase your chances of correctly answering the question.

Before you attempt to answer a question, break the question down into its components. First, read the stem. What is it actually asking? It may be helpful to paraphrase the stem to focus in on its content. Then, try to answer the question being asked in your own words before looking at the options. Hopefully, one of the options will be similar to your answer. Then, examine the other options and try to identify the correct answer. If you know, understand, and can apply the information being tested you can often recognize the correct answer. However, do not be tempted to rapidly select an option without careful thought. An option may contain accurate information, but it may not be correct because it does not answer the question asked in the stem. Be careful. Each option deserves equal consideration.

Use test-taking techniques for every question. The use of test-taking techniques becomes paramount when you are unsure of the answer because each distractor that you are able to eliminate will increase your chances of selecting the correct answer. Most students are able to reduce the number of plausible answers to two. However, contrary to popular belief, multiple-choice questions have only one correct answer. Use everything in your arsenal to conquer the multiple-choice–question test such as effective studying, a positive mental attitude, and last but not least, test-taking techniques.

The purpose of sample items in this chapter is for you to have an opportunity to apply test-taking strategies. The questions address content that is commonly presented in the supportive and introductory courses associated with the various healthcare disciplines. For your information the correct answers for the sample items in this chapter and the rationales for all the options are at the end of this chapter.

IDENTIFY KEY WORDS IN THE STEM THAT INDICATE NEGATIVE POLARITY

Read the stem slowly and precisely. Look for key words, such as "not, except, never, contraindicated, unacceptable, avoid, unrelated, violate, and least." These words indicate negative polarity, and the question being asked is probably concerned with what is false. Some words that have negative polarity are not as obvious as others. A negatively worded stem asks you to identify an exception, detect an error, or recognize actions that are unacceptable or contraindicated. If you read a stem and all the options appear correct, reread the stem because you may have missed a key negative word. These words are sometimes brought to your attention by an underline (not), italics (*except*), boldface (**never**), or capitals (VIOLATE). Many examinations avoid questions with negative polarity. However, examples of these items are included for your information.

SAMPLE ITEM 5–1	Which of the following actions would violate patient confidentiality and privacy?

(1) Writing patient statements in the progress notes
(2) Interviewing a patient in the presence of others
(3) Presenting the patient's problems at a team conference
(4) Sharing data about a patient at change-of-shift report

The key word in this item is "violate." This question is asking you to identify behavior that is unacceptable. Options one, three, and four are actions that are implemented by responsible healthcare providers.

SAMPLE ITEM 5–2	Which of the following signs is unrelated to hypoxia?

(1) Jaundice
(2) Cyanosis
(3) Pallor
(4) Dusky

The most important word in the stem is "unrelated." The word "unrelated" indicates negative polarity. The use of the word "unrelated" is not as obvious of negative polarity as the words "never" or "except." This negatively worded stem is asking you to identify a sign that is **not** associated with hypoxia. Options two, three, and four are all associated with assessments related to a lack of oxygenation. Jaundice is the only option that is not associated with oxygenation.

IDENTIFY KEY WORDS IN THE STEM THAT SET A PRIORITY

Read the stem carefully while looking for key words such as "first, initially, best, and most." These words modify what is being asked. This type of question requires you to put a value on each option and then place them in rank order. If the question asks what should be done first, what the initial action should be, or what the best response would be, then rank the options in order of importance from one to four with the most desirable option as number one and the least desirable option as number four. The correct answer would be the option that you ranked number one. If you are having difficulty ranking the options, eliminate the option that you believe is most wrong among all the options. Next, eliminate the option you believe is most wrong from among the remaining three options. At this point you are down to two options and your chance of selecting the correct answer is 50%. When key words such as "most important" are used, frequently all of the options may be appropriate for the situation; however, only one of the options is the most important. When all the options appear logical for the situation, reread the stem to identify a key word that asks you to place a priority on the options. These words are occasionally emphasized by an underline, *italics*, **boldface**, or CAPITALS.

SAMPLE ITEM 5–3

A healthcare provider observes another health team member treating a patient in an abusive manner. The *initial* action should be to:

(1) Become a role model for the other health team member
(2) Talk with the health team member about the incident
(3) Tell the supervisor and write a report
(4) Reassure and calm the patient

The key word in this stem is "initial." All of the options in this question are appropriate interventions for this situation. The stem is asking you to identify what should be done initially or first. Perhaps in your opinion all of the options presented would not be your first response. However, you must choose the correct answer from among the options presented. The question is testing your ability to recognize that the patient's physical and emotional safety is the priority.

SAMPLE ITEM 5–4

The **most** important rationale why the caregiver must understand the scientific reasons for the actions that constitute a procedure is because the caregiver should be able to:

(1) Document the care given
(2) Formulate a plan of care
(3) Implement the procedure safely
(4) Explain the procedure to the patient

The most important word in the stem is "most." The word "most" has been brought to your attention and is asking you to set a priority. All of the options are appropriate to performing a procedure. However, the most important reason for understanding why certain actions are performed is to implement the procedure safely. Maintaining patient safety is always the priority.

IDENTIFY CLUES IN THE STEM

A clue is the unintentional use of a word or phrase that leads you to the correct answer. Generally the stem is short and contains only the information needed to make it clear and specific. Therefore, a word or phrase in the stem may provide a hint for choosing the correct answer. A word that is a clue in the stem may be identical or similar to a word used in the correct answer. When a word is identical in the stem and the answer it is called a "clang association." A phrase that is a clue in the stem is usually paraphrased in or closely related to the correct answer.

SAMPLE ITEM 5–5	To help meet a patient's self-esteem needs the healthcare provider should: (1) Encourage the patient to perform self-care when able (2) Anticipate needs before the patient requests help (3) Assist the patient with the performance of care (4) Suggest that a family member provide the care An important word in the stem is "self-esteem." The word self-esteem is similar to the word "self-care." Thoughtfully examine option number one. An option that incorporates words that are similar to words in the stem is often the correct answer.

SAMPLE ITEM 5–6	The term dysuria denotes: (1) Glucose in the blood (2) Difficulty speaking (3) Pain on urination (4) Voiding at night An important word in the stem is "dys**uria**." If you know that "uria" is a suffix that denotes "urine" then you should recognize that the word "urination" is related. It is an unintentional clue that should provide a hint that option number three is the correct answer.

IDENTIFY PATIENT-CENTERED OPTIONS

Healthcare providers are involved with providing both physical and emotional care to people. Therefore, the focus of concern should be the patient. Items that test your ability to be patient-centered tend to explore patient feelings, identify patient preferences, empower the patient, afford the patient choices, or in some other way put emphasis on the patient. Because the patient is the center of the health team the patient is always the priority.

SAMPLE ITEM 5–7

A patient who has recently had an above-the-knee amputation starts to cry and says, "I am useless with only one leg." The best response would be:

(1) You still have one good leg.
(2) Losing a leg must be very difficult.
(3) A prosthesis would make a big difference.
(4) You will feel better when you can use crutches.

Option number two is patient-centered. It focuses on the patient's feelings by using the interviewing technique of reflection. Option one denies the patient's feelings and options three and four provide false reassurance. When a patient's feelings are ignored or minimized, the caregiver is not being patient-centered. To be patient-centered, the caregiver should concentrate on the patient's feelings.

SAMPLE ITEM 5–8

A patient who is incontinent of feces says, "This is disgusting. How can you stand this?" The caregiver's **best** response would be:

(1) You sound upset?
(2) This is disgusting?
(3) I am used to this by now.
(4) It is not as bad as you think.

Option one is patient-centered. It focuses on the patient's feelings and uses the interviewing technique of reflection. It identifies the emotional theme of the patient's statement. Options three and four focus on the caregiver rather than the patient. Although option two identifies the content of the patient's statement, it may reinforce negative feelings, which is not therapeutic.

IDENTIFY SPECIFIC DETERMINERS IN OPTIONS

A specific determiner is a word or statement that conveys a thought or concept that has no exceptions. Words such as "just, always, never, all, every, none, and only" are terms that are absolute and easy to identify. They place limits on a statement that would generally be considered correct. Statements that use all-inclusive terms frequently represent broad generalizations that are usually false. Because there are few absolutes in this world, options that contain specific determiners are usually incorrect and can be eliminated.

SAMPLE ITEM 5–9

Which of the following rules guides the building of medical terms?

(1) A compound word never uses more than one root word
(2) A combining vowel is always used before a suffix that begins with a vowel
(3) Suffixes, when added to root words, indicate the part of speech of the medical term
(4) A combining vowel is generally not used to link a root word to a suffix that begins with a consonant

The words "never" in option one and "always" in option two are specific determiners. They are absolute terms that allow for no exceptions. Generally, options that use all inclusive terms such as "never" and "always" can be eliminated after careful consideration. By eliminating options one and two you have increased your chances of selecting the correct answer to 50%.

SAMPLE ITEM 5–10

When providing care for patients that would expose caregivers to body secretions, the caregivers can most appropriately protect themselves from microorganisms by:

(1) Wearing clean gloves during care
(2) Washing their hands prior to giving care
(3) Encouraging patients to provide all of their own care
(4) Discarding contaminated materials into waste containers

In option three the word "all" is a specific determiner. It is a word that obviously includes everything. Expecting patients to provide all of their own care is unreasonable, unrealistic and could be unsafe. Option three can be eliminated. This raises your chances of choosing the correct answer because you only have to choose from among three options rather than four.

IDENTIFY OPPOSITES IN OPTIONS

Sometimes an item will contain two options that are opposite to each other. They can be single words that reflect extremes on a continuum, or they can be statements that convey converse messages. When opposites appear in the options they must be given serious consideration. One of them will be the correct answer, or they both can be eliminated from consideration. When one of the opposites is the correct answer, you are being asked to differentiate between two responses that incorporate extremes of a concept or principle. When the opposites are distractors, they are attempting to divert your attention from the correct answer. If you correctly evaluate opposite options, you can increase your chances of selecting the correct answer to 50% because you have reduced the plausible options to two.

SAMPLE ITEM 5–11	"Hyper," a medical word element, is a:

(1) Suffix
(2) Prefix
(3) Word root
(4) Combining form

Options one and two are opposites. Examine these options first. They are contrary to each other in relation to before or after a word root. One of these options will be the correct answer or they both can be eliminated. If you know that a combining form always ends in a vowel then you can eliminate option four. You have now raised your chances of getting this question correct to 33%. Now examine option three. If you know that a word root is the foundation of a word and that "hyper" is not preceded by any prefixes, then option three can be eliminated. Your next task is to select between options one and two. You have raised your chances of getting this question correct to 50%.

SAMPLE ITEM 5–12	In relation to extracellular body fluids, normal saline is:

(1) Hypertonic
(2) Hypotonic
(3) Isotonic
(4) Acidotic

Options one and two are opposites. Appraise these words in relation to each other and their relationship to body fluids and normal saline. They are extremes in the concentration of solutes. Because normal saline is equal to body fluids in the concentration of solutes, these options are probably distractors. Now examine options three and four. Normal body fluids have a neutral pH (between 7.35 to 7.45). Acidosis, which is referred to in option four, has a pH below 7.35. Option four can be deleted from consideration. By an efficient process of examination and elimination you have arrived at the correct answer, option three.

IDENTIFY EQUALLY PLAUSIBLE/UNIQUE OPTIONS

Items sometimes contain two or more options that are very similar. It is difficult to choose between them because they are comparable. One option is no better or worse than the other option in relation to the statement presented in the stem. Usually equally plausible options are distractors and can be eliminated from consideration. You have now improved your chances of selecting the correct answer to 50%. If you find three equally plausible options when initially examining the options, then the fourth option will probably be different from the others and appear unique. Children's activity books and a popular children's television program present a game based on this concept. Four pictures are presented and the child is asked to pick out the one that is different. Which one of these is not like the others? Which one of these is not the same? For example, the picture contains three types of fruit and one vegetable and the child is asked to identify which one is different. The correct answer to a test item can sometimes be identified by applying this concept of similarities and differences.

| SAMPLE ITEM 5–13 | When a patient is having a seizure the initial action should be to: |

(1) Restrain the patient
(2) Get portable oxygen for the patient
(3) Hold the patient's arms and legs securely
(4) Move objects away from around the patient

If you carefully examine options one and three you will notice that the concept inherent in both options are the same, controlling patient movement. Because equally plausible options are usually distractors, you can delete both these options. Now evaluate the remaining options. One of them is probably the correct answer.

| SAMPLE ITEM 5–14 | Before performing any patient procedure the caregiver should first: |

(1) Shut the door
(2) Wash the hands
(3) Close the curtain
(4) Drape the patient

Options one, three, and four are similar in that they all somehow enclose the patient and provide for patient privacy. They are all plausible interventions when providing patient care. It is difficult to choose the most correct answer from among these three options. Option two is different. It relates to microbiological safety rather than emotional safety. Since this option is unique in relation to the other options, it should be thoroughly examined in relation to the stem because it is likely to be the correct answer.

IDENTIFY DUPLICATE FACTS IN OPTIONS

Options sometimes contain two or more facts or statements that are identical or similar. When you can identify one part as being correct, you usually can eliminate at least two options that are distractors. By deleting two distractors, you have increased your chances of selecting the correct answer to 50%.

SAMPLE ITEM 5–15

The presenting symptoms associated with diabetes mellitus are:

(1) Polydipsia and polyuria
(2) Polydipsia and polyplegia
(3) Polycythemia and polyuria
(4) Polycythemia and polyplegia

This item is asking you to identify two symptoms that have a relationship with diabetes mellitus. Four medical terms are presented in different combinations. If you know that one of the terms is unrelated to diabetes mellitus, two options containing that word can be eliminated. If you know two terms that are unrelated to diabetes mellitus, you can eliminate the three distractors and arrive at the correct answer.

SAMPLE ITEM 5–16

A patient who is hemorrhaging would exhibit:

(1) Warm dry skin, hypotension, and a bounding pulse
(2) Hypertension, a bounding pulse, and cold clammy skin
(3) A weak thready pulse, hypertension, and warm dry skin
(4) Hypotension, cold clammy skin, and a weak thready pulse

This item is testing your knowledge about patient adaptations associated with hemorrhage. Three patient adaptations are presented: the condition of the skin, the blood pressure, and the characteristic of the pulse. Even if you only know one of these facts about hemorrhage you can reduce your final selection to between two options. If you know that hypotension is associated with hemorrhage then you can eliminate options two and three. If you know that cold clammy skin is related to hemorrhage then you can delete options one and three. If you know that a weak thready pulse is associated with hemorrhage then you can eliminate options one and two. If you know only one or two of the facts presented you can maximize the information you do possess in answering this type of item. Options that have three parts work to your advantage if you use the technique of identifying duplicate facts in options.

IDENTIFY OPTIONS THAT DENY PATIENT FEELINGS, CONCERNS, OR NEEDS

Because healthcare providers are concerned about their patients and primarily want their patients to get well, they often assume the roles of deliverer, champion, protector, or savior. However, by inappropriately adopting these roles, a person can often diminish patient concerns, provide false reassurance, and cut off further patient communication. To be a patient advocate you cannot always be a Pollyanna. (Pollyanna, the heroine of stories by Eleanor Hodgman Porter, was a person of irrepressible optimism who found good in everything.) Sometimes healthcare providers must focus on the negative rather than the positive, acknowledge that everything may not have the desired outcome, and recognize patient feelings as a priority. Options that imply everything will be all right, deny patient feelings, change the subject raised by the patient, encourage the patient to be cheerful, or abdicate responsibility to other members of the health team are usually distractors and can be eliminated from consideration.

SAMPLE ITEM 5–17	The night before surgery the patient says, "I am worried that I might die tomorrow." The best response would be: (1) Today surgery is really routine. (2) Have you told your doctor about this? (3) The thought of dying can be frightening. (4) Most people who have surgery survive. Options one and four dispute the patient's concerns because the messages imply that there is nothing to worry about; the surgery is routine and most patients survive. Option two avoids the opportunity to encourage a further discussion of the patient's feelings and surrenders this responsibility to the physician. After collecting more information, the physician can be informed of the patient's concern about death. Options one, two, and four deny the patient's feelings and can be eliminated because they are distractors. Option three is the correct answer because it encourages the patient to focus on the expressed feelings about death.

SAMPLE ITEM 5–18	Following surgery the patient complains of mild incisional pain while performing deep breathing and coughing exercises. The best response would be: (1) Each day it will hurt less and less. (2) This is an expected response after surgery.

(3) With a pillow apply pressure against the incision.
(4) I will get the nurse to give you pain medication.

Option one is a Pollyanna-like response that provides false reassurance. The caregiver does not know that the pain will get less and less for this patient. Option one can be deleted from consideration. Although option two is a true statement, it cuts off communication because it diminishes the patient's concern and does not explore a solution for minimizing the pain. Option two can be eliminated as a distractor. You now must choose between options three and four. Each time you can eliminate an option that denies a patient's feelings you raise your chances of selecting the correct answer. The correct answer is option three because it recognizes the pain and offers an intervention to help relieve the discomfort.

USE MULTIPLE TEST-TAKING TECHNIQUES

You have just been introduced to a variety of test-taking techniques. As you practice applying each of these techniques to test items you will become more skillful at being test-wise. As you become more proficient at applying test-taking techniques you can further maximize success in choosing the correct option if you use more than one test-taking technique within an item.

| SAMPLE ITEM 5–19 | The directional term that describes movement toward the midline of a structure is: |

(1) Adduction
(2) Visceral
(3) Abduction
(4) Lateral

Options one and three are opposites. They are contrary to each other in relation to a direction of movement. Examine these options first. One of them will be the correct answer or they will both be distractors. Now examine options two and four. Neither of these terms are related to movement and can therefore be eliminated. You have increased your chances of selecting the correct answer to 50%. This process has used the test-taking technique, identifying opposites. If you recognize that the words "movement toward" in the stem and the prefix "add" in the word "adduction" in option one reflect similar concepts, you have used the test-taking technique, identify clues in the stem. By using two test-taking techniques you can dramatically increase your chances of selecting the correct answer.

| SAMPLE ITEM 5–20 | When a patient is repositioned during a procedure to minimize physical discomfort the caregiver is meeting the patient's: |

(1) Safety needs
(2) Security needs
(3) Self-esteem needs
(4) Physiological needs

By thoughtfully reading the stem you should identify that the important words are "minimize physical discomfort." When reviewing the options you should recognize that the word "physiological" in option four is closely related to the word "physical" in the stem. Option four should be given serious consideration. This uses the test-taking technique, identify clues in the stem. Options one and two present the words "safety" and "security." They are comparable and choosing between them would be difficult. They probably are distractors. This uses the test-taking technique, identify equally plausible/unique options. The use of multiple test-taking techniques in an item can facilitate the deletion of distractors and the selection of the correct answer.

GENERAL TEST-TAKING TECHNIQUES

A general test-taking technique is a strategy that is utilized to conquer the challenge of an examination. To be in command of the situation, you must be able to manage your internal and external domains. The test-taker who approaches a test with physical, mental, and emotional authority is in a better position to regulate the testing situation, rather than have the testing situation dominate.

PRACTICE TAKING TESTS

Taking practice tests is an excellent way to improve the effectiveness of your test-taking techniques. Not only can you become more emotionally and physically comfortable in the testing situation but you can become more proficient at selecting the correct option when answering a multiple-choice question. Reviewing rationales for the right and wrong answers serves as an effective study technique. It reinforces learning and it can help you identify areas that require additional study.

As you practice test-taking it is advised that you gradually increase the number of questions on your practice tests. By doing this you can build stamina, enabling you to concentrate more effectively during a shorter test. Marathon runners have long recognized the value of building stamina and the need for practice to achieve a "groove" that enhances performance. Marathon runners also manage their practice so they "peak" on the day of the big event. The same principles can be applied to the student preparing for an important test. You are at your "peak" and can achieve a "groove" when you feel physically, emotionally, and intellectually ready for the important test.

FOLLOW YOUR REGULAR ROUTINE
THE NIGHT BEFORE A TEST

Follow your normal routine the night before a test. This is not the time to make changes that may disrupt your equilibrium. If you do not normally eat pepperoni pizza, exercise, or study until 2 AM, do not start now. Go to bed at your usual time. Avoid the temptation to have an all-night cram session. Studies have demonstrated that sleep deprivation decreases reaction times and cognitive skills. An adequate night's sleep is necessary to produce a rested mind and body, which provide the physical and emotional energy required to maximize performance on an examination.

ARRIVE ON TIME FOR THE EXAMINATION

Plan your schedule so that you arrive at the testing site approximately 15 to 30 minutes early. Arrange extra time for unexpected events associated with traveling. There may be a traffic jam, a road may have a detour, the car may not start, the train may be late, the bus could break down, or you may have to park in the farthest lot from the testing site. If the location of the testing site or classroom is unfamiliar to you, it would be wise to take a practice run and locate the room. On the day of the examination you want to avoid getting lost.

By arriving early you have an opportunity to visit the rest room, survey the situation, and collect your thoughts. Because anxiety is associated with an autonomic nervous system response, you may have urgency (the urge to urinate), frequency (the need to urinate frequently), or increased intestinal peristalsis. Visit the rest room before the test to avoid using test time to meet physical needs. The test may or may not be administered in the room in which the content is taught. Arriving early allows you to survey the situation and become more comfortable in the testing environment. Decide where you want to sit if seats are not assigned. Students have preferences such as sitting by a window, being in the back of the room, or surrounding themselves with friends. Selecting your own seat allows you to manipulate one aspect of your environment. In addition, this time before the test provides you with an opportunity to collect your thoughts. You may desire to review content on a flash card, perform relaxation exercises, or reinforce your positive mental attitude. However, avoid comparing notes with other students. They may have inaccurate information or be anxious. Remember anxiety is contagious. If you are the type who is readily affected by the anxiety of other people, evade these people until after the test.

BRING THE APPROPRIATE TOOLS

To perform a task, you need adequate tools. Pens, pencils, and an eraser are essential. A pen is usually required to complete the identifying information on the answer sheet. A pencil is usually necessary to record your answers on the answer sheet if it is a computer answer form. Use number two pencils because they have soft lead that facilitate the computer scoring of the answer sheet. Bring at least two pens and two or more pencils. Backup equipment is advisable because ink can run out and points can break. Sharpen all your pencils and bring a small, self-contained pencil sharpener if you prefer to work with a sharp point on your pencil. Have at least one eraser. You may decide to change an answer or need to erase extraneous marks that you make on the question book or the answer sheet. A watch is also a necessary tool for every test. Some proctors will announce time frames as the test progresses and others will not. Bringing your own watch provides you with a sense of independence and control. Depending on your individual needs, other tools might include eyeglasses, a hearing aid, or a calculator. Assemble all your equipment the night before the test and be sure to take them with you to the testing site.

UNDERSTAND ALL THE DIRECTIONS FOR THE TEST BEFORE STARTING

It is essential to understand the instructions before beginning the test. On some tests you are responsible for independently reading the instructions whereas on other tests the proctor verbally announces the instructions. However, more often than not you will have a written copy of the instructions while the proctor reads them aloud. In this instance do not read ahead of the proctor. The proctor may elaborate on the written instructions and you do not want to miss any of the additional directions. If you do not understand a particular part of the instructions immediately request the proctor explain them again. You must completely understand the instructions before beginning the examination.

MANAGE THE ALLOTTED TIME TO YOUR ADVANTAGE

All tests have a time limit. Some tests have severe time restrictions in which most test-takers do not complete all the questions on the examination. These are known as "speed tests." Other tests have a generous time frame in which the majority of test-takers have ample time to answer every question on the examination. These are known as "power tests." The purpose of tests is to identify how much information the test-taker possesses about the topic being evaluated. Most examinations in the various healthcare disciplines are power tests. Regardless of the type of test, you must use your time well.

To manage your time on an examination you must determine how much time you have to answer each item while leaving some time for review at the end of the testing period. To ascertain how much time you should allot for each item on a multiple-choice test, divide the total time you have for the test by the number of items on the test. For example, if you have 90 minutes to take a test that has 50 items, divide 90 by 50. This allots 1 minute and 48 seconds for each item. If you actually allot 1.5 minutes per item you will leave 15 minutes for a final review. Be aware of the time as you progress through a test. If you determine that you have approximately 1.5 minutes for each question, then by the time you have completed 10 items, 15 minutes should have passed. Pace yourself so that you do not spend more than 1.5 minutes on an item if possible. If you answer an item in less than 1.5 minutes, then you can use the excess time for another item that may take slightly longer than 1.5 minutes or add this time to the end for review. The allocation of time for test completion depends on the complexity of the content, the difficulty of the reading level, and the number of options presented in the items. Multiple-choice examinations generally allot 1 minute per item when there are four options.

Use all the time allocated for the examination. The test constructors calculated that the time parameters for the test were appropriate for a thoughtful review of the items. Read the items slowly and carefully. If you process items too quickly you may overlook important words, become careless, or arrive at impulsive conclusions. Work at your own pace. Do not be influenced by the actions of other test-takers. If other test-takers complete the examination early ignore them and do not become concerned. Just because they finish early does not indicate that they will score well on the test. They may be imprudent speed demons. A cautious, discriminating, and judicious approach is to your advantage. Be your own person, and remember that time can be your ally rather than your adversary.

CONCENTRATE ON THE SIMPLE BEFORE THE COMPLEX

Answer the easy questions before the difficult questions. This uses the basic teaching-learning principle of moving from the simple to the complex. By doing this you can maximize your use of time and maintain a positive mental attitude. Begin answering questions. When you confront a difficult item, and you have already used your allotted time to answer it, and you still do not know the answer, then skip over this item and move on to the next item. Make a notation on scrap paper, next to the item in the question booklet, or next to the number of the skipped item on the answer sheet so that you can return to this item later in the test. Making a mark on the answer sheet should prevent you from making the error of recording the next answer in the previous item's location on the answer sheet. These and any other extraneous marks must be erased from the answer sheet before handing it in to the proctor. Extraneous marks confuse the computer, and you will probably lose credit because it will be scored as an incorrect answer. When you reach the end of the test, return to those items that you reserved for the end. You should have more time to spend on these items, and you may have accessed information from other items that can assist you in answering these questions. Concentrating on the simple before the complex permits you to answer the maximal number of items in the time allocated for the examination.

MAKE EDUCATED GUESSES

An educated guess occurs when you select an option without knowing for certain that it is actually the correct answer. The selection is based on partial knowledge. When you reduce the final selection to two options, it is usually to your advantage to reassess these options in context of the knowledge you do possess and make an educated guess. Making a wild guess by flipping a coin or choosing your favorite number should depend on whether or not the test has a penalty for guessing.

Some examinations assign credit when you select a correct answer and do not allocate credit when you select one of the distractors. The instructions for these examinations may state in the directions that only correct answers will receive credit, you should answer every question, you should not leave any blanks, or that there are no penalties for guessing. In these tests it is to your advantage to answer every question. First select answers based on knowledge. If you are unsure of the correct answer, reduce the number of options and then make an educated guess. If you have absolutely no idea what the answer can be, then make a wild guess because you will not be penalized for a wrong answer.

Some tests will assign credit when you select a correct answer and will subtract credit when you select a distractor. The instructions for these examinations may inform you not to guess, that credit will be subtracted for incorrect answers, or there is a penalty for guessing. In these tests a statistical manipulation is performed to mathematically limit the advantage of guessing. When taking these tests, it is still to your advantage to make an educated guess if through knowledge you can reduce your final selection to two options. However, wild guessing is not to your advantage because you are penalized for guessing.

MAINTAIN A POSITIVE MENTAL ATTITUDE

It is important that you foster a positive mental attitude and a sense of relaxation. A little apprehension can be motivating but when it rises too much it can interfere with your attention, concentration, and problem-solving ability. Use positive techniques that you have practiced and that work for you to enhance relaxation and a positive mental attitude. For example, feel in control by skipping the difficult questions; enhance relaxation by employing diaphragmatic breathing for several deep breaths, rotating your shoulders, or flexing and hyperextending your head; foster a positive mental attitude by telling yourself, "I am prepared to do this well!" or "I know I have studied hard and I will be successful!"

CHECK YOUR ANSWERS AND ANSWER SHEET

Most examinations incorporate time at the end of the testing period for review. Reassess your answers, particularly for those items in which you made an educated guess. Subsequent questions may contain content that is helpful to answering a previous question, you may access information you did not remember originally, or you may be less anxious and are able to assess the question with more objectivity. Be aware of your success in changing answers on previous tests. Every time you review a test, evaluate your accuracy in changing answers. Keep score of how many answers you change from wrong to right and how many you change from right to wrong. If the number of items you changed from wrong to right is greater than the number of items you changed from right to wrong, then it would probably be to your advantage to change answers you ultimately believe you answered incorrectly. On the other hand, if you change more answers from right to wrong then you should avoid changing your answers unless you are positive that your second choice is the correct choice.

Review your answer sheet for accuracy. Make sure that you have answered every question, especially on tests that do not penalize for guessing. On computer-scored answer sheets each item has numbers or letters that represent the corresponding options within the item. Make sure that every mark is within the lines, heavy and full, and in the appropriate space. Erase any extraneous marks on the answer sheet. Additional pencil marks, inadequately erased answers, and marks outside the lines will confuse the computer and alter your score. An effective and thorough review should leave you with a feeling of control and a sense of closure at the end of the examination.

ANSWERS AND RATIONALES FOR SAMPLE ITEMS IN CHAPTER FIVE

An asterisk is in front of the rationale that explains the correct answer.

5–1   (1) This is an acceptable practice; the purpose of progress notes is to share and communicate data about the patient.
   * (2) This violates confidentiality; others may overhear information that should be kept confidential.
   (3) This is an acceptable practice; a team conference enables professionals to share and communicate important information about patients.
   (4) This is an appropriate practice; sharing information at report notifies other health team members of the patient's changing status.

5–2   * (1) This is a yellow-orange discoloration of the skin, mucous membranes of the oral cavity, and sclera caused by elevated blood levels of bilirubin, which deposits bile pigments into tissues.
   (2) This is a blue discoloration of the skin and mucous membranes caused by deoxygenated hemoglobin in the capillaries; it is a late sign of hypoxia.
   (3) This is an unnatural paleness or decreased color in the skin caused by reduced amounts of oxyhemoglobin.
   (4) This is a grayish discoloration of the skin, which frequently indicates deoxygenated hemoglobin in the capillaries in people with dark skin.

5–3   (1) This would be done later; the observer's first action is to support the patient.
   (2) Same as answer number one.
   (3) Same as answer number one.
   * (4) The patient is the priority; once the patient is protected and safe the actions of the abusive health team member can be addressed.

5–4   (1) The caregiver generally does not document the scientific rationale for care provided, but rather that it was implemented along with the patient's response.
   (2) Patient safety takes priority; however, healthcare providers also need to understand scientific rationales to appropriately plan care.
   * (3) Safety of the patient always takes priority; the healthcare provider must only perform skills that are understood and practiced.
   (4) Although it is important to explain all procedures to the patient, safety takes priority; healthcare providers need to have a strong scientific foundation to provide safe care.

5–5   * (1) This encourages independence, which increases self-esteem.
   (2) When a person is dependent on another person it often lowers self-esteem.
   (3) Same as answer number two.
   (4) This would meet the patient's needs for love and belonging, not self-esteem. It also promotes dependence.

5–6   (1) This is hyperglycemia.
   (2) This is dysarthria.
   * (3) Dysuria is defined as pain or discomfort when urinating.
   (4) This is nocturia.

5–7   (1) This denies the patient's feelings.
           * (2) This focuses on the patient's feelings by the use of reflection.
             (3) This is false reassurance.
             (4) Same as answer number three.

5–8   * (1) This is an example of reflective technique; it focuses on the patient's feelings and encourages verbalization.
             (2) Although this may encourage the patient to talk more, it focuses on the content of what the patient said rather than the emotional theme.
             (3) This denies the patient's feelings.
             (4) Same as answer number three.

5–9   (1) This is not true. Many medical terms use more than one root word. For example, leukocytopenia has two root words, "leuk" and "cyt." "Penia" is a suffix. In leukocytopenia the root words and suffix are joined by using the combining vowel "o."
             (2) This is not true. A combining vowel is not used before a suffix that begins with a vowel. For example, "hepat" (the root word for "liver") can be combined with "ic" (the suffix for "pertaining to") to produce "hepatic" without using a combining vowel.
           * (3) This is true. For example, "ic" in gastric is an adjective ending and "ia" in gastria is a noun ending.
             (4) This is not true. A combining vowel is used to link a root word to a suffix that begins with a consonant. This reduces the awkwardness of pronunciation. For example, "lithotripsy" is easier to pronounce than "lithtripsy."

5–10   * (1) Gloves are a barrier against body secretions and are used with universal (standard) precautions.
             (2) This protects the patient from the caregiver.
             (3) This is unreasonable and inappropriate; some patients need assistance with meeting their needs.
             (4) This is unsafe; the caregiver is still exposed to body secretions if not wearing gloves.

5–11   (1) A suffix is added to the end, not the beginning, of a word root or combining form to alter its meaning. For example, the suffix "ism" can be combined with the word root "alcohol" to form the word "alcoholism." Hyper is a prefix, not a suffix.
           * (2) Hyper is a prefix. A prefix is added to the beginning of a word root to alter its meaning or create a new word. For example, the prefix "hyper" can be combined with "tension" to form the word "hypertension."
             (3) A word root is the foundation of a word. "Hyper," a prefix, would precede a word root to alter its meaning or create a new word. For example, in the word "preoperative," "pre" is the prefix and "operative" is the word root.
             (4) A combining form is a word root plus a vowel which has been added to another word root or suffix to make the word easier to pronounce. For example, in the word "colonoscopy," "colon" is the word root and "o" is the combining vowel. Together they are the combining form "colono." When the combining form "colono" is joined with the suffix "scopy" it forms the word "colonoscopy."

5–12   (1) A solution is hypertonic when the total electrolyte content is 375 mEq/L or greater.

(2) A solution is hypotonic when the total electrolyte content is below 250 mEq/L.

* (3) A solution is isotonic when the total electrolyte content is approximately 310 mEq/L; normal saline (sodium chloride) is isotonic.

(4) This refers to excessive levels of hydrogen ions in the blood affecting pH values and is not directly related to sodium.

5–13   (1) This is unsafe; restriction of movement or manipulation of limbs during the tonic-clonic phase of a seizure could result in fractures or soft tissue damage.

(2) The patient will not breathe until the tonic-clonic phase of the seizure is over. Physical safety is the priority at this time.

(3) Same as answer number one.

* (4) Physical safety is the priority. The patient's uncontrolled movements could result in injury if environmental obstacles are not removed from the patient's immediate vicinity.

5–14   (1) This provides for privacy, but if the caregiver's hands are not clean they will contaminate the door.

* (2) Between patients and before providing care, the caregiver must wash the hands to remove dirt and microorganisms, otherwise equipment and the patient will be affected by cross contamination; medical asepsis is a priority.

(3) This provides for privacy, but if the caregiver's hands are not clean they will contaminate the curtain.

(4) This provides for privacy and prevents chilling, but if the caregiver's hands are not clean they will contaminate the linen and patient.

5–15   * (1) Polydipsia (excessive thirst) and polyuria (excessive excretion of urine) are both associated with diabetes mellitus (DM).

(2) Polydipsia is associated with DM; however, polyplegia (paralysis of several muscles) is not related to DM.

(3) Polyuria is associated with DM; however, polycythemia (an increase in the total red blood cell mass) is not related to DM.

(4) Both polycythemia and polyplegia are unrelated to DM.

5–16   (1) With hemorrhage the skin would be cold and clammy, not warm and dry, and the pulse would be weak and thready, not bounding.

(2) Because of the reduced blood volume associated with hemorrhage the blood pressure would be decreased, not increased, and the pulse would be weak and thready, not bounding.

(3) With hemorrhage the blood pressure would be decreased, not increased, and the skin would be cold and clammy, not warm and dry.

* (4) Because of the decreased blood volume associated with hemorrhage, there would be a reduced blood pressure and weak thready pulse; because of the autonomic nervous system response and the constriction of peripheral blood vessels, the skin would become cold and clammy.

5–17   (1) This denies the patient's feelings about death and cuts off further communication.

(2) This abdicates the responsibility to explore the patient's feelings to the physician; it cuts off communication and does not meet the patient's immediate need to discuss fears of death.

* (3) This uses reflective technique because it focuses on the underlying feeling expressed in the patient's statement.

(4) Same as answer number one.

5–18   (1) This is a Pollyanna-like response that provides false reassurance.

(2) Although this is a true statement, it cuts off communication and does not present an intervention to help limit the discomfort.

* (3) This recognizes the pain and offers an intervention to help limit the discomfort.

(4) This would be inappropriate at this time; analgesics should be administered if the pain is acute or continues after the exercises are completed; also the caregiver does not know if pain medication was given before the coughing and deep breathing to make this activity more tolerable for the patient.

5–19   * (1) This is correct. When a body extremity is being adducted it is being moved toward the midline of the body (medial or midsagittal plane).

(2) Visceral pertains to the covering of an organ, not to movement toward the midline of the body.

(3) Abduction pertains to movement away from the midline of the body.

(4) Lateral pertains to a side of a structure.

5–20   (1) Safety and security needs, the second level of needs according to Maslow, are met when the patient is protected from harm.

(2) Same as answer number one.

(3) Self-esteem needs are met when the patient is treated with dignity and respect.

* (4) Being free from pain or discomfort is a basic physiological need; changing position reduces muscle tension, reduces pressure, increases local circulation, and limits pain or discomfort.

6

Testing Formats Other Than Multiple-Choice Questions

In previous chapters, the multiple-choice question was discussed in detail. In this chapter testing formats other than multiple-choice questions are presented. Test questions can be classified as structured-response questions, restricted-response questions, extended essay questions, or performance appraisals. A **structured-response question** requires you to select the correct answer from among available alternatives. Multiple-choice, true-false, and matching items are examples of structured-response questions. A **restricted-response question** requires you to write a short answer. The response is expected to be a word, phrase, or sentence. Short-answer and completion items are examples of restricted-response questions. An **extended essay question** requires you to generate the answer, via a free-response format, in reply to a question or problem that is presented. A **performance appraisal** presents a structured situation and requires you to demonstrate a skill. When the teacher formulates these questions and when the student is challenged to respond to these questions decisions must be made.

Teachers make many decisions that influence students. Some decisions are instructional decisions. What teaching strategies should be used to teach certain content? Some decisions are curricular decisions. What information should be included in a unit of instruction? The decisions that teachers make that precipitate the most anxiety for most students are the measurement and evaluation decisions. What does the student know? What can the student do? To make these decisions, teachers use tests to appraise progress toward curricular goals, assess mastery of a skill, or evaluate knowledge of what was taught in a course. Three factors are involved in making measurement and evaluation decisions.

- What is the knowledge or ability that is to be measured? Generally, that which is most important or relevant is measured. Examples include the range of normal vital signs in an adult, the principles of patient teaching, legal and ethical implications of health-care delivery, obtaining a blood pressure, and patient safety. You can usually surmise what is most significant by the emphasis placed on the material. Content in a textbook that is highlighted, boldfaced, capitalized, or repeated several times is usually important. Information that appears in the textbook and is incorporated into the teacher's classroom instruction is also significant. Concepts that are introduced in the classroom setting and then applied in a classroom laboratory or clinical setting are critical concepts. You can often predict the content that will be on a test and therefore use your study time more efficiently.

- How can the identified knowledge or ability be measured? A set of operations must be devised to isolate and display the knowledge or ability that is to be measured. Examples include multiple-choice questions, true-false questions, completion items, matching columns, extended essay questions, and the performance of a procedure. To feel in control when taking tests you should be familiar with the various testing formats. Dealing with a particular test format is a skill and to develop a skill you must practice. Student workbooks, practice questions at the end of chapters, and books devoted to testing usually contain practice questions. Practice answering these questions. Experience promotes learning and practice makes perfect.

- How can the results of the devised operations be measured or expressed in quantitative terms? In other words, the unit of measure that indicates a passing grade or an acceptable performance must be identified by the instructor. Examples of acceptable results include a grade within 10% of the average grade in the class, a grade of 80%, or the correct performance of previously identified steps (critical elements) of a procedure. When taking tests, you should be aware of the criteria for scoring the test. A variety of questions can be asked. What is the passing grade? How many points are allocated to each question? Can partial credit be received for an answer? Is there a penalty for guessing? What are the critical steps in a procedure? Answers to these and other questions can help you make decisions such as how much time to devote to certain questions or whether or not to guess at an answer.

When confronted by tests with a variety of testing formats, you must make decisions. First, to make informed decisions when answering test questions, you must build a body of knowledge and understand the principles and concepts related to the content being tested. Second, it is important for you to understand the different testing formats to apply this knowledge effectively.

STRUCTURED-RESPONSE QUESTIONS

A structured-response item is one that asks a question and requires you to select an answer from among the options presented. These items include multiple-choice, true-false, and matching-column questions. They usually are efficient, dependable, and objective. Because multiple-choice questions are discussed elsewhere in the book, just true-false and matching-column questions will be presented here.

TRUE-FALSE QUESTIONS

A true-false question is known as an alternate-response item. You are presented with a question but only two choices are given from which to select an answer. This item frequently is used to test knowledge of facts because the response must be unequivocally true or false. It can be a challenging question because no frame of reference is supplied. The question is usually constructed out of context and the truth or falsity of the statement can be difficult to evaluate. However, true-false questions can be to your advantage because you have a 50% chance of getting the answer right. If you do not know the answer and there is no penalty for guessing, make a guess based on partial knowledge or flip a coin. Never leave a blank answer if there is no penalty for guessing.

SAMPLE ITEM 6–1	Antihypertensive medications reduce blood pressure. True _____ False _____

SAMPLE ITEM 6–2	A wound heals by primary intention when the wound's edges are approximated. True _____ False _____

SAMPLE ITEM 6–3	When blood leaves the left ventricle it enters the ascending vena cava. True _____ False _____

SAMPLE ITEM 6–4	Battery is a deliberate attempt or threat to touch another person without consent. True _____ False _____

Variations of true-false items have been developed to increase clarity, obtain more information about what you know, and limit guessing. **Highlighting a word or phrase in the question** is a simple variation that helps to reduce ambiguity and increase clarity. This technique also can be used by you when answering true-false questions that are not highlighted. Underlining key words as well as words that modify key words focuses attention on the most important part of the statement.

| SAMPLE ITEM 6–5 | Antiseptics **kill** bacteria.
True _____ False _____ |

| SAMPLE ITEM 6–6 | When placed in the supine position patients should be **lying on their backs**.
True _____ False _____ |

Grouping short true-false items under a common question is a variation of the true-false question that attempts to cluster related information together. It is an efficient way to assess knowledge about related categories, classifications, or characteristics. Each statement that is being evaluated as to whether it is true or false must be considered in relation to the original question. This variation increases clarity because it reduces the amount of reading and provides a greater frame of reference for evaluating each statement.

| SAMPLE ITEM 6–7 | Indicate if the following choices are true or false in relation to the introductory statement. A person infected with the AIDS virus (HIV) can transmit the virus to another person when:

(1) Sneezing and coughing
　　True _____ False _____
(2) Shaking hands
　　True _____ False _____
(3) Having sexual intercourse
　　True _____ False _____
(4) Breastfeeding
　　True _____ False _____ |

| SAMPLE ITEM 6–8 | Signify whether or not each of the following procedures uses the principle of gravity.

(1) A sterile dressing
　　True _____ False _____
(2) The high-Fowler's position
　　True _____ False _____
(3) Oral-pharyngeal suctioning
　　True _____ False _____
(4) A urinary catheter (Foley catheter)
　　True _____ False _____ |

Requiring the test taker to correct false statements is another variation of the true-false question. In this type of question, you are instructed to rewrite the question whenever the statement is identified as false. This approach ensures that you understand the information underlying a false statement. It also reduces guessing because you will get credit only if able to revise the question to make it an accurate statement. This variation is sometimes combined with the true-false variation that highlights a word or phase in the original question.

SAMPLE ITEM 6–9	If you signify that a statement is false, revise the statement so that it is accurate. The normal range of respirations for an adult is 17 to 22 breaths per minute. True _____ False _____

SAMPLE ITEM 6–10	Correct the underlined word if the statement is false. The organ of Corti is concerned with <u>sight</u>. True _____ False _____

True-false items can be asked in relation to specific stimulus material presented along with the question. This variation of the true-false question provides a frame of reference for you by including a stimulus such as a graft, map, chart, or table. Straight memorization of facts usually is not adequate for answering these types of questions because they test comprehension, interpretation, application, and reasoning abilities rather than just the recall of information.

SAMPLE ITEM 6–11	The accompanying line drawing represents ECG inflections. Determine if each statement is true or false in relation to the graft.

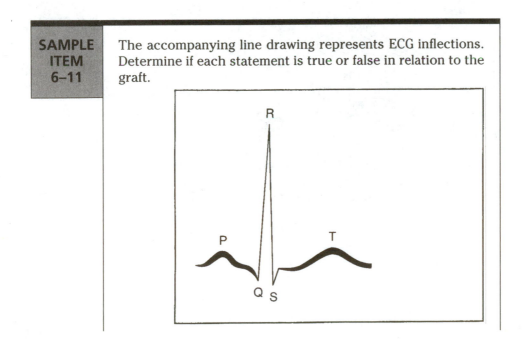

(1) The inflection marked P represents atrial contraction.
True _____ False _____

(2) The length of the QRS complex is within normal limits.
True _____ False _____

(3) The T wave should occur between the P and Q inflections, not the S and P inflections.
True _____ False _____

SAMPLE ITEM 6–12

The picture illustrates the Food Guide Pyramid: a guide to daily food choices. Identify if the following statements accurately or inaccurately reflect the information presented in the pyramid.

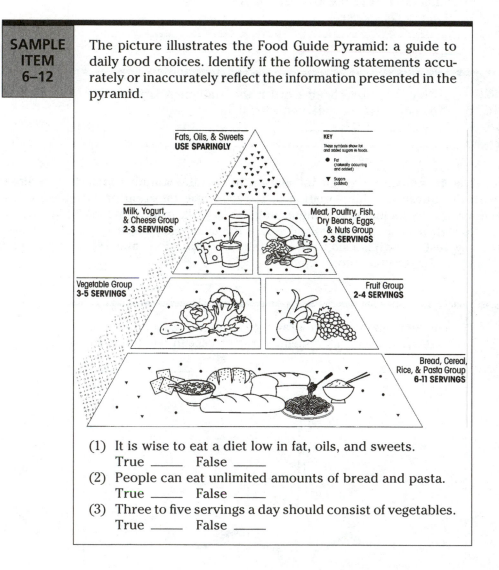

(1) It is wise to eat a diet low in fat, oils, and sweets.
True _____ False _____

(2) People can eat unlimited amounts of bread and pasta.
True _____ False _____

(3) Three to five servings a day should consist of vegetables.
True _____ False _____

MATCHING QUESTIONS

A matching question uses a double-column format. It presents several problem statements in one column and then requires you to select an answer for each statement from a common list of possible options. Sometimes the items in the two columns are equal in number and other times one column will have more options than the other column. There are unique problems when the columns are equal in length. For example, if the columns have six items each and you know five of the answers then you will automatically get the last answer correct, whether or not the information is understood. On the other hand, if you make an incorrect choice then you will automatically get two answers wrong. These problems can be minimized if the response column has more options than the question column. The matching question is a relatively superficial measurement technique that lends itself to factual information. The statements in the first column may be unrelated but more often than not the questions usually assess knowledge about related categories, classifications, or characteristics. You must read the directions carefully because the basis for the matching should be specified. For example, you should be directed where to place the correct answer and told the number of times an option can be selected.

SAMPLE ITEM 6–13

Column I contains abbreviations commonly used in the delivery of health care. Match the abbreviation to its correct meaning in column II. Place the number you select from column II on the line at the right of the abbreviation in column I. Use each letter and number only once.

Column I	*Column II*
a. b.i.d. _____	1. Three times a day
b. ad lib. _____	2. Nothing by mouth
c. t.i.d. _____	3. Freely, as desired
d. NPO _____	4. Twice a day
e. a.c. _____	5. When required
f. p.r.n. _____	6. Before meals
	7. Immediately

SAMPLE ITEM 6–14

Column I lists parts of the body associated with digestion. Match a part of the body with its **secretion**. Indicate in the space provided the number from column I that matches the letter in column II. Options from column I can be used more than once.

Column I	*Column II*	
1. Liver	a. Bile	_____
2. Stomach	b. Insulin	_____
3. Pancreas	c. Trypsin	_____
4. Gallbladder	d. Ptyalin	_____
5. Small intestine	e. Secretin	_____
6. Salivary gland	f. Cholecystokinin-pancreozymin	_____

To best answer matching questions you should first match items that are clearly recognized as correct matches. This eliminates options that you have correctly matched leaving a reduced list on which to focus. Now assess the remaining options moving from the simple to the complex as determined by your frame of reference. Another strategy would be to cover one column and try to identify the correct answer without being cued by the second column. By doing this you may become less confused or distracted by the list of options. If you do not know the answer and there is no penalty for guessing, make an educated guess.

RESTRICTED-RESPONSE QUESTIONS

Restricted-response questions, also known as free-response items, require you to produce the response to the question or problem that is proposed. The response can be a word, a phrase, or even several sentences in length. Short-answer or completion questions are examples of restricted-response questions. These types of questions usually have an uncomplicated, direct format and are most effective for evaluating the comprehension of simple concepts, the definition of terms, the knowledge of facts, and the ability to solve quantitative problems.

COMPLETION QUESTIONS

A completion question is usually a short statement with one or more blanks that have to be filled in. In a completion question, the key word or words are omitted. You are directed to focus on the important concept addressed in the question rather than trivia. This type of question does not permit much flexibility in the response. The question is expecting a particular word or phrase that will produce an accurate statement.

SAMPLE ITEM 6–15	The purpose of the gallbladder is to store _____ .

SAMPLE ITEM 6–16	An otoscope is an instrument used to inspect the _____ .

SAMPLE ITEM 6–17	When performing one-person cardiopulmonary resuscitation the rescuer provides _____ external cardiac compressions coordinated with _____ breaths.

The **provision of two possible answers to fill in the blank** is a simple variation of a completion question. When this format is used it mimics an alternate-response question because you are presented with a question and two choices are given from which to select an answer. This type of question is to your advantage because the words presented jog the memory and the chance of selecting the correct response is 50%.

SAMPLE ITEM 6–18	Washing the hands is an example of (surgical/medical) asepsis.

SAMPLE ITEM 6–19	The pulse (deficit/pressure) is the difference between the apical and radial pulse rates.

SHORT-ANSWER QUESTIONS

A short-answer question is a free-response question because it asks a question and expects you to formulate the answer. This type of question provides some flexibility because the response does not have to complete a sentence or fill in a blank. You usually can use anywhere from one word to several sentences to answer the question. By being able to include more information in the response, you can better demonstrate understanding of the content being tested. When a short-answer question needs only a word or a phrase to answer the question it is similar to a completion question, but the question is a complete sentence rather than an incomplete sentence. When a short-answer question requires several sentences to answer the question, it goes beyond the requirements of a completion question but it still focuses on the knowledge of facts, terminology, simple concepts, and the ability to perform mathematical manipulations. Completion questions and short-answer questions can be used interchangeably to address the same content. When reviewing the sample items in this section compare Sample Items 6–15 through 6–19 with Sample Items 6–20 through 6–24, respectively.

SAMPLE ITEM 6–20	What purpose does the gallbladder serve in the human body?

SAMPLE ITEM 6–21	What instrument can be used to inspect the ear canal and tympanic membrane?

SAMPLE ITEM 6–22	What is the ratio of external cardiac compressions to rescue breaths when performing one-person cardiopulmonary resuscitation?

SAMPLE ITEM 6–23	Washing the hands is an example of what kind of asepsis?

SAMPLE ITEM 6–24	How does a healthcare provider determine if a patient has a pulse deficit?

SAMPLE ITEM 6–25	The physician orders aspirin grains $\times$ po t.i.d. for a patient with the diagnosis of rheumatoid arthritis. Each aspirin tablet contains 5 grains. How many tablets should be administered?

SAMPLE ITEM 6–26	Define the term *tachycardia*.

SAMPLE ITEM 6–27	How do open-ended questions promote communication?

Completion questions do not lend themselves to test-taking strategies. However, write as much as the format permits in the hope that what you include answers the question and contains the information desired by the teacher. If there is no penalty for guessing, it is to your advantage to make an educated guess.

EXTENDED ESSAY QUESTIONS

An extended essay is a free-response question because the answer is formulated by you in response to a question. Essay questions require you to select, arrange, organize, integrate, synthesize, compare, or contrast information. Also, they require an ability to use language effectively, to be creative when solving problems, and to utilize cognitive skills at the application and analysis levels. The extended essay is most appropriate for evaluating mastery of complex material.

When writing responses to extended essay questions, it is wise to follow a three-part format when possible. The introduction should, in a general way, indicate what will be discussed. The central part of the answer should explore all the information that is being presented to answer the question. The summary should recap what was discussed and come to a conclusion. When organizing the information to be included in the central part of the answer, make a topical outline of the important facts. This promotes a sequential flow, ensures that important information is included, and prevents tangents.

Generally, instructors look at your writing from the perspective of "writing for evaluation." Instructors evaluate the acquisition of knowledge via assessment of an end product, the term paper or essay question on an examination. However, for you to improve your writing you need to view writing from the perspectives of **learning to write** and **writing to learn**. You need to practice writing by writing to explore, express, analyze, and critique without an end product as the goal but with a **focus on the process**. There is no easy way to acquire effective writing skills without practice. Most postsecondary institutions today have writing centers that provide specialized faculty to assist you with activities associated with learning to write and writing to learn.

When **learning to write** you learn the techniques of brainstorming, drafting, revising, and editing to eventually improve the end product. You also must focus on organizational and analytical skills that enable you to inform, instruct, argue a point of view, challenge new and old theories, and evaluate. Stated simply, you need to develop critical thinking. Critical thinking is an essential skill needed to process the composition that is to be written. Free-writing promotes critical thinking and the ability to write. Brainstorming is a form of free-writing. Making lists of words or phrases that relate to a topic allows writers to explore a topic and their perspectives of the topic. For example, when students were asked to make a list of everything and anything relevant to patient progress notes, interesting insights developed. Some students were content oriented, listing all those things a healthcare provider should include in progress notes such as vital signs, specific care provided, and patients' responses to care. Other students were process oriented, stating notes should be specific, legible, and comprehensive. This activity can be carried a step further and involves analyzing and ranking the items on the list to develop prioritizing skills. Writing a journal (diary) is another form of free-writing. When using this strategy the focus should be on the use of words, the expression of ideas, and the documentation of activities and no emphasis should be placed on format, grammar, or punctuation. Another writing activity involves analyzing and revising previously written compositions. The hardest thing to overcome when engaging in learning-to-write activities is the feeling that because you may not have necessarily completed a product, you have not learned. It would be wise to explore with a faculty member in the writing center at your institution how you can enhance your ability to write.

When **writing to learn** you go well beyond the process of writing. You also learn the course content you are writing about and discover what you know, what you need to know, and what you think about certain topics. When you are writing to learn, you are writing for yourself and what you learn is the end product. In early education you may have written spelling words 10 times to promote memorization through writing. When learning more complex material there are various activities that promote writing to learn. Journals can be written to summarize reactions to clinical experiences or compare clinical experiences with classroom instruction. Class notes on one side of a page can be augmented by adding relevant information from the textbook to the other side of the page. Lists can be written to identify commonalities and differences among curricular content. Posing and answering questions can lead to a better understanding of the content as well as improve your critical thinking skills. When writing to learn you learn content by the very act of writing.

SAMPLE ITEM 6–28	Compare and contrast medical and surgical asepsis and give three examples of each.

PERFORMANCE APPRAISAL

A performance appraisal evaluates the ability to execute a procedure. Psychomotor skills, the motor effects of mental processes, are most appropriately assessed by performance appraisals. Measuring a blood pressure, obtaining a blood specimen, removing contaminated gloves, and performing cardiopulmonary resuscitation are examples of psychomotor skills. When these skills are tested, the criteria for passing should be identified before you attempt the procedure. For example, when obtaining a blood pressure reading the criteria might be that you must obtain accurate systolic and diastolic readings. In another testing situation the criteria for passing might be previously identified steps of the procedure such as washes hands, checks functioning of equipment, identifies the patient, evenly places cuff around the upper arm, palpates brachial artery, places stethoscope over brachial artery, inflates cuff 20 mm Hg above palpated systolic reading, deflates cuff at 2 to 3 mm Hg per second, obtains accurate systolic reading, obtains accurate diastolic reading, and waits 2 minutes before reinflating cuff if procedure needs to be performed a second time. It may be required to perform one or more of these steps (critical elements) or additional steps identified by the evaluator to receive a passing score. These criteria are very specific. Other criteria may be more general. For example, when obtaining a blood pressure reading you must maintain medical asepsis, provide for physical safety, and ensure privacy. These requirements are less specific because there are numerous ways to meet each of these criteria. For example, privacy can be provided by closing a door, pulling a curtain, or using adequate draping. Performance appraisals should be objective and the criteria for an acceptable performance identified. Clinical techniques and skills textbooks are helpful when practicing procedures and preparing for performance appraisals. A clinical-skills check list of step-by-step-elements can be used by another student to assess your performance of a psychomotor skill in a laboratory setting. This is a nonthreatening way to practice and it supports reciprocal study relationships. It also provides an opportunity to simulate a testing situation and helps with desensitization, which may promote a feeling of control.

SUMMARY

To increase success when confronted by an examination with a variety of testing formats, it is wise to be familiar with the different formats. Structured-response, restricted-response, extended essay, and performance appraisal formats have some commonalities but each is unique. Pre-tests and post-tests that are presented within chapters in textbooks, student workbooks that accompany textbooks, and textbooks that help students prepare for examinations should be used to practice test-taking skills. Understanding the commonalities and differences in testing formats and employing various test-taking strategies enhance a feeling of control, which contributes to a positive mental attitude.

ANSWERS AND RATIONALES FOR SAMPLE ITEMS IN CHAPTER 6

6–1   True—Antihypertensive agents, such as vasodilators, reduce blood pressure by reducing resistance to blood flow via relaxation of peripheral blood vessels.

6–2   True—Primary intention healing, also known as primary union or first intention healing, occurs when the tissue surfaces are close together.

6–3   False—When blood leaves the left ventricle it enters the arch of the aorta.

6–4   False—Battery is the deliberate touching of another person against his or her will. In relation to healthcare delivery, the deliberate attempt or threat to touch another person without consent is known as assault.

6–5   False—Antiseptics are chemical substances that inhibit the growth of bacteria. Germicides and sterilization techniques kill bacteria.

6–6   True—The supine position, also known as the back-lying or dorsal position, requires the person to be lying on the back with the arms extended along the sides of the body.

6–7   (1) False—Although the HIV has been found in saliva it is not transmitted via the airborne route.
        (2) False—The HIV is transmitted via certain body secretions not just by touching.
        (3) True—The HIV is found in semen and vaginal secretions and sexual intercourse is one of the main routes of transmission of HIV.
        (4) True—The HIV is found in breast milk and studies have demonstrated transmission from mother to infant via this route.

6–8   (1) False—The application of a sterile dressing follows the principles of surgical asepsis.
        (2) True—When in the high-Fowler's position the head and trunk are raised 90 degrees and the abdominal organs drop by gravity, limiting pressure against the diaphragm. Gravity also pulls the diaphragm downward, facilitating greater expansion of the lungs.

(3) False—Suctioning uses negative pressure to remove fluid from the body.

(4) True—A urinary catheter, also known as a retention or indwelling catheter, is inserted through the urethra into the urinary bladder and left in the bladder to drain urine into a collection bag. It uses gravity, the force that draws all masses in the earth's sphere toward the center of the earth.

6–9   False—The statement can be revised two different ways. The normal range of respirations for a child 10 to 14 years of age is 17 to 22 breaths per minute or the normal range of respirations for an adult is 15 to 20 breaths per minute. Either of these revisions would result in an accurate statement.

6–10   False—To revise this question as directed, the word "sight" must be changed to "hearing." You would not receive credit for this question if "organ of Corti" was changed to "optic nerve." Although this statement would be accurate, it did not follow the instructions for revising the statement.

6–11   (1) True—The P wave arises from a stimulus from the sinoatrial (SA) node and represents atrial muscle depolarization (atrial contraction).

(2) False—The QRS complex represents ventricular muscle depolarization (ventricular contraction) and is normally 0.04 to 0.10 second in duration. The QRS complex depicted in the line drawing exceeds this length.

(3) False—The T wave normally occurs between the QRS complex and the next P wave. The T wave represents ventricular muscle repolarization. The T wave could not occur between the P and Q inflections because the ventricles have not yet depolarized.

6–12   (1) True—The US Department of Agriculture advocates that fat, oils, and sweets should be used sparingly in a healthy diet. This group of food appears at the apex of the pyramid.

(2) False—The Food Guide Pyramid suggests that a healthy diet should include a daily intake of 6 to 11, not unlimited, servings of bread, cereal, rice, and pasta. This group of food is the foundation of the pyramid.

(3) True—The guide to daily food choices advises people to eat three to five servings of vegetables per day. This food group, along with the fruit group, forms the second level of the pyramid.

6–13   a. __4__ b.i.d. means *bis in die* or two times a day.
b. __3__ ad lib. means *ad libitum* or freely as desired.
c. __1__ t.i.d. means *ter in die* or three times a day
d. __2__ NPO means *nil per os* or nothing by mouth
e. __6__ a.c. means *ante cibum* or before meals
f. __5__ p.r.n. means *pro re nata* or when required
Stat, which means *statim* or immediately (option seven) was an extra option included in column II that did not have a matching abbreviation in column I.

6–14   a. (1) Bile, secreted by the liver and stored in the gallbladder, emulsifies ingested fats and facilitates their digestion and absorption.

b. (3) Insulin is secreted by the beta cells of the islets of Langerhans in the pancreas. Insulin regulates the metabolism of glucose, proteins, carbohydrates, and fats.

c. (3) Trypsin, a pancreatic digestive enzyme, aids in the digestion of starch.

    d. (6) Ptyalin, also known as salivary amylase, is an enzyme in saliva that is secreted by the salivary glands.

    e. (5) Secretin is secreted by the mucosa in the upper portion of the small intestine. Secretin stimulates the secretion of bicarbonate in pancreatic juice and inhibits the secretion of gastric acid.

    f. (5) Cholecystokinin-pancreozymin (CCK-PZ) is released from the cells in the upper small intestine and causes contraction of the gallbladder and releases digestive enzymes from the pancreas.

The gallbladder in column I did not match any of the options in column II because it does not secrete bile, it just serves as a storage depot for bile.

6–15   **Bile** is the only acceptable answer to this question. The gallbladder, a pear-shaped organ located below the liver, serves as a storage place for bile.

6–16   The **ear**, **ear canal**, or **tympanic membrane** would all be acceptable answers to this question. An otoscope is an instrument, which has an internal light source and various sizes of specula, that can be used to visualize the ear canal and tympanic membrane.

6–17   The correct answers for this question are **15** and **2**. The American Heart Association guidelines for single-rescuer cardiopulmonary resuscitation indicate that there should be a ratio of 15 external cardiac compressions to two rescue breaths.

6–18   The correct answer is medical asepsis. Medical asepsis limits the number, growth, and transmission of microorganisms. Surgical asepsis renders or maintains objects or sites free of all microorganisms and their spores.

6–19   The correct answer is pulse deficit. The difference between the apical and radial pulse rates is known as the pulse deficit. A pulse deficit usually indicates the presence of a dysrhythmia. The pulse pressure is the difference between the systolic and diastolic pressures of a blood pressure reading. A widening pulse pressure may indicate increasing intracranial pressure.

6–20   Acceptable answers include: the gallbladder stores bile; the gallbladder stores bile that is secreted by the liver. Compare this item with Sample Item 6–15.

6–21   Acceptable answers include: an otoscope; an otoscope with a light source. Compare this item with Sample Item 6–16.

6–22   Acceptable answers include: 15:2; 15 cardiac compressions 1.5 to 2 inches in depth must be coordinated with two rescue breaths. Compare this item with Sample Item 6–17.

6–23   Acceptable answers include: medical asepsis; washing the hands is an example of medical asepsis, which limits the number and transmission of microorganisms. Compare this item with Sample Item 6–18.

6–24   Acceptable answers include: by determining if there is a difference between the apical and radial pulses; auscultate the apical pulse and palpate the radial pulse and if the number for the radial pulse is less than the number for the apical pulse then the patient has a pulse deficit. Compare this item with Sample Item 6–19.

6–25 To arrive at the correct answer you would have to perform the following calculation. Using ratio and proportion:

$$\frac{\text{Desired}}{\text{Have}} \quad \frac{10 \text{ grains}}{5 \text{ grains}} \quad \frac{x \text{ tablets}}{1 \text{ tablet}}$$

$$5x = 10$$

$$x = \frac{10}{5}$$

$$x = 2 \text{ tablets}$$

6–26 The following is an example of an answer that you might write: *Tachycardia is a dysrhythmia characterized by a rapid but regular heart rate in excess of 90 beats per minute. Tachycardia is precipitated by physical and emotional stress and may indicate cardiopulmonary disease.* There can be numerous variations of this answer but the important facts to include in the definition of tachycardia are that it is a dysrhythmia, it has a regular rhythm, and it has a heart rate greater than 90 beats per minute.

6–27 The following is an example of an answer that you might write: *Open-ended questions promote communication because they are nonjudgmental, nondirected questions that invite patients to explore, elaborate, or clarify their concerns or feelings. These questions give patients control over the topics being discussed and the extent of information they reveal.* There can be a variety of answers to this question but important concepts to include are nondirective questions are used by the interviewer, patients are encouraged to explore personal concerns, and patients can discuss concerns to the extent they decide is appropriate.

6–28 To answer this question use the three part format.

INTRODUCTION: The introduction actually introduces the topic to be discussed. It functions as a preface or prologue for what will follow.
The chain of infection has six links: the microorganism; the source of the microorganism; the portal of exit from the source; the mode of transmission; the portal of entry into the body; and a susceptible host. Medical and surgical asepsis are techniques that can be used to interrupt this chain of infection and prevent disease. The commonalities and differences of medical and surgical asepsis will be discussed and examples of each will be presented.

CENTRAL PART: The central part of the answer presents and explores the information necessary to answer the question. Make a topical outline of the facts to be included and then write a narrative that incorporates and elaborates on the information in the outline.
Definition of asepsis
*   Free from infection*
*   Free from infectious material*
Definition of medical asepsis
*   Confines microorganisms to a specific area*
*   Limits the number, growth, and transmission of microorganisms*
*   Concepts of clean and dirty*

Examples of medical aseptic techniques and rationales for why they are effective

    Universal (standard) precautions

    Wearing a mask for respiratory isolation (droplet and airborne precautions)

    Placing a container lid upside down on the counter

Definition of surgical asepsis

    Destroys all microorganisms and their spores

    Keeps an area or object free of microorganisms

Examples of surgical aseptic techniques and rationales for why they are effective

    A sterile field must be kept within view

    Objects placed on a sterile field must be sterile

    Packages containing sterile objects must be dry and intact

SUMMARY: The summary should briefly recap or review the general tone of the discussion and come to one or more conclusions. It serves to formally close the response to the essay question.

Microorganisms are constantly in our environment and therefore patients and healthcare providers are continuously at risk. To break the chain of infection, medical and surgical aseptic techniques need to be employed in the delivery of health care. Preventing infection and maintaining the health of patients, their families, and healthcare providers are priorities.

Computer Applications in Education and Practice

The embracing of computers in American society in industry, educational settings, and private homes makes it imperative that people have a basic fluency in the use of a computer to survive in today's world. It is clear that emerging healthcare reform initiatives will accelerate the use of computers in the healthcare setting to plan, facilitate, and manage professional clinical practice. Students preparing for a healthcare profession should have at least a basic knowledge of computers to take advantage of computer-assisted instruction offered within the educational setting, know how computers are presently being used within their own discipline, have the basic skills to manage computers in a comfortable manner, and be willing to be a learner to keep pace with rapidly advancing computer technology. Also, in the future licensing and certification examinations required by specific healthcare disciplines could become computerized. In 1994 the profession of nursing moved to a computer adaptive testing format for the evaluation of graduate nurses seeking licensure (NCLEX-RN) in the United States and its territories.

Computing across the curriculum is not new in the educational setting. Educators have long recognized the potential of interactive technology to enhance teaching and learning. Programmed instructional textbooks were the forerunner of computer programs in which frames of information contained a narrative text that generally required a successful response for the learner to move on to the next narrative frame. Computers enabled the programmed approach to become more interactive by increasing the potential, richness, and variety of frame styles that improved the effectiveness of the lesson. Graphics and the use of color and sound grab the attention of the learner in a way that programmed instruction textbooks were unable to do because of the limitations of the written format.

Students generally enjoy working with computer programs to enhance learning because programs hold their attention, support classroom material, require active participation, provide immediate feedback, challenge the student, make learning fun, are accessible, and never become impatient. The greatest advantage of computer-assisted instruction is that the learner becomes an active participant and is not just a passive spectator. However, the use of computer-assisted instruction will be only as valuable as the student is successful. Most computer-assisted instructional programs require a simple understanding of a few essential keyboard keys. Also, students must be committed to learning and willing to be active participants in their own learning. In some disciplines the potential for learning via a computer is limited by the availability of computer hardware and appropriate software. The availability of programs depends on administrators and faculty members recognizing the potential of computer-assisted instruction within specific disciplines, demonstrating a commitment to seeking funds to procure or create programs, providing accessibility to program use, and committing to evaluating the effectiveness of programs. Programs need to be evaluated in terms of cost and benefits, which inherently includes whether or not students achieve the learning objectives. Administrators and faculty members must take an active role in this process if computer-assisted instructional materials are to be made available to students. Computer-assisted instruction is not designed to replace the more traditional forms of instruction but to augment learning methods to encourage students to review difficult material at their own rate, increase creative inquiry and experimentation, and provide opportunities for independent study. Computer-assisted instruction has generally been well received in the educational setting, however, there are a few disadvantages. Some students' learning styles do not lend themselves to linear and structured learning, that is, information presented in one dimension. Other students cannot maintain the level of concentration necessary to generate the attention to detail that is required to complete the task of a program. And in some disciplines, programs are limited in number or may not present the depth and breadth of content desired by faculty or students.

The following are examples of how computers can be used in the educational and practice settings. The computer can be used to develop student skills by teaching the material, using simulation programs, accessing professional resources, or using the computer to manage information.

THE COMPUTER AS AN INSTRUCTOR

Computer-assisted instruction (CAI) can present principles and theory, enhance comprehension, and provide for self-assessment and learning through a testing format.

Programs designed to transmit factual information and theory present frames that contain textual information, charts, tables, and so on. Questions may appear throughout the program to encourage the user to apply learned concepts and principles. Feedback may be provided to ensure that material has been integrated and comprehended in response to the student's answers. Some programs are designed in a linear way and others in a branching format. A linear format goes from the beginning of the program to the end of the program without deviating. The linear format presents information on a straight line with one beginning and one end. Every student is exposed to the same information.

The branching format allows students to select an individual path that focuses on information relevant to the assignment or the interest of the user.

Practice and evaluation programs also present principles and theory and enhance comprehension; however, they extend beyond the learning of information to the application of information. This type of program is sometimes called a drill and practice program.

Self-assessment programs designed in a testing format are programs that generally contain both a learning mode and a self-assessment testing mode. In the **learning mode** the student is presented with a multiple-choice question with four options and is asked to select the correct answer. Once the student selects an option the program provides immediate feedback regarding the correctness of the choice. Immediate feedback with rationales for the correct and wrong answers is provided depending on how the program is designed. The learning mode that provides rationales for all the choices has the potential to promote new learning or reinforce previous learning. The **testing mode** enables the student to conduct a self-assessment of test-taking abilities regarding a specific body of knowledge addressed in the program. The testing mode also enables the student to simulate a testing situation. Some programs provide rationales for all the options at the completion of the program. Self-assessment test-taking programs are particularly successful because they focus on competency and provide immediate feedback.

THE COMPUTER AS A SIMULATOR

Computer simulations are designed to enhance problem-solving skills. Problem-solving skills necessary to relate and integrate information into a meaningful frame of reference require competencies in the area of information processing, critical thinking, and decision making. The role of the teacher is to assist students to move beyond mere memorization of facts to the development of problem-solving and integrative skills. Simulation programs assist learners to achieve these skills.

Simulations may focus on the application of information processing skills, which assist the learner to select sources of data that are most appropriate, classify data, cluster and sequence data, and even evaluate data. Simulations may focus on components of critical thinking. A program addressing critical thinking may explore activities such as identifying relationships, recognizing commonalities and differences, and using deductive and inductive reasoning to support inferences. Simulation programs may be designed to enhance decision making by encouraging the learner to recognize the nature of the problem, choose the most appropriate of the potential alternative interventions, establish priorities, and evaluate the outcome of the final decision. Learners must recognize that because the steps of problem solving are interrelated with the components of integrated critical thinking, some of the steps overlap in nature. Simulation programs may be designed specifically to focus only on one step or all the steps of problem solving and other programs may require application of competencies related to one component or all the components of critical thinking. Computer simulators have long been used in disciplines, such as aeronautics and the use of the flight simulator, but it is in its infancy in simulating experiences within the healthcare professions. Computer-assisted instructional programs can present a patient database that requires the student to input, sort, and retrieve data. It also can present clinical events that would be difficult to present in a classroom setting or an event that the student may not have had the opportunity to experience in the clinical setting. The disadvantage of simulation programs in healthcare disciplines is that they lack sophistication to include unpredictable variables that occur in real-life situations. As software technology advances, the computer as a simulator will provide learning opportunities that replicate, as closely as possible, actual clinical situations. One of the newer advances in technology is CD-ROM (compact disk read-only memory) technology that uses a compact disk read by a laser player steered by computer software. To understand the potential of CD-ROM technology recognize that one CD-ROM disk can retain approximately three million pages of text. The future use of CD-ROM technology in the educational setting is unlimited. How this technology will be applied to the service sector still remains to be seen. Curricula cannot guarantee that each and every student will have an opportunity to experience each and every event that may be important to learning. However, computer simulation using CD-ROM technology may be able to fill this gap.

THE COMPUTER AS A RESOURCE TOOL

The computer as a resource tool enables students to acquire and send information. Databases, library resources, and networks can increase students' contact with sources of data within their field. Modems (communication devices) can connect students with learning environments that reach beyond their own home, school, or agency. Databases require the user to have an understanding of how to implement specific protocols to gain access to the desired systems. Cost is also a factor because fees are involved when maintaining telephone lines to transmit and receive information and when initiating computer searches of specific databases. The user has to decide whether these activities are cost-effective when time saved is measured against money spent. Without careful planning to identify word parameters clearly when conducting computer searches and accessing databases, a user could incur fees beyond the financial means of the average student.

THE COMPUTER AS INFORMATION MANAGER

The computer can be used for word processing, setting up spreadsheets, data processing, graphing data, and so on. Some students report that they no longer write on anything but the computer. With the use of sophisticated software the student can manipulate data, words, images, and so on to easily complete academic assignments. Healthcare agencies are already relying on computers to manage many aspects of professional service and practice, including the planning and documenting of healthcare interventions. As computers are used more frequently in the clinical setting, medical records may become completely computerized. The challenge is that users must learn the commands and functions of the systems employed by the agency. However "user friendly" programs are becoming more frequent, especially those that use touch, a stylus, or a mouse. A mouse is an instrument that permits the user to instruct the computer with a directional arrow that points to on screen commands without having the need to have strong keyboard skills.

SUMMARY

Computers are causing major changes in the traditional way things have been done in the educational and healthcare arenas. Computers have permitted the manipulation of data to become more sophisticated than ever before. In the computer age some certainties exist: computers are here to stay, computers will be used more extensively in the educational and practice settings in the future, healthcare providers must be computer literate, and if healthcare providers are to survive in the technological world in which they live they must be willing to learn about new computer technology as it emerges. The most important implication of computer applications in learning and practice is that individuals can use the computer to increase the efficiency of work and study, thereby leaving more time to interact with instructors, peers, and clients.

Practice Questions with Answers and Rationales

HEALTHCARE DELIVERY AND LEGAL ISSUES

This section encompasses factors that influence the delivery of health care. Questions address values, ethics, legal issues, patients' rights, steps in the problem-solving process (assessment, planning, implementation, and evaluation), trends in health care, and the responsibilities associated with the delivery of health care and the supervision of subordinates.

QUESTIONS

1. The person in charge directs a team member to perform a specific procedure with a patient. It has been a long time since the team member has performed this procedure. To ensure the safety of the patient, the person in charge should:
   (1) Assign the patient to someone else
   (2) Explain to the team member how to perform the procedure
   (3) Ask the team member to demonstrate how to perform the procedure
   (4) Request another team member to assist with the procedure

2. When working with patients who have dementia, are verbally and physically abusive, and are suspicious and distrustful of others, the caregiver should always:

    (1) Administer care as quickly as possible
    (2) Explain everything that is to be done
    (3) Tell patients what they want to hear
    (4) Tell patients how nice they look

3. Which of the following is a right of patients in a hospital?
    (1) Being able to smoke in their rooms
    (2) Requesting meals at the times they prefer
    (3) Refusing treatments ordered by their physician
    (4) Demanding that they be moved to private rooms

4. A caregiver breaks a patient's eyeglasses because of carelessness. What specific legal term applies to this action?
    (1) Battery
    (2) Assault
    (3) Negligence
    (4) Malpractice

5. Informed consent is a component of the Patient's Bill of Rights. Informed consent would have to be obtained from the next of kin when the patient is:
    (1) An extremely elderly woman
    (2) A 16-year-old married woman
    (3) An illiterate 48-year-old man
    (4) A very depressed 55-year-old man

6. Which of the following statements is true concerning the role of a healthcare provider in relation to a motor vehicle accident?
    (1) Legal immunity is extended to healthcare providers by the Good Samaritan law.
    (2) Healthcare providers must stop to meet the legal trust required by their professions.
    (3) Healthcare providers are responsible for the care they provide at the scene of an accident.
    (4) Immunity from prosecution is extended to healthcare providers because a contract does not exist.

7. A healthcare provider says to a patient, "You should get a second opinion because your physician is not the best." The healthcare provider could be sued for:
    (1) Libel
    (2) Assault
    (3) Slander
    (4) Negligence

8. The signature of a witness on an informed consent document indicates that the:
    (1) Physician described the procedure and its risks
    (2) Patient actually signed the consent form
    (3) Physician is protected from being sued
    (4) Patient understands the procedure

9. When obtaining a formal or informal health history the healthcare provider is performing which step in the problem-solving process?
    (1) Planning
    (2) Analysis

(3) Assessment

(4) Evaluation

10. When identifying that a patient is having difficulty breathing after an intervention, the healthcare provider has performed which step of the problem-solving process?

(1) Analysis

(2) Assessment

(3) Evaluation

(4) Implementation

11. The healthcare provider needs to recognize the patient's health beliefs prior to giving care. Therefore, the healthcare provider should first:

(1) Identify the patient's level of wellness

(2) Understand the patient's frame of reference

(3) Individualize the patient's plan of care

(4) Teach the patient acceptable values related to health

12. Ethics is specifically concerned with:

(1) Preventing a crime

(2) Protecting civil law

(3) Determining right or wrong

(4) Potentially negligent actions

13. Which of the following would support a patient's right to privacy?

(1) Leaving a crying patient alone

(2) Addressing a patient by the last name

(3) Providing information about patient care

(4) Closing the door when interviewing the patient

RATIONALES

1.   (1) This does not address the team member's need to know how to safely perform the procedure.

(2) This is unsafe; this teaching method does not take into consideration the need for the team member to practice psychomotor skills associated with this task. Explaining is not enough; a demonstration and return demonstration, meeting all the critical elements regarding principles of the procedure should be done before a person can be considered capable of performing the procedure safely.

* (3) Demonstration is the safest way to assess whether a person has the knowledge and skill to safely perform a procedure. The individual providing the care, as well as the person delegating the care, can be held responsible for a negligent act performed by the caregiver. A superior delegating care is responsible for ensuring that the person implementing the care is legally qualified and competent.

(4) A peer should not be held accountable for the care assigned to another team member; the person in charge is directly responsible for ensuring that delegated care is safely delivered to patients.

2.   (1) This does not address the right of the patient to know what is being done and why; rushing may increase the patient's anxiety.

* (2) This supports every patient's legal right to know what care is being given and why; understanding increases compliance; this is especially important with people who are paranoid.

(3) This is patronizing; when patients feel they are being humored, trust deteriorates.

(4) This may not be true; trust is based on honesty.

3.
(1) Some hospitals provide designated smoking areas. The Joint Commission on Accreditation of Healthcare Organizations, the agency responsible for accrediting hospitals, identified a new standard to be effective January 1, 1993; as of this date healthcare organizations seeking Joint Commission accreditation were required to be smoke free.

(2) Meals are generally scheduled during regular meal times. It is impractical to serve meals any time a patient prefers; however, if a special need arises an attempt should be made to individualize care.

* (3) The patient has a right to refuse care against medical advice; the physician needs to explain to the patient the risks involved in lack of treatment.

(4) A private room is generally a privilege, not a right, that is provided at extra expense; it is not automatically provided on demand. However, a patient requiring isolation may be transferred to a private room.

4.
(1) Battery is the purposeful, angry, or negligent touching of a patient without consent.

(2) Assault is an act intended to provoke fear in a patient.

* (3) Negligence occurs when the caregiver's actions do not meet appropriate standards and result in injury to another; negligence can occur with acts of omission or commission.

(4) Malpractice is professional misconduct performed in professional practice that results in harm to another.

5.
(1) The ability to understand the procedure and its implications and alternatives is related to emotional and mental stability, not age.

(2) An under-legal-age person with a valid marriage certificate can sign an informed consent form.

(3) A patient who is illiterate can receive verbal explanations and sign by making a mark on the consent form; a witness attests that the mark was made by the patient.

* (4) A patient must be mentally and emotionally competent to sign a consent form; depression can interfere with cognitive processes and comprehension.

6.
(1) The Good Samaritan law does not provide legal immunity; healthcare providers can still be held accountable for gross departure from acceptable standards of practice or willful wrong doing.

(2) Assistance at the scene of an accident is an ethical, not a legal, duty.

* (3) Healthcare providers are responsible for their own actions, and the care provided must be what any reasonably prudent peer would do under similar circumstances.

(4) A contract does not have to exist for a healthcare provider to commit negligence.

7. (1) Libel is defamation of character via print, writing, or pictures, not words.
    (2) Assault is an attempt or threat to touch another person unjustifiably.
  * (3) Slander is defamation of character by spoken words.
    (4) Negligence is the omission to do something a reasonably prudent health-care provider would do under similar circumstances or the commission of an act that a reasonably prudent peer would not do under similar circumstances.

8. (1) The signature of a witness only attests that the patient's signature on the form is that of the patient. It is the physician's legal responsibility to ensure that the patient is informed and understands the procedure and its risks.
  * (2) The witness only attests that the patient, not someone else, actually signed the consent form.
    (3) This is untrue; reasonable prudent practice protects the physician from successfully being sued.
    (4) Same as answer number one.

9. (1) Planning is involved with setting goals, establishing priorities, identifying expected outcomes, and planning interventions.
    (2) Analysis is involved with interpreting data and determining the significance.
  * (3) Collecting information, regardless of whether it is done formally or informally, is part of the assessment phase of the problem-solving process.
    (4) Evaluation is involved with identifying a patient's response to interventions, comparing the patient's actual response with the expected outcomes, and drawing conclusions about the effectiveness of specific interventions.

10. (1) In the analysis step of the problem-solving process, a person interprets and determines the significance of data.
    (2) Collection of data about the status of an individual is part of the assessment phase of the problem-solving process; this occurs before any intervention.
  * (3) Evaluation involves determining a patient's response to an intervention; it may include identifying if goals and outcomes are met and revising the plan of care if necessary.
    (4) Implementation involves carrying out the planned intervention and documenting the interventions provided.

11. (1) This occurs after understanding the variables influencing the patient's attitudes, beliefs, and practices.
  * (2) Attitudes and beliefs influence health practices and how one perceives self-health; caregivers must always "begin care where the patient is."
    (3) Same as answer number one.
    (4) This is judgmental; people perceive their values as acceptable.

12. (1) Criminal law is concerned with crimes.
    (2) Civil law is concerned with wrongs committed by one person against another.
  * (3) Ethics is concerned with value judgments such as right and wrong or behavior that is acceptable or unacceptable.
    (4) Negligence is concerned with a careless act of commission or omission that results in injury to another.

13.   (1) Leaving a crying patient would abandon the patient and is not an acceptable intervention; a crying patient needs support, not isolation.

    (2) Properly addressing a patient supports the patient's need for identity, dignity, and respect, not privacy.

    (3) Providing patient-care information supports the patient's right to know what is going to be done and why, not privacy.

* (4) Closing the door during an interview provides a personal, secluded environment for a confidential discussion.

COMMON THEORIES RELATED TO MEETING PATIENTS' BASIC HUMAN NEEDS

This section encompasses questions related to the work of theorists Maslow, Kubler-Ross, and Erikson. Also it includes questions related to the principles of teaching, motivation, growth and development, and stress and adaptation.

QUESTIONS

1. A mentally disadvantaged (retarded) adult patient is to receive health care. To motivate this patient, the most appropriate intervention by the healthcare provider would be to:
   (1) Verbally recognize when goals are met
   (2) Use candy as a reward when goals are met
   (3) Set a variety of short-term goals to be met
   (4) Disregard the behavior when goals are not met

2. According to Maslow, which action would meet a patient's safety needs?
   (1) Calling the patient by name
   (2) Conversing with the patient
   (3) Providing rest periods
   (4) Explaining procedures

3. The process of growth and development within an individual can generally be described as:
   (1) Plodding
   (2) Unique
   (3) Simple
   (4) Even

4. A patient draws pictures and hangs them on the wall. According to Maslow's Hierarchy of Needs, the basic human need being met by this action is:
   (1) Physiological
   (2) Self-esteem
   (3) Security
   (4) Love

5. Growth and development follows a pattern that:
   (1) Is unpredictable
   (2) Relies on motivation
   (3) Is based on the previous step
   (4) Depends on personal strengths

6. When planning to teach self-care for a temporary problem to a young adult, the health-care professional should initially:
   (1) Identify the individual's interest in self-care
   (2) Determine the individual's usual habits
   (3) Reinforce that this is only temporary
   (4) Establish goals for the teaching plan

7. Considering theories about stress, which of the following generally precipitates the highest degree of stress?
   (1) Retirement
   (2) Relocation
   (3) Pregnancy
   (4) Marriage

8. The most appropriate way to teach a person a skill would be through a:
   (1) Demonstration
   (2) Discussion
   (3) Movie
   (4) Book

9. Which of the following is most relevant when predicting success of a teaching program regarding the learning of a skill?
   (1) The learner's cognitive ability
   (2) The extent of family support
   (3) The interest of the learner
   (4) The amount of reinforcement

10. An elderly female patient reminisces extensively and attempts to keep the caregiver from leaving the room. The **most** therapeutic response would be:
    (1) Encouraging her to focus on the present and future
    (2) Limiting the amount of time she talks about the past
    (3) Suggesting that she reminisce with people her own age
    (4) Setting aside some time to listen to her stories.

11. A patient, who has cancer and is receiving chemotherapy, says, "I just want to be well enough to enjoy the holidays." According to Kubler-Ross, this patient is in the stage of grieving known as:
    (1) Denial
    (2) Acceptance
    (3) Bargaining
    (4) Depression

12. A true statement about Kubler-Ross' theory on death and dying is that, people:
    (1) Ultimately reach the stage of acceptance
    (2) Can move back and forth between the stages
    (3) Generally pass smoothly through the stages
    (4) Should move progressively forward through the stages

13. Growth and development progress at a rate that can be described as:
    (1) Fast
    (2) Slow
    (3) Smooth
    (4) Irregular

14. An elderly person says, "I am now 1 inch shorter than when I was young." The caregiver should:
    (1) Explain that people do not usually lose height
    (2) Recognize this as part of growth and development
    (3) Understand that this could be the sign of a problem
    (4) Identify that the patient is worried about losing height

15. The patient is terminally ill. Which of the following is an **unexpected** behavior associated with the usual process of grieving?
    (1) Talking about the illness
    (2) Becoming angry with people
    (3) Attempting to commit suicide
    (4) Seeking alternative therapies

16. According to Maslow's Hierarchy of Needs, which of the following actions would help meet a patient's basic need for security and safety?
    (1) Addressing the patient by name
    (2) Ensuring that the patient is warm
    (3) Explaining what is going to be done
    (4) Accepting a patient's angry behavior

17. According to Maslow's Hierarchy of Needs, when planning care for several patients the caregiver should first assist the patient who needs to:
    (1) Void
    (2) Talk
    (3) Walk
    (4) Know

RATIONALES

1.   * (1) Verbal recognition would support feelings of self-esteem and independence; it provides external reinforcement and promotes internal reinforcement.
       (2) Praise is a more acceptable reward than candy. Concentrated sweets may be contraindicated on certain diets.
       (3) A mentally disadvantaged person generally can focus on only one goal at a time; several goals may be overwhelming.
       (4) A patient's behavior should never be disregarded; all behavior should be addressed in a nonjudgmental and appropriate manner.

2.   (1) Calling the patient by name relates to the need for self-esteem, the fourth level in Maslow's Hierarchy of Needs.
       (2) Conversing with the patient relates to the need for love and belonging, the third level in Maslow's Hierarchy of Needs.

(3) Providing rest relates to the physiological need to balance rest and exercise; this reflects the first level in Maslow's Hierarchy of Needs.

* (4) Explaining procedures relates to the need for safety and security; patients have a right to know what is happening to them and why.

3. (1) Some stages are faster and some are slower.

* (2) While a general pattern is followed, each individual grows and develops at a different rate or extent.

(3) This is an extremely complex process based on many influencing variables.

(4) Just the opposite is true; some stages are faster and some are slower depending on the stage and the individual.

4. (1) "Physiological" relates to meeting basic physical needs such as the need for oxygen, food, water, rest, sleep, and elimination, not self-esteem.

* (2) The situation illustrated in this item meets "self-esteem" needs; control, self-respect, and competence are reflected when a person hangs self-made pictures in a room for the enjoyment of self and others.

(3) "Security" refers to shelter, clothing, and the need to feel comfortable with the rules of the society, community, and hospital.

(4) "Love" refers to the need for bonds of affection and a sense of belonging.

5. (1) While growth and development progress through some stages slower or faster than others, they still follow a basic predictable pattern.

(2) Motivation may influence the achievement of tasks in some stages of growth and development; however, growth and development do not rely on motivation.

* (3) Success or failure of task achievement in one stage of development influences succeeding stages; failure to resolve a crisis at one stage damages the ego, which makes the resolution of the following stages more difficult.

(4) Personal strengths may assist a person to more easily achieve a particular developmental task; however, growth and development do not directly depend on personal strengths.

6. * (1) Determining the individual's readiness for learning and point of reference are the priorities.

(2) This would be done after a readiness for learning is established.

(3) Same as answer number two.

(4) Same as answer number two.

7. (1) Stress units for life events have been determined based on the readjustment required by an individual to adapt to a particular situation or event; the mean stress unit for retirement is 45 and is less than marriage, which is 50.

(2) The mean stress unit for a change in residence is 20.

(3) The mean stress unit for pregnancy is 40.

* (4) The mean stress unit for marriage is 50, which is higher than the other options presented.

8. * (1) Observing a demonstration and manipulating equipment promote learning a skill; a demonstration uses a variety of senses such as sight, hearing, and touch. It is most useful in the psychomotor domain.

(2) Learning via discussion is appropriate for the cognitive and affective domains.

(3) Although this can be used for learning a psychomotor skill, it is not as effective as demonstration and return demonstration; it is more appropriate for learning in the cognitive domain.

(4) Same as answer number three.

9. (1) Although a teaching program must be designed within the patient's developmental and cognitive abilities, it is useless unless the patient recognizes the value of what is to be learned and has a desire to learn.

(2) Although this is important, the patient's interest and readiness to learn are the priorities for the successful learning of a skill; some patients do not have a family support system.

* (3) The motivation of the learner to acquire new attitudes, information, or skills is the most important component for successful learning; motivation exists when the learner recognizes the future benefits of learning.

(4) Although this is important, self-motivation is the most significant factor in learning.

10. (1) Encouraging the patient to focus on the present and future is inappropriate; the developmental task of the elderly is to perform a life review.

(2) Same as answer number one.

(3) Patients should not be responsible for meeting each other's needs.

* (4) Healthcare providers should use opportunities to assist patients to meet their developmental needs. In the elderly, a life review assists the person to come to terms with past events and to attempt some degree of closure.

11. (1) Denial is the first stage of disbelief, where the person avoids reality, is noncompliant, and uses emotional energy to deny the truth.

(2) Acceptance is the fifth and final stage, where the person reminisces about the past, completes financial arrangements, and accepts death.

* (3) Bargaining is the third stage where the person is willing to do anything to change the prognosis, accepts new forms of therapies, and negotiates for more time.

(4) Depression is the fourth stage where the person recognizes the future loss, withdraws from relationships, and has feelings of loneliness.

12. (1) Reaching the stage of acceptance does not always occur; some people never progress past denial. Kubler-Ross' theory of grieving is behaviorally oriented.

* (2) The stages are not concrete, and the patient's behavior changes as different levels of awareness or coping occur.

(3) Although some people pass smoothly through the stages, it is not true for most individuals. The intensity and speed of progression depend on many factors such as extent of loss, level of growth and development, cultural and spiritual beliefs, gender roles, and relationships with significant others.

(4) Not all patients move progressively forward through the stages; patients tend to move back and forth among stages or may remain in one stage.

13. (1) Growth and development are not continuously fast, although infants and adolescents experience growth spurts.

(2) Growth and development are not continuously slow, although adults and the elderly may experience slower periods of growth.

(3) Growth and development reflect change, and change is rarely smooth.

* (4) Growth and development as a whole is uneven; some stages are faster than others and people move through the stages at their own pace. The commonalities of growth and development are predictable, but a specific individual's changes are unpredictable.

14. (1) This could precipitate anxiety because it implies that getting shorter means that there is a problem. People generally do get shorter as they age.
* (2) People do get slightly shorter as they age because of compression of the vertebral column.
   (3) This is not true; it is a developmental response to aging.
   (4) The patient has made a declarative statement that does not indicate the presence of anxiety.

15. (1) Although this behavior occurs throughout the grieving response, it is most expected during the early stage of denial and disbelief ("No, not me").
   (2) Anger is expected and occurs when there is a developing awareness of the impending loss ("Why me").
* (3) Although some people who are terminally ill attempt suicide, it is not a normal expected response to loss.
   (4) This behavior occurs most often during the stage of bargaining ("Yes me, but").

16. (1) This meets the patient's need for self-esteem.
   (2) This meets basic physiological, not safety and security, needs.
* (3) Knowing what will happen and why provides for security needs; it is also a patient's right; the unknown can be frightening.
   (4) Same as answer number one.

17. * (1) When setting priorities, usually the most basic physiologic needs must be met first. Voiding is a basic physiologic need.
   (2) Although important, basic physiologic needs must be met first.
   (3) Same as answer number two.
   (4) Same as answer number two.

COMMUNICATION AND MEETING PATIENTS' EMOTIONAL NEEDS

This section encompasses questions related to assessing and meeting patients' psychological needs. It includes questions that focus on the principles of communication, communication skills, communicating with confused patients, and interventions that support patients' emotional needs. Additional questions focus on patterns of behavior in response to illness, caring for the dying patient's emotional needs, and responding to the crying patient.

QUESTIONS

1. A patient is angry because of feelings of dependency related to not being able to participate in self-care. To best reduce this anger, the caregiver should:

(1) Offer choices about care
(2) Disregard the angry behavior
(3) Gently set limits on the behavior
(4) Encourage recognition of limitations

2. A patient's son has just died. The patient states, "I can't believe that I have lost my son. Can you believe it?" The BEST response is to:
   (1) Touch the patient's hand and say, "I am very sorry."
   (2) Say, "It is sad. I can't believe it either."
   (3) Leave the room and allow the patient to grieve privately.
   (4) Encourage a family member to stay and provide support.

3. Which intervention would be *least* effective in meeting a patient's psychosocial needs?
   (1) Addressing a patient by name
   (2) Assisting a patient with an activity
   (3) Identifying achievement of goals
   (4) Explaining care prior to it being given

4. Which is a true statement about communication?
   (1) A patient with expressive aphasia cannot communicate
   (2) Progress notes are a form of nonverbal communication
   (3) Touch has various meanings to different people
   (4) Words have the same meaning for all people

5. A man has a history of verbally aggressive behavior. One afternoon he starts to shout at another patient. The best response would be:
   (1) "Stop what you are doing."
   (2) "Let's go talk in another room."
   (3) "Please sit down and be calm."
   (4) "What seems to be the problem?"

6. A patient is soon to be admitted to a nursing home. The patient says, "I feel that nobody cares about me." The *best* response would be:
   (1) "You sound angry at your family."
   (2) "You feel as though nobody cares?"
   (3) "We all care about you and are concerned."
   (4) "Your family doesn't have the skills to care for you."

7. A patient who is usually verbal appears sad and withdrawn. The caregiver should:
   (1) Describe the behavior to the patient
   (2) Continue to observe the patient's behavior
   (3) Ensure that the patient has time to be alone
   (4) Attempt to engage the patient in cheerful conversation

8. A patient with a terminal illness appears sad and withdrawn. The caregiver should be:
   (1) Demonstrative
   (2) Cheerful
   (3) Present
   (4) Aloof

9. A patient with a terminal illness is depressed. Which of the following behaviors would support this conclusion?
   (1) Wishing to attend a nephew's wedding
   (2) Evading activities of daily living

    (3) Seeking second medical opinions

    (4) Being sarcastic to caregivers

10. A patient, who has been withdrawn, says, "When I have the opportunity, I am going to commit suicide." The **best** response would be:

    (1) "You have a lovely family. They need you."

    (2) "Let's explore the reasons you have for living."

    (3) "You must feel overwhelmed to want to kill yourself."

    (4) "Suicide does not solve problems. Tell me what is wrong."

11. A patient who is hard of hearing tells the caregiver he cannot hear what people say to him. The caregiver should:

    (1) Shout to him with a loud voice in the better ear

    (2) Ask questions that require a yes or no answer

    (3) Provide pencil and paper for communication

    (4) Encourage him to use gestures when talking

12. A patient is confused and disoriented. The route of communication used by the caregiver that would be most effective would be:

    (1) Touch

    (2) Writing

    (3) Talking

    (4) Pictures

13. A patient is crying. The best response would be:

    (1) "Sometimes it helps to talk about it."

    (2) "I hope things will get better by tomorrow."

    (3) "Deep breathing may help you regain control."

    (4) "Crying helps because it gets it out of your system."

14. The sense that is most important for a patient who appears to be in a coma is:

    (1) Taste

    (2) Touch

    (3) Smell

    (4) Hearing

15. A patient has difficulty communicating verbally because of a stroke (aphasia). To increase the patient's ability to communicate the caregiver should:

    (1) Encourage the patient to also use gestures

    (2) Talk to the patient, but not expect a response

    (3) Anticipate the patient's needs to reduce frustration

    (4) Ask the patient questions that require a yes or no response

16. A dying patient is withdrawn and depressed. The action that would be most therapeutic would be:

    (1) Assisting the patient in focusing on positive thoughts

    (2) Explaining that the patient still can accomplish goals

    (3) Accepting the patient's behavioral adaptation

    (4) Offering the patient advice when appropriate

17. The factor that **most** upsets adults who are incontinent is the feeling of:

    (1) Dependence

    (2) Regression

    (3) Loneliness
    (4) Wetness

18. One factor common to all communication is the:
    (1) Direction of the message
    (2) Fact that there is a message
    (3) Transmission route
    (4) Use of words

19. A patient is disoriented to time and place and has impaired cognitive ability because of extensive brain damage following a motor vehicle accident. When communicating with the patient the caregiver should:
    (1) Offer basic choices
    (2) Explain care in detail
    (3) Provide simple verbal directions
    (4) Use just nonverbal techniques when communicating

20. A female patient, whose husband recently died, begins to cry. The best response would be to:
    (1) Sit down next to her
    (2) Look away when she cries
    (3) Arrange for grief counseling
    (4) Explain that being sad is normal

21. Several times a day, every day, a male patient asks when he will be getting his therapy. He receives this therapy at the same time every day. The most therapeutic intervention would be to:
    (1) Tell him to go to the nurse when it is time for his therapy.
    (2) Encourage him to remember when he should have his therapy.
    (3) Inform him when he is scheduled for his next therapy.
    (4) Make a sign for his room indicating the time for therapy.

22. A preoperative patient verbalizes fear of the pain experienced with prior surgery. To help the patient deal with this fear the caregiver should:
    (1) Encourage the patient not to be afraid
    (2) Teach the patient relaxation techniques
    (3) Listen to the patient's concerns about pain
    (4) Inform the patient that pain medication is available

23. A patient with a terminal illness says, "Do you believe in life after death?" The most therapeutic response would be:
    (1) "I don't know."
    (2) "What do you think?"
    (3) "Why are you asking?"
    (4) "That's a difficult question."

24. A male patient has been told by his physician that he has metastatic lung cancer and he is seriously ill. After a severe episode of coughing and shortness of breath he says, "This is just a cold. I'll be fine once I get over it." The best response would be:
    (1) "Remember what the doctor told you."
    (2) "The doctor had some bad news for you today."
    (3) "It's not a cold, it's lung cancer."
    (4) "Tell me more about your illness."

25. A hospitalized, male patient appears to be asleep but does not react when his name is called. The caregiver should:
    (1) Inform the nurse immediately about the patient's condition
    (2) Tell the patient, "Squeeze my hand."
    (3) Gently touch the patient and softly call his name
    (4) Loudly call the patient's name and say, "Wake up."

26. A hospitalized male patient is crying and the only word that is understandable is "wife." What would be the best response?
    (1) "I'm sure that your wife is fine."
    (2) "You are concerned about your wife?"
    (3) "What did your wife do to upset you?"
    (4) "Do you expect your wife to visit today?"

27. A patient has significant short term memory loss and does not remember daily caregivers. When the patient asks, "Who are you?", the most appropriate response would be:
    (1) "You know me. You see me every day during the week."
    (2) Say nothing, because it would only upset the patient.
    (3) "Don't worry. I'm the same person you had yesterday."
    (4) State your name and say, "I am here to take care of you."

RATIONALES

1.   * (1) Making decisions puts the patient in control and supports feelings of independence.
      (2) Behavior should not be disregarded or ignored; all behavior has meaning and requires recognition.
      (3) Setting limits will only make the patient more angry because it is a controlling intervention.
      (4) Recognizing limitations will only intensify feelings of dependence.

2.   * (1) Touch denotes caring; this statement is direct and supportive yet does not reinforce denial.
      (2) Although this statement identifies feelings, it supports denial.
      (3) Leaving the room is abandonment.
      (4) Although this may be done later, the patient needs immediate support.

3.   (1) Addressing the patient by name individualizes care and supports dignity and self-esteem.
      * (2) For an adult, assistance with an activity may precipitate feelings of dependence and regression.
        (3) Identifying goal achievements is motivating and supports independence, self-esteem, and self-actualization.
        (4) Explaining care provides emotional support because it reduces fear of the unknown and involves the patient in care.

4.   (1) Patient's with expressive aphasia often can communicate using nonverbal behaviors, a picture board, or written messages.
        (2) Words, whether they are spoken or written, are verbal communication.

* (3) Touch is a form of nonverbal communication that sends a variety of messages depending on the person's culture, gender, age, past experiences, and present situation; touch also invades a person's personal space.
(4) Words do not have the same meaning for all people. People from different cultures and people in subgroups within the same culture place different values on words.

5.
(1) This is a command that may demean the patient; it challenges the patient and may precipitate more abusive behavior.
* (2) This interrupts the behavior and protects the other patient; walking to another room uses energy and talking promotes verbalization of feelings and concerns.
(3) This is judgmental; this implies the patient is not calm; an agitated patient has too much energy to sit quietly.
(4) This is inappropriate because it challenges the patient and puts the patient on the defensive; this is a direct question that the patient may or may not be able to answer.

6.
(1) Patients who are angry strike out with verbal abuse or sarcasm; this patient's statement reflects feelings of sadness and isolation.
* (2) Repeating the patient's statement allows the patient to focus on what was said, validates what was said, and encourages communication.
(3) This may or may not be true and denies the patient's feelings.
(4) Same as answer number three.

7.
* (1) Pointing out the patient's behavior brings it to the attention of the patient and provides an opportunity to explore feelings.
(2) The patient's behavior needs to be addressed more fully than would be possible with only continued observation.
(3) This would be abandonment; sad, withdrawn patients need to know that they are accepted and that support is available.
(4) Cheerful conversation denies the patient's feelings.

8.
(1) This is inappropriate; the patient is in the fourth stage of Kubler-Ross' Theory of Grieving, depression. During this stage people become quiet and withdrawn; caregivers should be quiet and available, not demonstrative.
(2) This is inappropriate; cheerfulness denies the patient's feelings and cuts off communication.
* (3) The patient is developing a full awareness of the impact of dying and is expressing sorrow; this stage of coping should be supported by the quiet presence of caregivers.
(4) This would be a form of abandonment; caregivers must be present and accessible.

9.
(1) This is future-oriented thinking and may be a form of bargaining for more time.
* (2) When patients are depressed, they may feel a loss of control, alone, and withdrawn; when a person is depressed there is little physical energy, a lack of concern about the activities of daily living, and a decreased interest in physical appearance.
(3) This behavior is associated with denial and bargaining.
(4) This behavior reflects feelings of anger.

10.   (1) This statement is inappropriate; the patient is unable to cope, is selecting the ultimate escape, and is not capable of meeting the needs of others; this response may also precipitate feelings such as guilt.
        (2) This denies the patient's feelings; the patient must focus on the negatives before exploring the positives.
      * (3) This statement identifies feelings and invites further communication.
        (4) This is a judgmental response that may cut off communication. This response is too direct, and the patient may not consciously know what is wrong.

11.   (1) Shouting is demeaning and unnecessary; enunciating the words slowly and directly in front of the patient supports communication.
        (2) This is unrealistic. Communication is a two-way process; the patient is not having difficulty sending a message but rather is having difficulty receiving a message. This intervention is more appropriate for a patient with expressive aphasia.
      * (3) Communication can be promoted in a written, rather than a verbal, form; this reduces social isolation and promotes communication.
        (4) The patient is having difficulty with receiving, not sending, messages.

12.   * (1) Touch is a simple form of communication that is easily understood even by confused, disoriented, or mentally incapacitated individuals.
        (2) This requires interpretation of symbols, which is a more complex form of communication than touch.
        (3) Same as answer number two.
        (4) Same as answer number two.

13.   * (1) This response recognizes the patient's behavior and provides an opportunity to verbalize feelings and concerns.
        (2) This is false reassurance.
        (3) This statement is inappropriate; it implies the patient is out of control. This interferes with the patient's coping mechanisms and may not help the patient regain control.
        (4) This is false reassurance; crying may or may not help this patient.

14.   (1) Although all the senses are important, food should not be given to an unconscious patient because aspiration can occur.
        (2) Although all the senses are important, this sense is not as important as hearing for a patient in a coma.
        (3) Same as answer number two.
      * (4) Hearing is the most important sense to an unconscious patient because it is believed it is the last sense that is lost; the senses receive stimuli from the environment and hearing keeps one in contact with others.

15.   * (1) Communication can be both verbal and nonverbal; this encourages communication.
        (2) Communication is a two-way process, and the patient should be involved; the patient should be encouraged to respond in some way.
        (3) Although this may be done occasionally, it does not increase the patient's ability to communicate.
        (4) Although this may be done occasionally, it does not increase the patient's ability to communicate; a yes or no response is too limited.

16.   (1) Focusing on positive thoughts is inappropriate because it denies the patient's feelings; the patient needs to focus on the future loss.
    (2) Same as answer number one.
* (3) Depression is the fourth stage of dying according to Kubler-Ross; patients become withdrawn and noncommunicative when feeling a loss of control and recognizing future losses. The nurse should accept the behavior and be available if the patient wants to verbalize feelings.
    (4) It is never appropriate to offer advice; people must explore their alternatives and come to their own conclusions.

17.   (1) Not all people who are incontinent are dependent on others; many people are capable of cleaning themselves.
* (2) Incontinence is often associated with childlike behavior; most cultures value control over one's bodily functions, which is usually accomplished early in life.
    (3) Although incontinence is embarrassing, which may result in social isolation and loneliness, it is the feeling of being like a child that causes the most concern.
    (4) Although being wet and soiled are uncomfortable, it is the feelings associated with regression that are most upsetting.

18.   (1) Messages go in a variety of directions (e.g., from the caregiver to the patient, from the patient to the caregiver).
* (2) Communication is the transfer of information from one person to another; in communication there is always a message.
    (3) A message can be transmitted via a variety of routes (e.g., verbal, nonverbal).
    (4) Communication can be nonverbal (e.g., touch, a smile).

19.   (1) Offering choices is too challenging a task for a person with extensive brain damage.
    (2) Patients with extensive brain damage lack the cognitive ability to integrate details or comprehend "cause and effect."
* (3) Simple, short statements with a single message are the easiest to integrate intellectually.
    (4) Nonverbal behaviors require an interpretive ability and are too limited an approach; simple, short statements with a single message are the easiest to understand.

20.   * (1) Sitting down with her communicates acceptance and caring.
    (2) Looking away may give the patient the message that it is not acceptable to cry.
    (3) Grief counseling may be done later, the patient needs immediate support.
    (4) Although this statement is often true, it is making the assumption that the patient is sad; not knowing the patient-spouse relationship, the tears may indicate other feelings such as relief or joy.

21.   (1) The patient probably would not be capable of this task; too challenging a task can be frustrating.
    (2) Same as answer number one.
    (3) Although this might be done, it is not the most therapeutic intervention because it only addresses the next therapy session.

* (4) This promotes independence and does not demean the patient; the patient can refer to the schedule when necessary.

22. (1) Encouraging the patient not to be afraid, denies the patient's fears.
    (2) Teaching relaxation techniques may eventually be done, it does not allow the patient to discuss fears.
    * (3) Listening to the patient's concerns supports the patient's need to verbalize fears.
    (4) Offering pain medication is false reassurance and cuts off communication; it does not recognize the patient's need to verbalize fears.

23. (1) Although this is a direct response to the patient's question, it does not focus on the patient's concern.
    * (2) This focuses on the patient's concern and provides an opportunity for the patient to verbalize further.
    (3) This is too confrontational and may cut off communication.
    (4) This side-steps the patient's question and may or may not promote further dialogue.

24. (1) This response would take away the patient's coping mechanism, is demeaning, and could cut off communication; the patient is using denial to cope with the diagnosis.
    (2) Same as answer number one.
    (3) Same as answer number one.
    * (4) This provides an opportunity to discuss the illness; eventually a developing awareness will occur, and the patient will move on to other coping mechanisms.

25. (1) The patient needs to be assessed further before informing the nurse.
    (2) The patient's attention must first be obtained before giving a direction.
    * (3) Touch is the first step to further assess this patient; touch and sound stimulate two senses while using the patient's name is individualizing care.
    (4) Speaking loudly could frighten the patient; an additional sense should be stimulated because the patient previously has not responded to a verbal intervention.

26. (1) This statement is false reassurance and draws a conclusion based on insufficient information.
    * (2) This response encourages further communication which is necessary to obtain more information about what is upsetting the patient.
    (3) This is a judgmental statement not based on fact.
    (4) This response focuses on one thought and may cut off further communication; this is not an open-ended question that allows the patient to express concerns.

27. (1) This is a demeaning response and does not answer the patient's question.
    (2) Not responding would make the patient more upset; the patient has a right to know who is providing care.
    (3) This denies the patient's concern and does not answer the question.
    * (4) This answers the question which meets the patient's right to know; it is also a respectful response.

PHYSICAL ASSESSMENT

This section encompasses questions related to various aspects of physical assessment. Questions focus on the use of common physical examination techniques and the assessment of temperature, pulse, respirations, blood pressure, level of consciousness, and pain. Additional questions focus on whether assessment data are subjective or objective in nature, whether sources are primary or secondary, the responsibilities regarding the data collected during assessment, the use of equipment to accurately collect data, principles related to specimen collection and the general adaptation syndrome.

QUESTIONS

1. When assessing how a patient feels the only primary source would be the:
   (1) Physician
   (2) Roommate
   (3) Patient
   (4) Nurse

2. An individual's body temperature would be at its lowest at:
   (1) 6 AM
   (2) 10 AM
   (3) 5 PM
   (4) 9 PM

3. When entering a room a patient is found lying in bed with their eyes closed. The caregiver should:
   (1) Suspect that the patient is feeling withdrawn
   (2) Return in 30 minutes to check on the patient
   (3) Collect more information about the patient
   (4) Allow the patient to continue sleeping

4. To assess if patients are oriented the caregiver should:
   (1) Ask them to state where they are and the time of day
   (2) Ascertain if they can follow simple directions
   (3) Inquire if they remember the caregiver's name
   (4) Determine if their eyes follow movement

5. Which range for a resting pulse is normal for the elderly?
   (1) 50 to 60 beats per minute
   (2) 80 to 90 beats per minute
   (3) 105 to 115 beats per minute
   (4) 120 to 130 beats per minute

6. Which of the following rectal temperatures is within the normal range?
   (1) 96.4°F
   (2) 97.6°F
   (3) 99.8°F
   (4) 101.2°F

7. To assess for orthostatic hypotension, a patient's blood pressure should be measured:
   (1) Between meals
   (2) After standing
   (3) During activity
   (4) First thing in the morning

8. Bloody drainage from a patient's wound is called:
   (1) Sanguineous
   (2) Hemoptysis
   (3) Purulent
   (4) Serous

9. An example of subjective data is the patient:
   (1) Appears jaundiced
   (2) Has a headache
   (3) Looks tired
   (4) Is crying

10. The diastolic blood pressure reflects which of the following physiological actions?
    (1) Contraction of the ventricles
    (2) Resting arterial pressure
    (3) Volume of cardiac output
    (4) Pulse pressure

11. When assessing a patient for an emotional response to stress, the patient should be monitored for:
    (1) Anorexia
    (2) Headaches
    (3) Irritability
    (4) Hypertension

12. A pedal pulse reflects the function of a patient's:
    (1) Vein
    (2) Heart
    (3) Blood
    (4) Artery

13. Which physical examination technique would elicit the most significant information concerning a patient's respiratory system:
    (1) Palpation
    (2) Percussion
    (3) Inspection
    (4) Auscultation

14. Which blood pressure reading would be considered the most hypertensive?
    (1) 90/70 mm Hg
    (2) 120/80 mm Hg
    (3) 150/115 mm Hg
    (4) 160/90 mm Hg

15. When assessing the results of a culture and sensitivity report, the sensitivity part of the test directly indicates the:

(1) Type of microorganisms present
(2) Virility of the organisms in the culture
(3) Antibiotics that would be effective treatment
(4) Extent of the patient's response to the pathogens

16. When auscultating the lungs, bubbling sounds produced by air entering alveoli that contain secretions are called:
    (1) Crackles
    (2) Stridor
    (3) Wheezes
    (4) Rhonchi

17. Patients with chronic pain often have psychological adaptations. A psychological reaction to pain is:
    (1) Dyspnea
    (2) Depression
    (3) Hypertension
    (4) Self-splinting

18. A behavioral response to moderate pain is:
    (1) Rapid, irregular breathing
    (2) Increased muscle tension
    (3) Self-splinting
    (4) Fatigue

19. Pain perception is **most** influenced by the:
    (1) Duration of the stimulus
    (2) Characteristics of the pain
    (3) Activity of the cerebral cortex
    (4) Level of endorphins in the blood

20. A patient adaptation that may first indicate internal abdominal bleeding would be:
    (1) An increased body temperature
    (2) Pain in the bleeding area
    (3) Slow, deep respirations
    (4) An accelerated heart rate

21. Which of the following clinical signs is indicative of internal hemorrhage?
    (1) Decreased respiratory rate
    (2) Fall in blood pressure
    (3) Warm clammy skin
    (4) Bradycardia

22. An elderly patient with a history of obstructive respiratory disease begins to have difficulty breathing. The assessment that would indicate the most serious complication would be:
    (1) Wheezing sounds on expiration
    (2) Mucus tinged with frank red streaks
    (3) Orthostatic hypotension when rising
    (4) The need to sit in the orthopneic position

23. Pulse oximetry is primarily done to assess the patient's:
    (1) Heart rate
    (2) Vital signs

(3) Blood pressure
(4) Oxygen saturation

24. When assessing a patient's breath sounds, wheezes are heard. Wheezes occur when:
    (1) There is fluid in the alveoli
    (2) Air moves through a narrowed airway
    (3) The patient sits in the orthopneic position
    (4) The pleural sack rubs against the lung surface

25. Which assessment would BEST evaluate peripheral circulation in a lower extremity:
    (1) Capillary refill in the toenails
    (2) Blood pressure in the extremity
    (3) Lack of hair on the toes
    (4) Color of the affected foot

26. The adequacy of the lungs ability to oxygenate blood and remove excess carbon dioxide is most accurately measured by:
    (1) Hemoglobin levels
    (2) Hematocrit values
    (3) Arterial blood gases
    (4) Pulmonary function tests

27. When a patient's breathing pattern alternates between periods of apnea and progressively deeper breaths it is known as:
    (1) Kussmaul respirations
    (2) Apneustic respirations
    (3) Paradoxical respiration
    (4) Cheyne-Stokes respirations

28. When applying a pulse oximetry sensor to the patient's finger the caregiver should:
    (1) Remove frosted nail polish from the patient's nails
    (2) Send the patient's rings home with a family member
    (3) Keep the hand continuously elevated on a pillow
    (4) Shave any hair that might be on the finger

29. Dorsiflexion of the great toe and fanning of the other toes when stroking the lateral aspect of the sole of the foot is known as:
    (1) Babinski's reflex
    (2) Romberg's sign
    (3) Achilles reflex
    (4) Rovsing's sign

30. Black tarry-colored stools are related to:
    (1) An overproduction of bile
    (2) Gastrointestinal bleeding
    (3) A decreased absorption of fat
    (4) An insufficient amount of pancreatic enzymes

31. Which of the following should be assessed further?
    (1) A pulse rate that is 68 beats per minute and regular
    (2) A respiratory rate of 28 breaths per minute
    (3) A blood pressure reading of 120/88 mm Hg
    (4) A rectal temperature of 99.8°F

32. A patient's vital signs are oral temperature 99°F, pulse 84 beats per minute with a regular rhythm, respirations 16 breaths per minute and deep, and blood pressure 180/110 mm Hg. The sign that should cause the most concern would be the:
    (1) Pulse
    (2) Temperature
    (3) Respirations
    (4) Blood pressure

33. The location and characteristics of pain are important to explore when determining its:
    (1) Etiology
    (2) Duration
    (3) Threshold
    (4) Intensity

34. Which is an example of objective data?
    (1) Pain
    (2) Fever
    (3) Nausea
    (4) Fatigue

RATIONALES

1. (1) This is a secondary source; this individual may not be totally aware of how well the patient slept.
    (2) Patients should not be held responsible for other patients.
  * (3) The patient is the primary source and the only source able to provide subjective data concerning how she or he slept.
    (4) Same as answer number one.

2. * (1) A person's body temperature is at its lowest in the early morning; core temperatures vary with a predictable pattern over 24 hours (diurnal or circadian temperature variations) because of hormonal variations.
    (2) It is not at its lowest temperature at this time; body temperatures steadily rise as the day progresses.
    (3) Body temperatures peak between 4 and 7 PM.
    (4) It is not at its lowest temperature at this time; the temperature is still falling from its peak.

3. (1) This is an assumption based on insufficient data.
    (2) This is unsafe; more data need to be collected at this time.
  * (3) More information must be collected to make a complete assessment and come to an accurate conclusion.
    (4) This is unsafe; this is an assumption based on insufficient data; a further assessment should be performed.

4. * (1) Questions related to time, place, in addition to person, are essential when assessing patients' levels of orientation.
    (2) This is inaccurate; this can be done by confused, disoriented patients.
    (3) This assesses recent (short term) memory, not orientation.
    (4) Same as answer number two.

5. (1) Fifty to 60 beats per minute is below the normal range of a pulse rate in an elderly adult.
    * (2) The normal heart rate in an elderly adult is between 60 to 100 beats per minute.
    (3) One hundred and five to 115 beats per minute is too high for a heart rate taken at rest; this would be expected during exercise.
    (4) One hundred and twenty to 130 beats per minute is too high for a heart rate taken at rest.

6. (1) This is outside the normal range for a rectal temperature; this is too low.
    (2) Same as answer number one.
    * (3) This is within the normal range of 98.6°F to 100.6°F for a rectal temperature.
    (4) A fever is indicated at 101.2°F.

7. (1) This is untrue; meals are unrelated to positional changes.
    * (2) Blood pressures taken before and after standing reflect the effectiveness of the automatic vasoconstriction that occurs in the lower half of the body when a patient moves from a horizontal to a vertical position; delayed vasoconstriction when standing, resulting in a decreased blood pressure, indicates orthostatic hypotension.
    (3) This is done during a stress test.
    (4) This is a blood pressure at rest.

8. * (1) Sanguineous, or bloody drainage, indicates fresh bleeding or hemorrhage.
    (2) Hemoptysis is coughing up blood from the respiratory tract.
    (3) Purulent drainage contains pus and indicates the presence of infection.
    (4) Serous drainage consists of clear, watery plasma.

9. (1) This is an example of objective data; objective data require the use of a sense to collect the data. Jaundice is a human response that is measured using the sense of vision and the assessment technique of inspection.
    * (2) Subjective data are data that can be described or verified only by the patient; a patient's descriptions of pain, concerns, feelings, or sensations are additional examples of subjective data.
    (3) This is a conclusion. A group of data could eventually lead to this conclusion.
    (4) This is objective information. The patient can be observed crying.

10. (1) Contraction of the ventricles is reflected by the systolic pressure.
    * (2) Diastole is the period when the ventricles are relaxed and reflects the pressure in the arteries when the heart is at rest.
    (3) The volume of cardiac output is computed by multiplying the stroke volume by the number of heart beats per minute.
    (4) Pulse pressure is the difference between the systolic and diastolic pressures.

11. (1) Anorexia is a physiological response to stress.
    (2) Headaches are physiological responses to stress.
    * (3) Irritability is a behavioral/emotional response; the individual is using physical and emotional energy to reduce stress.
    (4) Hypertension is a physiological response to stress.

12.   (1) Veins do not have a pulse.

          (2) A radial, carotid, or apical pulse more readily assesses heart function.

          (3) Laboratory tests assess blood and its components.

    * (4) The presence, absence, or quality of a pedal pulse reflects the patency of the dorsalis pedis artery; peripheral pulses should be present, equal, and symmetrical.

13.   (1) Although the chest wall is palpated for bulges, tenderness, respiratory excursion, and vocal fremitus, which provide valuable information, auscultation of breath sounds provides the most significant information concerning a patient's respiratory system.

          (2) Although percussion of the thorax determines whether underlying tissue is filled with air, liquid, or solid material and identifies the boundaries of the lung, auscultation of breath sounds provides the most significant information concerning a patient's respiratory system.

          (3) Although inspection assesses the pattern of respirations, condition of the skin, and shape and symmetry of the thorax, auscultation of breath sounds provides the most significant information concerning a patient's respiratory system.

    * (4) Auscultation of the chest includes assessment of breath sounds (normal, diminished, absent); adventitious breath sounds (crackles or rales, rhonchi, wheeze, friction rub); and vocal resonance (bronchophony, whispered pectoriloquy, egophony). This information is the most significant for assessing the patient's respiratory system.

14.   (1) A blood pressure reading of 90/70 mm Hg is hypotensive.

          (2) A blood pressure reading of 120/80 mm Hg is within the normal range for blood pressure; the normal range for the systolic pressure is 100 to 140 and the diastolic pressure is 60 to 90.

    * (3) A blood pressure with a higher diastolic pressure is more hypertensive than a blood pressure with a higher systolic pressure but lower diastolic pressure. The diastolic pressure is the pressure exerted against the arterial walls when the ventricles are at rest; the higher the diastolic, the more dangerous the situation.

          (4) Although this systolic reading is high and needs to be reported to the physician, a blood pressure with a higher diastolic reading is more dangerous.

15.   (1) Examination of a specimen under a microscope identifies the microorganisms present.

          (2) The ability to produce disease (virulence) is not determined by the sensitivity portion of a culture and sensitivity; virulence is determined by statistical data concerning morbidity and mortality associated with the microorganism.

    * (3) Areas of lack of microorganism growth surrounding an antibiotic on a culture medium indicate that the microorganism is sensitive to the antibiotic and the antibiotic is capable of destroying the microorganism.

          (4) The sensitivity part of a culture and sensitivity test refers to the ability of an antibiotic to destroy a microorganism, not an individual's susceptibility to or extent of response to the microorganism.

16.   * (1) Crackles, also known as rales, is an adventitious sound heard on auscultation of the base of the lungs. Crackles make a bubbling noise heard at the height of inspiration as air passes through serous secretions in the distal bronchioles or alveoli. Crackles cannot be cleared by coughing.
       (2) Stridor is an abnormal breath sound caused by an obstruction of the trachea or larynx characterized by a high pitched musical sound, not a crackling sound known as crackles.
       (3) Wheezes are high pitched musical sounds caused by a high velocity flow of air through a narrowed airway. Although wheezes can be heard throughout the ventilatory cycle, they are more pronounced during expiration.
       (4) Rhonchi are rumbling sounds that are most pronounced during expiration. They are caused by respiratory obstruction precipitated by thick secretions, muscular spasm, neoplasms, or external pressure. Rhonchi usually can be cleared by coughing.

17.   (1) Dyspnea is a physiological adaptation to a stress.
    * (2) Patients with chronic pain commonly experience depression; this is an adaptation to lack of control over relentless pain.
       (3) Hypertension is a physiological adaptation to a stress.
       (4) Self-splinting is a physical attempt to minimize pain.

18.   (1) Rapid, irregular breathing is a physiological response to pain; pain generally activates the fight-or-flight mechanism of the general adaption syndrome (GAS).
       (2) The GAS stimulates the sympathetic branch of the autonomic nervous system, which results in this symptom; it is a physiological response that prepares the muscles for action.
    * (3) Self-splinting is a behavioral attempt to protect and minimize stress and strain to the area. Supporting the area or leaning in the direction of the pain are examples of self-splinting.
       (4) Fatigue is a physiological response to pain; pain uses physical and emotional energy which leaves a person fatigued.

19.   (1) Duration is one component of a description of pain once it is perceived.
       (2) Characteristics of pain are the components of the description of pain once it is perceived.
    * (3) The cerebral cortex controls the higher levels of the perceptual aspects of pain.
       (4) Although endorphin levels influence pain perception, it is the activity of the cerebral cortex that controls the higher levels of the perceptual aspects of pain.

20.   (1) An increased body temperature is not an initial sign of hemorrhage.
       (2) Pain in the bleeding area would be a later sign because enough blood would have to collect to cause distention of tissues and organ displacement.
       (3) Initially the respirations would be rapid and deep; as hypovolemia progresses then the respirations would become rapid and shallow.
    * (4) Because of the loss of red blood cells with bleeding, there is a decreased oxygen-carrying capacity of the blood; the body attempts to meet oxygen needs by increasing the heart rate and cardiac output.

21. (1) The respiratory rate would increase in an effort to bring more oxygen to body cells.
   * (2) The patient will become hypotensive with the loss of blood because of hypovolemia.
   (3) The skin will be cool and clammy because of the sympathetic nervous system response.
   (4) The heart rate would increase, not decrease, in an effort to increase cardiac output and bring more oxygen to body cells.

22. (1) Expiratory wheezing is not uncommon for patients with chronic respiratory disease; however, if it continues or progresses, it should be reported.
   * (2) Blood in sputum is not a common response to chronic respiratory disease and should be reported immediately.
   (3) Orthostatic hypotension is a common response to rising in the elderly because of slowed peripheral vasoconstriction.
   (4) The need to sit in the orthopneic position is a common response of individuals with chronic respiratory disease; elevating the head helps breathing by lowering the abdominal organs by gravity which allows the diaphragm to contract more efficiently on inspiration.

23. (1) Although pulse oximetry will obtain a pulse rate, it is primarily done to obtain the oxygen saturation of the blood. The heart rate can simply be obtained when palpating a peripheral pulse or auscultating the apical pulse.
   (2) Vital signs are temperature, pulse, respirations, and blood pressure, not oxygen saturation.
   (3) Blood pressure is one of the vital signs, and it reflects the pressures exerted by the blood as it pulsates through the arteries.
   * (4) Oxygen saturation via pulse oximetry measures the degree to which hemoglobin is saturated with oxygen; it provides some indication of the efficiency of lung ventilation.

24. (1) Sounds caused by fluid in the alveoli are called crackles (rales), and sounds caused by fluid or resistance in the bronchi are called rhonchi.
   * (2) Wheezes occur as air passes through air passages narrowed by secretions, edema, or tumors; these high-pitched squeaky musical sounds are best heard on expiration and are usually not changed by coughing.
   (3) Positioning is unrelated to adventitious sounds (abnormal breath sounds).
   (4) Pleural friction rub is when the pleural sac rubs against the lung surface. It is a superficial grating sound heard particularly at the height of inspiration and not relieved by coughing; it is caused by rubbing together of inflamed pleural surfaces.

25. * (1) Applying pressure to a toenail causes blanching. When the pressure is released, the normal color should quickly return (within 1 to 2 seconds), indicating adequate arterial perfusion.
   (2) Blood pressure reflects the pressure exerted by the blood as it pulsates through the arteries. Although people with arteriosclerosis may have increased resistance and therefore hypertension, a blood pressure does not evaluate peripheral circulation in the lower extremities as does inspection and palpation.

(3) Although lack of hair on the feet and lower legs may indicate prolonged hypoxia, other factors such as genetic endowment may cause a lack of hair.

(4) Assessing the color of one foot is inadequate; both feet must be assessed and compared.

26.

(1) Although hemoglobin is the red pigment in red blood cells that carries oxygen, it is not an accurate test for measuring the lungs ability to oxygenate blood and remove excess carbon dioxide. A low hemoglobin level is evidence of iron-deficiency anemia or bleeding.

(2) Although hematocrit is the percentage of red blood cell mass in proportion to whole blood, it is not an accurate test for measuring the lungs ability to oxygenate blood and remove excess carbon dioxide. A low hematocrit level may indicate possible water intoxication, and an elevated hematocrit may indicate dehydration.

* (3) Arterial blood gases include the partial pressures of oxygen and carbon dioxide; they determine the adequacy of alveolar gas exchange and the ability of the lungs and kidneys to maintain the acid-base balance of body fluids.

(4) Pulmonary function tests measure lung volume and capacity; although these provide valuable data they do not provide specific data about the lungs ability to oxygenate blood and remove excess carbon dioxide.

27.

(1) Kussmaul respirations have an increased rate and depth; this is associated with metabolic acidosis and renal failure.

(2) Apneustic respirations have a prolonged gasping inspiration followed by a short, inefficient expiration; this is associated with central nervous system disorders.

(3) With paradoxical respirations the chest wall balloons on expiration and is depressed or pulled downward on inspiration; this is associated with flail chest as a result of fractured ribs.

* (4) Cheyne-Stokes breathing has a rhythmic waxing and waning of respirations. The breaths vary from very deep to very shallow followed by a brief period of apnea; this is associated with brain damage, increased intracranial pressure, and cardiac failure.

28.

* (1) The ingredients in acrylic nails or black, blue, green, metallic, or frosted nail polish will interfere with an accurate reading.

(2) Rings can be worn, or the reading can be taken on a finger without a ring; metal jewelry does not interfere with the reading.

(3) It is unnecessary to elevate the site being monitored; however, the pulse oximeter may identify motion as arterial pulsations. It may be necessary to immobilize, not elevate, the monitoring site to achieve accurate readings.

(4) The removal of body hair is unnecessary to achieve an accurate reading.

29.

* (1) The Babinski's reflex, also known as the plantar reflex, is a normal reflex in newborns but may indicate a lesion in the pyramidal tract of children and adults.

(2) Romberg's sign is the loss of the sense of position when the eyes are closed and the feet are close together.

     (3) The Achilles reflex is assessed by striking a blow directly to the Achilles tendon just above the heel; it should produce a normal plantar flexion of the foot.

     (4) Rovsing's sign is elicited by palpating the left lower quadrant, causing pain in the right lower quadrant in the patient with appendicitis.

30.   (1) Bile pigments color the stool brown; in the absence of bile pigments, the stool has a clay color.

    * (2) Digestive acids and enzymes act on blood in the gastrointestinal system, causing the stool to become black or tarry in color.

     (3) In the absence of pancreatic enzymes there is a decreased absorption of fat resulting in stool that contains white globules of fat and is foul smelling.

     (4) Same as answer number three.

31.   (1) This is within the normal pulse range of 60 to 80 beats per minute and the rhythm is regular, indicating no abnormalities.

    * (2) This is above the normal respiratory rate of 14 to 20 breaths per minute and is abnormal.

     (3) This is within the normal blood pressure range of 100 to 140 mm Hg for the systolic reading and 60 to 90 mm Hg for the diastolic reading, indicating no abnormalities.

     (4) This is within the normal rectal temperature range of 97.6°F to 99.8°F for a rectal temperature, indicating no abnormalities.

32.   (1) Although this is slightly outside the normal pulse rate of 60 to 80 beats per minute, the rhythm is regular; the patient should be assessed further and the information compared to the patient's baseline data.

     (2) This is within the normal temperature range of 97.6°F to 99.6°F for an oral temperature.

     (3) This is within the normal respiratory rate of 14 to 20 breaths per minute.

    * (4) The blood pressure is above the normal range of 100 to 140 mm Hg for the systolic reading and 60 to 90 mm Hg for the diastolic reading and should cause the most concern of the options presented.

33.   * (1) The location of pain is often related to the underlying disease or illness. The quality or subjective characteristics of pain often have common descriptions related to specific illness, such as burning pain associated with gastric ulcers and crushing chest pain associated with myocardial infarctions.

     (2) The duration of the pain is not as significant as its location and characteristics in determining its etiology.

     (3) Pain threshold is totally individual and unreliable for determining relationships among characteristics, location, or etiology of pain.

     (4) Intensity of pain is totally individual and unreliable for determining relationships among characteristics, location, or etiology of pain.

34.   (1) This is subjective; subjective data are a patient's perceptions, feelings, sensations, or ideas.

    * (2) This is objective because it can be measured with a thermometer.

     (3) Same as answer number one.

     (4) Same as answer number one.

MEETING PATIENTS' SAFETY NEEDS

This section encompasses questions related to maintaining patients' safety. A particular emphasis is placed on concepts of surgical and medical asepsis (including isolation/precautions), the use of restraints, prevention of injury, fire safety, physical safety (including interventions to protect a patient having a seizure), electrical safety, and safety related to the use of oxygen.

QUESTIONS

1. The *main* reason for accidents in hospitals is:
    (1) Patients sneak cigarettes
    (2) Equipment breaks unexpectedly
    (3) People do not recognize hazards
    (4) Safety precautions take extra time

2. A patient sitting in a wheelchair begins to have a tonic-clonic (grand mal) seizure. The patient should be:
    (1) Moved to the floor to prevent injury
    (2) Wheeled immediately to a private area
    (3) Returned to bed to provide a soft surface
    (4) Secured in the wheelchair to prevent falling

3. Disoriented, confused patients who are restrained often struggle against restraints primarily because they are:
    (1) Unable to understand what is occurring
    (2) Trying to manipulate the staff
    (3) Responding to the discomfort
    (4) Attempting to gain control

4. The most effective method to prevent a confused patient from falling out of bed is:
    (1) Using sedatives
    (2) Raising of the bedside rails
    (3) Lowering the height of the bed
    (4) Applying a vest restraint

5. Which of the following actions is appropriate after a patient vomits:
    (1) Contain vomitus in a medical waste container
    (2) Discard the vomitus in the toilet and flush
    (3) Save a specimen for the physician
    (4) Pour the vomitus down the sink

6. Which of the following would have the greatest impact on limiting the spread of microorganisms?
    (1) Disposable equipment
    (2) Double-bagging
    (3) Handwashing
    (4) Gloves

7. To provide for physical safety when administering oxygen, it is most important to recognize that oxygen:

(1) Must have its flow rate adjusted
(2) Is drying to the nasal mucosa
(3) Should be humidified
(4) Supports combustion

8. Which action is specific to caring for a patient with a communicable respiratory infection?
(1) Keeping the patient's door closed
(2) Wearing disposable gloves at all times
(3) Donning a gown when standing in the room
(4) Instructing the patient to wear a mask when receiving care

9. Sterile technique is best maintained when the person performing the procedure:
(1) Holds a wet 4×4 gauze pad upward until ready for use
(2) Changes the gloves if they are positioned below the waist
(3) Wipes a wound in a circular motion from the outside inward
(4) Drops a sterile item onto a sterile field from a 2 inch height

10. When ambulating a patient with an indwelling urinary catheter the caregiver should:
(1) Hang the collection bag below the patient's hips
(2) Maintain multiple dependent loops in the tubing
(3) Clamp the urinary tube before ambulating
(4) Detach the tube from the collection bag

11. A person is visually impaired and is afraid to walk at home because of a fear of falling. The **best** intervention would be to have a family member:
(1) Describe the environment
(2) Assist the person with ambulating
(3) Ensure that prescribed eye glasses are worn
(4) Encourage the person to walk only around their bed

12. A patient with one-sided weakness (hemiparesis) needs help transferring to a chair. To do this safely, the caregiver should:
(1) Stand on the patient's weak side
(2) Keep the patient's feet together
(3) Pivot the patient on the strong leg
(4) Hold the patient under both forearms

13. To promote safety when putting a sweater on or off a patient with a hemiparesis, the caregiver should:
(1) Flex the patient's wrist and elbow on the affected side
(2) Remove the sweater from the weaker side first
(3) Support the joints when removing the sweater
(4) Put the sweater on the stronger side first

14. The best action when assisting a blind person to walk would be to:
(1) Walk on the side while holding the person's elbow
(2) Stand behind the person and provide directions
(3) Walk alongside while the person uses a cane
(4) Instruct the person to hold onto your arm

15. When assisting a patient to move from a sitting to a standing position, the patient should stand in place a minute primarily to:

(1) Enable the body to adapt to the temporary drop in blood pressure
(2) Allow the patient to regain the energy expended while moving
(3) Provide time for the heart rate to return to normal
(4) Permit the patient to take several deep breaths

16. The most effective method to prevent the spread of microorganisms to all the patients in a hospital is:
    (1) Medical asepsis
    (2) Surgical asepsis
    (3) Transmission-based precautions
    (4) The use of antibiotics

17. When a fire is discovered in a dirty utility room, the FIRST action should be to:
    (1) Close the fire doors on the unit
    (2) Move patients toward the stairs
    (3) Attempt to put out the fire
    (4) Pull the fire alarm

18. When moving from a lying to a sitting position, the patient complains of dizziness. The initial response should be to:
    (1) Position the patient's head between the knees
    (2) Transfer the patient to a chair quickly
    (3) Instruct the patient to remain seated
    (4) Tell the patient to lie back down

19. To effectively put out a fire, the spray from the fire extinguisher should be directed across the:
    (1) Middle of the flames
    (2) Edge of the flames
    (3) Base of the flames
    (4) Top of the flames

20. When transferring a patient who is weak on the right side, from the bed to a chair the caregiver should:
    (1) Place the feet of the patient close together
    (2) Hold the patient under the elbows during the transfer
    (3) Instruct the patient to bear weight equally on both legs
    (4) Put the right arm of the chair against the left side of the patient's bed

21. Which of the following actions uses poor body mechanics?
    (1) Flexing the knees when lifting an object from the floor
    (2) Holding clean equipment close to the body when walking
    (3) Placing the feet apart when transferring a patient
    (4) Bending from the waist when providing patient care

22. A class A fire extinguisher can put out a fire in a:
    (1) Maintenance closet
    (2) Waste paper basket
    (3) Desk top computer
    (4) Microwave oven

23. A patient who is debilitated and unsteady when standing, insists on walking to the bathroom without calling for assistance. This behavior reflects a need to be:

(1) Alone
(2) Accepted
(3) Independent
(4) Manipulative

24. When an individual has an indwelling urinary catheter (Foley catheter) the collection bag should be:
(1) Carried at waist level when ambulating
(2) Kept below the level of the pelvis
(3) Emptied prior to ambulating
(4) Clamped when out of bed

RATIONALES

1.
(1) Statistics do not support smoking as the main reason for accidents in hospitals. Most hospitals are smoke free.
(2) Equipment is usually monitored for preventive maintenance; equipment generally shows wear and tear before it breaks.
* (3) Patients can be cognitively impaired, deny their physical impairments, or have limited perception, all of which can impede their ability to recognize hazards.
(4) Safety precautions do not take extra time; it often takes the same amount of time to do something correctly than it takes to do it incorrectly.

2.
* (1) Moving the patient to the floor is the safest action; it provides for free movement on a supported surface.
(2) Physical safety is the priority, not the need for privacy.
(3) Keeping the patient in the wheelchair while being transported could cause muscle strain, bones to fracture, or other injury; this should be done once the seizure is over.
(4) Securing the patient in a wheelchair could cause serious injury; moving the patient to the floor is the safest action.

3.
* (1) This is true; disoriented and confused patients do not have the cognitive ability to always understand what is happening to them.
(2) A patient usually struggles against a restraint to get free, not to manipulate staff.
(3) A restraint should not cause discomfort if it is applied correctly and checked frequently.
(4) Confused, disoriented patients who are restrained may become agitated and respond in a reflexlike way; attempts to gain control require problem solving, which confused, disoriented patients usually are unable to perform.

4.
(1) Sedation should not be used as a restraint.
(2) The patient can still climb over the rail and fall.
(3) Lowering the height of the bed may be done but it will not prevent a fall.
* (4) Of all the options offered, the vest restraint is the method that provides the most security to prevent a fall.

5.
(1) Containing the vomitus in a medical waste container is unnecessary if the vomitus can be flushed down a toilet.

* (2) Flushing the vomitus down the toilet is the safest and most practical action when disposing of vomitus; it dilutes, contains, and removes the vomitus.

(3) Saving a specimen is usually unnecessary; although a physician may request that vomitus be assessed, it is rarely saved to be assessed by the physician.

(4) Vomitus should not be poured down a sink, but rather a toilet.

6. (1) Disposable equipment helps reduce the spread of microorganisms, it still needs to be safely handled once used; handwashing is the most effective measure to reduce the spread of microorganisms.

(2) Double bagging is used to dispose of infectious waste; it limits the spread of infection, but handwashing is the most effective measure to reduce the spread of microorganisms.

* (3) Handwashing is the most effective measure to reduce the spread of infection because it removes microorganisms from the hands.

(4) Gloves protect the wearer; however, even when gloves are used hands must be washed before and after use to prevent the spread of microorganisms.

7. (1) Although this is true, prevention of fire is the priority when concerned about physical safety.

(2) This relates to physiological safety, not physical safety.

(3) Same as answer number two.

* (4) Although oxygen by itself will not burn or explode, it facilitates combustion; the greater the concentration of oxygen the more rapidly fires start and burn.

8. * (1) Keeping the door closed prevents the spread of microorganisms suspended in the air.

(2) Gloves are needed only when there is a likelihood of touching respiratory secretions.

(3) When just standing in the room only masks are necessary.

(4) The individual providing care wears a mask for self-protection, not the patient.

9. (1) This is incorrect technique; fluid from the wet 4×4 gauze pad can run down the upraised hand. When the hand is repositioned with the fingers downward, the fluid that runs back down the hand may be contaminated, which in turn will contaminate the 4×4 gauze pad.

* (2) When sterile gloves are accidentally positioned below the waist, they are considered out of the line of sight and must be changed because they may have become inadvertently contaminated.

(3) An inward circular motion can move contaminated material from a more contaminated section to a less contaminated section of a wound. The center of a wound is considered less contaminated than the edges of the wound or the surrounding skin; therefore, the wound should be wiped moving from the center outward using one gauze pad per stroke.

(4) From this height the unsterile portion of the wrapper should not contaminate the sterile field; however, a distance of 6 inches is preferred to prevent accidental contamination.

10. * (1) Hanging the bag below the patient's hips prevents the reflux of urine back up the tubing into the bladder.

(2) Loops of tubing should not be in a dependent position; dependent loops can cause urine to collect, stagnate, and back up into the bladder.

(3) This is unnecessary; this can be unsafe for patients recovering from surgery of the bladder.

(4) Urinary drainage systems should always remain intact; closed systems reduce infection by preventing pathogens from entering the system.

11.   (1) Describing the environment will help but it will not prevent an accident; it does not address the person's fear.

* (2) This will reduce fear because a family member is providing for the person's physical safety.

(3) Although glasses may help improve vision, this action does not address the person's fear.

(4) This is limiting; the problem is not mobility but fear of falling.

12.   (1) Standing on the patients weak side is unsafe; when transferring a patient the caregiver should stand in from of the patient.

(2) Keeping the patients feet together is unsafe; keeping the feet apart provides a wide base of support, which improves stability.

* (3) This is a safe method to transfer a patient; it avoids extra unnecessary movement by directly transferring a patient to the chair while supporting body weight on the stronger leg.

(4) Just using the arms places strain on the pectoral (shoulder) girdles and is unsafe. When not using a transfer belt, place both arms under the patient's axillary areas and the hands around the scapulae.

13.   (1) This should not be done without supporting the joints. Supported they can be flexed but this option does not indicate that the joints are being supported.

(2) This is an incorrect action; the stronger side usually has greater range of motion and should be dressed last and undressed first.

* (3) Joints should always be supported when moving to reduce unnecessary strain; moving an unsupported joint can cause an injury to that joint.

(4) Same as answer number two.

14.   (1) Walking on the side while holding the person's elbow is unsafe; the person cannot see and should not lead.

(2) Standing behind the person and providing directions is the method used to assist a person with a walker who has a mobility deficit.

(3) This does not allow for physical contact between the caregiver and the blind person and is unsafe; this method does not inspire confidence.

* (4) Instructing the person to hold onto your arm allows the caregiver to provide guidance and the blind person to follow; it supports comfort and contributes to confidence.

15.   * (1) Orthostatic hypotension is a condition that contributes to impaired stability. When moving from a sitting to a standing position, venous return is temporarily impeded; standing for a minute allows the circulation time to adjust to the change in position.

(2) Moving from a sitting to a standing position does not require an excessive amount of energy.

     (3) Moving from a sitting to a standing position does not require an excessive amount of energy; the heart rate should not be significantly elevated.

     (4) Although the patient might do this, it is not the main reason for waiting for a minute after standing.

16.   * (1) All patients in a hospital require care that employs medical aseptic techniques; procedures that break the chain of infection help control the transmission of microorganisms.

     (2) Not all patients require care that necessitates this specific intervention.

     (3) Same as answer number two.

     (4) Same as answer number two.

17.   (1) This may eventually be done, but it is not the priority.

     (2) Same as answer number one.

     (3) Same as answer number one.

    * (4) Of the options presented, pulling the fire alarm would be the first action; this alerts other health team members and the fire department that help is needed.

18.   (1) Positioning the patient's head between the knees is unsafe; it moves the patient's center of gravity forward, and the patient could fall.

     (2) Transferring the patient to a chair is unsafe; this would not permit time for the patient's vasomotor response to compensate for the change in position, and the patient could fall.

    * (3) Orthostatic or postural hypotension occurs because the ability of the autonomic nervous system to equalize the blood supply is diminished; when rising, blood pools in the lower extremities until the sympathetic nervous system causes peripheral vasoconstriction; sitting for a few minutes gives the body time to adjust.

     (4) Telling the patient to lie down is unnecessary.

19.   (1) Spraying the middle of the flames is unsafe; this could scatter the burning debris which would intensify the fire.

     (2) Spraying the edge of the flames is unsafe; this could scatter the burning debris, which would intensify the fire.

    * (3) The source of the fire is at its base where the fuel (e.g., linens, paper, flammable liquids) is burning.

     (4) Spraying the top of the flames is ineffective; this is too far from the source of the burning material.

20.   (1) Placing the patient's feet close together eliminates a wide base of support and raises the center of gravity, which promotes falls.

     (2) Holding the patient under the elbows is unsafe because it provides inadequate support. The patient should be supported with the caregiver's arms under the patient's arms and the caregiver's hands should be gripping the patient's back at the height of the scapulae.

     (3) This is unrealistic and unsafe; the side with the hemiparesis cannot bear as much weight as the unaffected side.

    * (4) The patient with a hemiparesis should get out of bed by leading with the unaffected side; this allows the stronger arm and leg to lead the movement into a chair. A patient with a right hemiparesis should get out of the left side of the bed.

21.
   (1) Flexing the knees when lifting from the floor is desirable because the strong muscles of the legs carry the load, which helps prevent back strain.
   (2) This is desirable because the weight is being carried close to the center of gravity, which helps maintain balance.
   (3) The wider the base of support and the lower the center of gravity, the greater the stability of the nurse.
 * (4) This puts too much stress on the vertebrae and muscles of the back because it does not distribute the work among the largest and strongest muscle groups of the legs.

22.
   (1) A maintenance closet usually contains flammable materials; water is contraindicated because it dilutes flammable liquids, which spreads the fire.
 * (2) A class A fire extinguisher contains water, which safely and effectively puts out fires consisting of wood, paper, or cloth.
   (3) A class A fire extinguisher contains water and is contraindicated in an electrical fire because water conducts electricity.
   (4) Water should not be used because a microwave oven is an electrical appliance.

23.
   (1) The patient is seeking independence, not trying to be left alone.
   (2) The primary motivation for this behavior is to feel independent, not to belong or be accepted.
 * (3) This is correct; the patient is attempting to perform self-care to demonstrate the ability to be self-sufficient.
   (4) The patient is seeking independence, not trying to manipulate the staff.

24.
   (1) This is too high; it allows urine to flow back into the bladder, which can cause a urinary tract infection.
 * (2) This prevents urine from flowing back into the bladder; urine flows away from the bladder by gravity.
   (3) This is unnecessary; urine in the collection bag will not interfere with ambulation.
   (4) This is unnecessary; this is unsafe for some patients.

ABBREVIATIONS AND SYMBOLS

This section encompasses questions that address the shortened or abridged form of medical terms. Questions focus on the identification of symbols or letters that refer to such topics as a disease, times of medication administration, activities, and commonly used phrases found in the medical record.

QUESTIONS

1. The abbreviation that indicates a disease of the central nervous system is:
   (1) CBC
   (2) CVA
   (3) CAD
   (4) CHF

2. A blood test used to measure the circulating glucose level after a 12-hour fast is the:
   (1) FHR
   (2) FSH
   (3) FBS
   (4) FUO

3. The abbreviation for a test that measures kidney function is the:
   (1) ICF
   (2) IVP
   (3) ICU
   (4) IUD

4. The abbreviation for a test that measures the electrical activity of the brain is:
   (1) ECG
   (2) ENT
   (3) EEG
   (4) EMG

5. The abbreviation that stands for a vaccine that protects an individual from three childhood diseases is:
   (1) DUB
   (2) DTP
   (3) DNA
   (4) DVT

6. The abbreviation that stands for "right eye" is:
   (1) OA
   (2) OB
   (3) OC
   (4) OD

7. The abbreviation for a test that is performed regularly to manage patients who are undergoing anticoagulant therapy is:
   (1) PT
   (2) PA
   (3) PBI
   (4) PID

8. An abbreviation that indicates temporary cerebrovascular insufficiency is:
   (1) TKA
   (2) TPN
   (3) TIA
   (4) TUR

9. What does the abbreviation "NPO" represent?
   (1) Whenever necessary
   (2) No people allowed
   (3) Nothing by mouth
   (4) Not permitted

10. What does the symbol s̄ represent?
    (1) Without
    (2) One half

    (3) Normal saline
    (4) Swish and swallow

11. A frequently used symbol is   . What does this symbol represent?
    (1) Dram
    (2) Pint
    (3) Ounce
    (4) Liter

12. A commonly accepted symbol for indicating male is:
    (1) ♂
    (2) ∞
    (3) ♀
    (4) @

13. The symbol for the word "increase" is:
    (1) →
    (2) ↑
    (3) >
    (4) ↗

14. The initials that represent arteriosclerotic heart disease are:
    (1) AST
    (2) ASD
    (3) ARDS
    (4) ASHD

15. The initials q.i.d. mean:
    (1) Once a day
    (2) Twice a day
    (3) Three times a day
    (4) Four times a day

16. When measuring fluids, an equivalent abbreviation for cubic centimeter (cc) is:
    (1) ml
    (2) ac
    (3) c̄
    (4) cm

17. If a medication is to be taken when going to bed at night, the prescription will indicate this direction with the abbreviation:
    (1) g.d.
    (2) b.t.
    (3) h.s.
    (4) p.c.

18. The symbol Rx in a physician's order means:
    (1) Take
    (2) Rectally
    (3) Right eye
    (4) Repeat one time

19. The abbreviation that refers to activities that are performed every day to support well being is:
    (1) ABG
    (2) ADL
    (3) ADH
    (4) ACTH

20. When the cause of a person's illness is indicated by the initials MVA it means that the illness was caused by a:
    (1) Car accident
    (2) Retrovirus
    (3) Cardiac dysrhythmia
    (4) Mitral valve anomaly

21. A patient states, "I am not allergic to anything that I know of." This information can be charted by the abbreviation:
    (1) AKA
    (2) PCN
    (3) NKA
    (4) ANA

22. The abbreviation b.i.d. means:
    (1) Twice a day
    (2) Before meals
    (3) Bathroom privileges
    (4) Bowel movement every day

23. When a person's vital signs are inside the acceptable average range, this fact could be charted that the patient's vital signs are:
    (1) BMR
    (2) WNL
    (3) TPR
    (4) ADL

24. The abbreviation "ad lib." means:
    (1) If necessary
    (2) Every day
    (3) When required
    (4) Freely as directed

25. The abbreviation q2h means:
    (1) Repeat two times
    (2) Two times a day
    (3) Every other day
    (4) Every 2 hours

26. Which of the following represents a milligram?
    (1) mL
    (2) mg
    (3) mcg
    (4) mEq

27. When a physician writes a prescription and states that a medication should be administered p.o. it means that the drug should be taken:
    (1) By mouth
    (2) When required
    (3) After meals
    (4) Every day

28. When a person has a terminal illness and decides that cardiopulmonary resuscitation is not an option, the choice may be indicated on official documents by the abbreviation:
    (1) DOA
    (2) DNR
    (3) DTR
    (4) DNA

RATIONALES

1. (1) CBC denotes **c**omplete **b**lood **c**ount.
    * (2) CVA represents a **c**erebral **v**ascular **a**ccident. A CVA is caused by a cerebral hemorrhage, a thrombus, or an embolus that results in a lack of oxygen to brain tissue. The lay term for CVA is stroke.
    (3) CAD stands for **c**oronary **a**rtery **d**isease, which is a disease of the heart.
    (4) CHF denotes **c**ongestive **h**eart **f**ailure, which is a syndrome associated with cardiac insufficiency.

2. (1) FHR is the abbreviation for **f**etal **h**eart **r**ate.
    (2) FSH is the abbreviation for **f**ollicle-**s**timulating **h**ormone.
    * (3) FBS refers to **f**asting **b**lood **s**ugar and is also known as a fasting blood glucose. This routine test is done on blood drawn after a 12- to 14-hour fast to screen for diabetes mellitus when adaptations for this disease are present.
    (4) FUO is the abbreviation for **f**ever of **u**nknown **o**rigin.

3. (1) ICF is the abbreviation for **i**ntra**c**ellular **f**luid.
    * (2) IVP is the abbreviation for **i**ntra**v**enous **p**yelogram and is a radiologic technique for examining the structures and function of the urinary system.
    (3) ICU is the abbreviation for **i**ntensive **c**are **u**nit.
    (4) IUD is the abbreviation for **i**ntra**u**terine **d**evice.

4. (1) ECG, also known as EKG, is the abbreviation for **e**lectro**c**ardio**g**ram, which measures the function of the heart.
    (2) ENT is the abbreviation for "pertaining to **e**ar, **n**ose, and **t**hroat."
    * (3) This is correct. An **e**lectro**e**ncephalo**g**ram records the electrical potential produced by brain cells. The test is used to diagnose seizure disorders, focal lesions, impaired consciousness, brainstem disorders, or the presence of tumors.
    (4) EMG is the abbreviation for **e**lectro**m**yo**g**ram which is a test that records the electrical activity in a skeletal muscle. This test is done to diagnose neuromuscular problems.

5. (1) DUB is the abbreviation for **d**ysfunctional **u**terine **b**leeding.
    * (2) DTP stands for **d**iphtheria-**t**etanus-**p**ertussis vaccine, which is prescribed for the routine immunization of children against these diseases.
    (3) DNA is the abbreviation for **d**eoxyribo**n**ucleic **a**cid, which is the carrier of genetic information in living cells.
    (4) DVT is the abbreviation for **d**eep **v**ein **t**hrombosis.

6. (1) OA is the abbreviation for **o**ste**o**arthritis.
    (2) OB is the abbreviation for **ob**stetrics.
    (3) OC is the abbreviation for **o**ral **c**ontraceptive.
    * (4) OD stands for *oculus dexter* the Latin phrase for "right eye."

7. * (1) PT is the abbreviation for **p**rothrombin **t**ime. Prothrombin is essential for the clotting process.
    (2) PA is the abbreviation for **p**ostero**a**nterior view, indicating the direction x-ray beams travel through the body when the x-ray is taken from the back to the front. This is the usual view for chest radiographs.
    (3) PBI is the abbreviation for **p**rotein-**b**ound **i**odine, a test that measures thyroid gland activity.
    (4) PID is the abbreviation for **p**elvic **i**nflammatory **d**isease.

8. (1) TKA is the abbreviation for **t**otal **k**nee **a**rthroplasty.
    (2) TPN is the abbreviation for **t**otal **p**arenteral **n**utrition.
    * (3) TIA is the abbreviation for **t**ransient **i**schemic **a**ttack. Symptoms of a TIA vary depending on the area affected and the extent of the occlusion; the symptoms usually resolve within 24 hours.
    (4) TUR is the abbreviation for **t**rans**u**rethral **r**esection.

9. (1) "Whenever necessary" (*pro re nata*) is represented by the initials p.r.n.
    (2) There is no acceptable abbreviation for this phrase.
    * (3) "Nothing by mouth" (*non per ora*) represents NPO.
    (4) Same as answer number two.

10. * (1) "Without" (**s**ine) is represented by the symbol s̄.
    (2) "One half" (**semis**) is represented by the symbol s̄s̄.
    (3) "Normal **s**aline" is represented by the abbreviation NS.
    (4) There is no symbol for "swish and swallow." Some physicians will use the abbreviation **S&S** for swish and swallow; however, this could be confused with "swish and spit." Therefore these orders should be written in full to avoid confusion. This describes how an oral anesthetic is administered.

11. (1) "Dram" is represented by the symbol ∉.
    (2) "Pint" is represented by the symbol "O" or the abbreviation "pt."
    * (3) This is the symbol for the word "ounce." A way to remember this symbol is to close the first loop of the symbol so that it becomes a circle. The resulting symbol will be an "o" on top of a "z" which represents oz, the abbreviation for ounce.
    (4) "Liter" is represented by the abbreviation "L."

12. * (1) This is correct. The symbols for "male" are ♂ or □.
    (2) This is the symbol for "infinity."

(3) This is the symbol for "female."

(4) This symbol represents the word "at."

13.   (1) This symbol means "leads to" or "yields."

* (2) This is the symbol for "increase" or "increased."

(3) This symbol means "greater than."

(4) This symbol means "increasing."

14.   (1) These initials represent **A**sparate amino**t**ransferase, an enzyme found in the serum and certain body tissues such as the heart and liver.

(2) These initials represent **a**rterial **s**eptal **d**efect.

(3) These initials represent **a**cute **r**espiratory **d**istress **s**yndrome.

* (4) This is the correct abbreviation for **a**rterio**s**clerotic **h**eart **d**isease.

15.   (1) The abbreviation for once a day is "o.d." (*omni die*) or "q.d." (*quaque die*).

(2) The abbreviation for twice a day is "b.i.d." (**b**is **i**n **d**ie).

(3) The abbreviation for three times a day is "t.i.d." (**t**er **i**n **d**ie).

* (4) This is correct. The abbreviation for four times a day is "q.i.d." (**q**uater **i**n **d**ie).

16.   * (1) A milliliter, which contains 15 to 16 drops, is the approximate equivalent of a cubic centimeter.

(2) The abbreviation "a.c." represents the term "before meals" (*ante cibum*).

(3) The abbreviation "c̄" represents the word "with."

(4) The abbreviation "cm" represents the word "**c**enti**m**eter."

17.   (1) This abbreviation stands for "every day" (*quaque die*).

(2) There is no such abbreviation.

* (3) This is the abbreviation for "hour of sleep" (*hora somni*). The abbreviation "h.d." (*hora decubitus*) also means bedtime but it is rarely used.

(4) This abbreviation stands for "after meals" (*post cibum*).

18.   * (1) Rx, which was derived from the word recipe, means "take, treatment, or prescription."

(2) "Rectally" is represented by the abbreviations "Rect." or "p.r."

(3) "Right eye" is represented by the abbreviation "OD" (*oculus dexter*).

(4) "Let it be repeated" is abbreviated as "Rep" (*repetatur*).

19.   (1) ABG is the abbreviation that refers to **a**rterial **b**lood **g**ases.

* (2) ADL is the abbreviation that refers to **a**ctivities of **d**aily **l**iving. These activities include activities such as bathing, grooming, toileting, eating, dressing and undressing.

(3) ADH is the abbreviation that refers to **a**nti**d**iuretic **h**ormone.

(4) ACTH is the abbreviation that refers to **a**dreno**c**ortico**t**ropic **h**ormone.

20.   * (1) The initials MVA represents **m**otor **v**ehicle **a**ccident.

(2) MVA is unrelated to retroviruses. There are many retroviruses and they are referred to specifically.

(3) MVA is unrelated to dysrhythmias. There are many types of dysrhythmias and they are referred to specifically.

(4) MVA is unrelated to mitral valve disorders. There are a variety of mitral valve disorders and they are referred to specifically.

21.   (1) AKA stands for "an **a**bove the **k**nee **a**mputation" or "**a**lso **k**nown **a**s."

            (2) PCN stands for "**p**eni**c**illi**n**"; this is an antibiotic to which many people are allergic.

    * (3) NKA stands for "**n**o **k**nown **a**llergies."

            (4) ANA stands for "**a**nti**n**uclear **a**ntibodies" or "**A**merican **N**urses **A**ssociation."

22.   * (1) The abbreviation "b.i.d." (***bis in die***) means "twice daily."

            (2) The abbreviation for "before meals" is "a.c." (***ante cibum***).

            (3) The abbreviation for "**b**athroom **p**rivileges" is "BRP."

            (4) Although there is no specific abbreviation for this phrase, "**b**owel **m**ovement" is abbreviated "BM" or "bm" and "every day" is abbreviated as "q.d." (***quaque die***). Therefore, "BM q.d." represents "bowel movement every day."

23.   (1) The abbreviation BMR represents "**b**asal **m**etabolic **r**ate."

    * (2) The abbreviation WNL represents "**w**ithin **n**ormal **l**imits."

            (3) The abbreviation TPR represents "**t**emperature, **p**ulse and **r**espirations;" additional information, such as the degree of the temperature or rate of the pulse and respirations, would have to be included to make this note significant.

            (4) The abbreviation ADL represents "**a**ctivities of **d**aily **l**iving," which includes activities such as dressing, grooming, bathing, eating, and toileting.

24.   (1) The abbreviation s.o.s. (***si opus sit***) means "if necessary."

            (2) The abbreviations o.d. (***omni die***) or q.d. (***quaque die***) mean "every day."

            (3) The abbreviation p.r.n. (***pro re nata***) means "when required" or "when needed."

    * (4) The abbreviation ad lib. (***ad libibitum***) means "freely as desired."

25.   (1) There is no specific abbreviation for this phrase; the abbreviation for repeat is "Rep."

            (2) The abbreviation b.i.d. (***bis in die***) means "two times a day."

            (3) The abbreviation q.o.d. means "every other day."

    * (4) The abbreviation q.h. (***quaque hora***) means "every hour;" when the number 2 is inserted between "q." and "h." it represents "every 2 hours" (q2h).

26.   (1) This abbreviation represents a **m**illi**l**iter.

    * (2) This abbreviation represents a **m**illi**g**ram.

            (3) This abbreviation represents a **m**i**c**ro**g**ram.

            (4) This abbreviation represents a **m**illi**e**quivalent.

27.   * (1) The abbreviation p.o. (***per os***) means "orally" or "by mouth."

            (2) The abbreviation p.r.n. (***pro re nata***) means "when required."

            (3) The abbreviation p.c. (***post cibum***) means "after meals."

            (4) The abbreviations o.d. (***omni die***) and q.d. (***quaque die***) means "every day."

28.   (1) The abbreviation DOA represents "**d**ead **o**n **a**rrival."

    * (2) The abbreviation DNR represents "**d**o **n**ot **r**esuscitate."

            (3) The abbreviation DTR represents "**d**eep **t**endon **r**eflexes."

            (4) The abbreviation DNA represents "**d**eoxyribo**n**ucleic **a**cid."

PHARMACOLOGY AND ADMINISTRATION OF MEDICATIONS

This section encompasses questions related to the classification, physiological action, therapeutic effects, side effects, and toxic effects of drugs. Questions address allergies, developmental considerations, and peak and trough levels of medications. Also, it includes questions related to the principles associated with the administration of medications via the oral, parenteral (intravenous, intramuscular, intradermal, and subcutaneous), topical, ear, eye, vaginal, and rectal routes.

QUESTIONS

1. A pharmacological agent used to prevent or relieve itching is called an:
   (1) Antiseptic
   (2) Antifungal
   (3) Antipruritic
   (4) Antiarrhythmic

2. The classification of drugs that alter the activity of epinephrine and norepinephrine, causing a reduced work load of the heart is:
   (1) Peripheral vasodilators
   (2) Calcium channel blockers
   (3) Beta blockers
   (4) Cardiotonics

3. Which of the following pharmacological terms is correctly matched with the description of a drug classification?
   (1) Mucolytic: solidifies tenacious mucus
   (2) Expectorant: decreases mucus production
   (3) Antitussive: encourages coughing contributing to airway clearance
   (4) Bronchodilator: causes relaxation of smooth muscles of respiratory passageways

4. Narcotic analgesics limit pain by:
   (1) Diminishing peripheral pain reception
   (2) Competing with receptors for sensory input
   (3) Modifying the patient's perception of pain
   (4) Closing the gating mechanism for impulse transmission

5. Prior to administering a medication that is teratogenic, the patient should be asked:
   (1) "Have you ever had an anaphylactic reaction?"
   (2) "Were you ever addicted to drugs?"
   (3) "Do you have any allergies?"
   (4) "Are you pregnant?"

6. Besides its therapeutic effect of inhibiting microbial growth, a specific antibiotic may also depress the bone marrow. This response is classified as:
   (1) An overdose
   (2) A side effect
   (3) A drug toxicity
   (4) An idiosyncratic effect

7. When calculating dosages of medication for children, the **most** important factor to consider is their:
   (1) Age
   (2) Weight
   (3) Level of anxiety
   (4) Developmental level

8. A patient is receiving a drug every 4 hours. Because the drug has a narrow therapeutic window, the physician orders a peak blood level. A blood specimen should be obtained:
   (1) Immediately before administering a dose
   (2) Halfway between two scheduled doses
   (3) One hour after administering a dose
   (4) At 10 PM in the evening

9. Because of the physiological changes associated with aging, when administering drugs to the elderly, they should specifically be assessed for signs of:
   (1) Toxicity
   (2) Side effects
   (3) Allergic reactions
   (4) Drug-food interactions

10. A route of administration that is used only for its local therapeutic effect is the:
    (1) Rectum
    (2) Skin
    (3) Nose
    (4) Eye

11. When receiving an intradermal injection, the patient is at the highest risk for exhibiting an:
    (1) Overdose
    (2) Allergic response
    (3) Idiosyncratic reaction
    (4) Interaction with other drugs

12. To best protect the patient from aspiration when administering an oral medication the caregiver should:
    (1) Offer extra water
    (2) Crush the medication
    (3) Position the patient in a sitting position
    (4) Inspect the patient's mouth before swallowing

13. Which of the following routes for medication administration is considered to be the most accurate and safe?
    (1) By mouth
    (2) Topically
    (3) Intravenous
    (4) By injection

14. Which of the following is the most dangerous route for administering medication?
    (1) IV push
    (2) Piggyback

    (3) Injection

    (4) Inhalation

15. The physician orders peak and trough levels to monitor an antibiotic administered every 6 hours. To measure trough levels a blood specimen should be drawn:
    (1) One half hour before a scheduled dose
    (2) Halfway between scheduled doses
    (3) One hour after a scheduled dose
    (4) At 8 AM in the morning

16. The classification of medication associated with oncology that inhibits the formation of specific enzymes necessary for cell division are:
    (1) Antimetabolites
    (2) Cytotoxic drugs
    (3) Alkylating agents
    (4) Mitotic inhibitors

17. What action should be taken when a drop of blood appears at the insertion site after performing an IM injection?
    (1) Massage the area gently
    (2) Take the patient's vital signs
    (3) Apply pressure with an antiseptic swab
    (4) Document this reaction in the patient's chart

18. Most orally administered drugs are absorbed in the:
    (1) Liver
    (2) Stomach
    (3) Small intestine
    (4) Large intestine

RATIONALES

1.   (1) Antiseptics are topically applied agents that destroy bacteria.
       (2) Antifungals are administered topically or systemically to destroy fungi or disrupt their growth.
   * (3) An antipruritic is an agent that relieves, prevents, or counteracts itching.
       (4) Antiarrhythmics are effective in preventing or alleviating cardiac dysrhythmias.

2.   (1) Peripheral vasodilators expand blood vessels in the extremities, causing a decrease in blood pressure. They are used to treat inadequate circulation to the extremities.
       (2) Calcium channel blockers act by slowing the influx of calcium ions into muscle cells, thereby decreasing arterial resistance.
   * (3) Beta-adrenergic receptor blocking agents compete with the sympathetic neurotransmitters, epinephrine and norepinephrine, for beta-adrenergic receptor sites. These sites are located mainly in the heart.
       (4) Cardiotonics act by altering the force of cardiac contraction.

3.   (1) A mucolytic liquifies, not solidifies, tenacious mucus.
       (2) An expectorant increases, not decreases, mucus production, so that it promotes the coughing up and removal of mucus from the lungs.

      (3) An antitussive relieves, not encourages, coughing.

* (4) Once bronchi and bronchioles relax their lumens increase in diameter (bronchodilation) causing a decrease in airway resistance.

4.   (1) Local anesthetics, not narcotics, produce loss of localized sensation by inhibiting nerve conduction and thus the perception of pain.

      (2) This is the theory related to increasing distracting sensory input to inhibit painful stimuli perception.

* (3) Narcotics modify pain perception by acting on the higher centers of the brain to inhibit the perception of pain.

      (4) Narcotics do not close synaptic gates; stimulation of large nerve fibers via methods such as transcutaneous electrical stimulation close synaptic gates.

5.   (1) This question refers to a severe, systemic hypersensitivity to a drug, food, or chemical; a severe form of this reaction can be fatal.

      (2) This question refers to an uncontrollable craving for a chemical substance due to a physical or psychological dependence.

      (3) Allergies are unpredictable hypersensitivity reactions to allergens such as drugs; it can be a mild to severe reaction and can cause a rash, pruritus, rhinitis, wheezing, hives, and even an anaphylactic reaction.

* (4) "Teratogenic," when used in the context of medication, refers to a drug that can cause adverse effects in a fetus or embryo.

6.   (1) An overdose happens when a person receives a dosage larger than the usual recommended dose; this is rarely planned and is usually an accident.

* (2) A side effect is a secondary effect. It can be harmless or cause injury; if injurious, the drug is discontinued.

      (3) Toxicity occurs when a patient is on a drug for a long time or when a drug accumulates in the blood because of poor excretion or metabolism, causing excess amounts in the blood.

      (4) An idiosyncratic effect is an unexpected effect; it can be an overreaction, an underreaction, or an unusual reaction.

7.   (1) Age is not reliable for calculating a pediatric dose of medication; the weight of a child at any age can vary greatly.

* (2) Dosages depend on body mass; therefore, weight is the most important and objective factor for calculating medication dosages for children.

      (3) The level of anxiety does not influence dosage calculation of a child's medication.

      (4) The developmental level does not influence dosage calculation of a child's medication.

8.   (1) A specimen would be drawn immediately before the administration of the drug for a trough level.

      (2) Halfway between two scheduled doses would not provide an accurate result.

* (3) Most medications administered q4h have an accurate peak concentration about 1 hour following administration.

      (4) A blood specimen taken at 10 PM would provide inaccurate results unless the drug was administered at 9 PM; there is no information to indicate that the drug was administered at 9 PM.

9.   * (1) Although toxicity occurs in all ages, biotransformation of drugs is less efficient in the elderly than during younger developmental ages; when drugs are not fully metabolized and excreted from the body, toxic levels can accumulate.
   (2) Harmless or injurious secondary effects are common to all ages, not just the elderly.
   (3) Allergic reactions are common to all ages, not just the elderly.
   (4) Drug-food interactions are common to all ages, not just the elderly.

10.   (1) Medication can be administered via this route for either a local or systemic effect; medications can be absorbed through the rich vascular bed in the mucous membranes.
   (2) Medications can be administered via the skin for either a local or systemic effect.
   (3) Same as answer number one.
   * (4) Medications are instilled into the eye only for their local effect; part of the procedure for instillation of eye drops is to apply gentle pressure to the nasolacrimal duct for 10 to 15 seconds to prevent absorption of the medication into the systemic circulation.

11.   (1) Overdoses are a risk with all types of injections but are at the highest risk with the intravenous route, not the intradermal route.
   * (2) An intradermal injection is given under the skin to test for such things as allergies; these drugs can cause an anaphylactic reaction if absorbed by the circulation too quickly or if the person has a hypersensitivity to the solution.
   (3) Idiosyncratic reactions are unpredictable effects. They are usually under-reactions, overreactions, or reactions that are different from the expected reactions; idiosyncratic reactions are less likely to occur than allergic reactions with intradermal injections.
   (4) A drug interaction is when one drug alters the action of another drug; this is an impossible response to a singular intradermal injection.

12.   (1) Excessive water may promote aspiration.
   (2) Crushing the medication helps some people, it is not the consistency of medication but rather the amount of water taken with the medication that could promote aspiration. Also multiple crushed particles taken with water could stimulate the gag reflex; however, crushed medications if placed in applesauce would increase safety.
   * (3) A sitting position allows the patient to control the flow of fluid to the back of the oropharynx as well as promote the flow of fluid down the esophagus via gravity.
   (4) Inspecting the patient's mouth is important after, not before, administering medication.

13.   * (1) By mouth is the safest route because it is convenient, it does not break the skin barrier, it is slowly absorbed, and it usually does not cause physical or emotional stress.
   (2) Because absorption is affected by a variety of factors, such as extent of capillary network and condition of the skin, this is not the most accurate method of administration.

(3) Intravenous route carries the highest risk because it breaks the skin barrier and the medication is injected directly into the bloodstream.

(4) This route carries a high risk because the medication is rapidly absorbed and it breaks the skin barrier.

14. * (1) An IV push or bolus administration of medication is the instillation of a medication directly into a vein over a period of about 1 to 5 minutes; this rapid administration of a medication places the patient at highest risk for adverse effects.

(2) Although an IV piggyback is a dangerous route, the medication is generally diluted in 50 mL to 150 mL of fluid and it is infused over a time period of about 20 to 60 minutes.

(3) A solution instilled into a muscle is absorbed over a time period.

(4) Although inhaled medications can produce almost immediate local or systemic responses, this route is not as dangerous as an IV bolus medication.

15. * (1) "Trough level" refers to when a drug is at its lowest concentration in the blood in response to biotransformation; this usually occurs during the time period just prior to the next scheduled dose.

(2) Halfway between scheduled doses would not be a time period when a drug is at its lowest concentration in the blood.

(3) Many variables affect the time a drug reaches its peak plasma level within an individual; however, 1 hour after the administration of an antibiotic one could safely plot the antibiotic plasma level on the rising side of the curve of the plasma level profile, not within the trough.

(4) This is irrelevant; the peak and trough of a blood plasma level depends on the time the last dose was administered, not the time of day the specimen is drawn.

16. * (1) Antimetabolites are drugs that resemble normal human metabolites, which inhibit enzymes necessary for the formation of critical cellular elements.

(2) Cytotoxic drugs interfere with the proliferation of cells by inhibiting cellular division.

(3) Alkylating agents destroy parts of the DNA molecule. They may also destroy rapidly proliferating non-malignant cells. Certain cytotoxic drugs are also alkylating agents.

(4) Mitotic inhibitors work by preventing cell division during the mitosis phase of the cell growth cycle.

17. (1) Massaging the area is traumatic and could cause further bleeding.

(2) Taking the vital signs is unnecessary; the loss of a drop of blood would not influence vital signs.

* (3) Pressure constricts blood vessels, which will limit bleeding; an antiseptic swab will help prevent infection at the needle insertion site.

(4) Documenting this reaction is unnecessary; although this is not an expected therapeutic response, it does occasionally occur because the needle may pierce a tiny blood vessel.

18. (1) Most drugs are metabolized, not absorbed, in the liver by microsomal enzymes.

(2) The stomach has a small surface area and slow capillary blood flow and

therefore has poor absorptive potential. Most tablets and capsules are disintegrated and dissolved in the stomach.

* (3) The small intestine, consisting of the duodenum, jejunum, and ileum, is approximately 20 feet long and secretes enzymes that complete the digestive process. These structures provide a large surface area and have a rapid capillary blood flow facilitating absorption of orally administered drugs.

(4) The main function of the large intestine is to reabsorb water, not absorb oral medications.

MEDICAL TERMINOLOGY

This section encompasses questions related to medical terminology. Questions focus on the basic elements of a medical word, rules associated with building a medical term, and identifying suffixes, prefixes, and word elements that are included in medical words.

QUESTIONS

1. Which medical term correctly uses a combining vowel to link parts of the medical term?
   (1) Phlebtomy
   (2) Erythrocyte
   (3) Gastroectomy
   (4) Gastrenteritis

2. Which of the following parts of the medical term leuk/o/cyt/o/penia is the suffix?
   (1) leuk
   (2) o
   (3) cyt
   (4) penia

3. Which suffix denotes a surgical puncture?
   (1) -centesis
   (2) -plasty
   (3) -plegia
   (4) -lysis

4. Which of the following is a diagnostic, or symptomatic, suffix?
   (1) -algia
   (2) -desis
   (3) -tripsy
   (4) -ectomy

5. The suffix that denotes reconstructive surgery is?
   (1) -pexy
   (2) -tome
   (3) -emia
   (4) -ology

6. Which suffix means "dropping?"
    (1) -plasia
    (2) -ptosis
    (3) -phasia
    (4) -poiesis

7. The suffix "-pepsia" refers to:
    (1) Dilation
    (2) Digestion
    (3) Discharge
    (4) Difficulty

8. The suffix that means "formation or growth" is?
    (1) -phasia
    (2) -phagia
    (3) -plasia
    (4) -pathy

9. Which suffix means "flow or discharge?"
    (1) -rrhexis
    (2) -rrhophy
    (3) -rrhagia
    (4) -rrhea

10. "Hypo," "intra," and "supra" are examples of:
    (1) Suffixes
    (2) Prefixes
    (3) Word roots
    (4) Combining forms

11. Which of the following examples indicate the correct plural form of the words listed?
    (1) Bronchus/bronchae
    (2) Thorax/thoracia
    (3) Pleura/pleure
    (4) Lumen/lumina

12. A person who specializes in the study of blood is called a(n).
    (1) Immunologist
    (2) Hematologist
    (3) Pathologist
    (4) Internist

13. In relation to a chronic illness, exacerbation refers to:
    (1) A discharge of fluid, cells, or other substances
    (2) An escape of blood or serum into the tissues
    (3) An increase in the intensity of a disease
    (4) A progressive deterioration of health

14. The medical term that denotes "pertaining to the testes" is:
    (1) Orchidic
    (2) Orchialgia
    (3) Orchiodynia
    (4) Orchidalgia

15. The suffix "-penia" stands for:
    (1) Destroy
    (2) Dilation
    (3) Deficiency
    (4) Development

16. The medical word element "cholangio" stands for:
    (1) Bile
    (2) Bile duct
    (3) Bile vessel
    (4) Biliary system

17. An instrument used to cut is a:
    (1) -tome
    (2) -scope
    (3) -graph
    (4) -meter

18. The medical word element "hepat/o" stands for:
    (1) Lobe
    (2) Loins
    (3) Liver
    (4) Lymph

19. The medical word element "rhin/o" stands for:
    (1) Neck
    (2) Nose
    (3) Nerve
    (4) Nipple

20. Which medical word element stands for "protection?"
    (1) Phylaxis
    (2) Poiesis
    (3) Lympho
    (4) Globin

21. The medical word element "-desis" stands for:
    (1) Stabilization
    (2) Suspension
    (3) Stimulate
    (4) Straight

22. The medical word element "squamo" stands for:
    (1) Scanty
    (2) Saliva
    (3) Scaly
    (4) Same

23. The medical word element "philia" refers to:
    (1) Grow
    (2) Love
    (3) Break
    (4) Secrete

24. The medical word element that stands for "within" is:
    (1) Endo
    (2) Hydro
    (3) Gyneco
    (4) Hystero

25. The medical word element "bucco" stands for:
    (1) Beneath
    (2) Eyelid
    (3) Cheek
    (4) Slow

26. Which medical word element stands for "head?"
    (1) Cervico
    (2) Cephalo
    (3) Cheilo
    (4) Chromo

27. Which medical word element refers to "lip?"
    (1) Lipo
    (2) Lobo
    (3) Labio
    (4) Linguo

28. The medical word element for "bladder" is:
    (1) Vesico
    (2) Viscero
    (3) Vesiculo
    (4) Ventriculo

29. The word root and combining form that denotes "brain" is:
    (1) Endo
    (2) Cranio
    (3) Cerebro
    (4) Encephalo

30. The suffix that denotes "movement" is:
    (1) -plegia
    (2) -algesia
    (3) -kinesia
    (4) -esthesia

31. The suffix "-taxia" refers to:
    (1) Nourishment, development
    (2) Muscular coordination
    (3) Incomplete paralysis
    (4) Feeling, sensation

32. The inability to express oneself verbally because of damage to the speech center in the brain as a result of tissue ischemia is called:
    (1) Ataxia
    (2) Aphasia

(3) Asthenia

(4) Anesthesia

33. The medical term that denotes "incision of the skull" is:
    (1) Craniotomy
    (2) Craniectomy
    (3) Cerebrotomy
    (4) Cranioplasty

34. The medical term that denotes "disease of the brain" is:
    (1) Encephalopyosis
    (2) Encephalopathy
    (3) Encephalocele
    (4) Encephalogram

35. Pain in a nerve is indicated by the medical term:
    (1) Neuralgia
    (2) Neuroglial
    (3) Neurotripsy
    (4) Neurorrhaphy

36. The medical term "myringoplasty" denotes:
    (1) Surgical repair of the eardrum
    (2) Fungal infection of the eardrum
    (3) Incision into the tympanic membrane
    (4) Inflammation of the tympanum and mastoid cells

37. The medical term that denotes "ear wax" is:
    (1) Vertigo
    (2) Cerumen
    (3) Smegma
    (4) Sebum

38. The medical term that refers to "purulent discharge from the ear" is:
    (1) Otopyorrhea
    (2) Otorrhagia
    (3) Otodynia
    (4) Otalgia

39. Which term is related to rapidly growing cells?
    (1) Proliferate
    (2) Metastasis
    (3) Exacerbation
    (4) Infiltrating

40. An incision of the bladder is known as a:
    (1) Cystotomy
    (2) Colectomy
    (3) Mastectomy
    (4) Phlebotomy

41. Surgical fixation of the uterus is known as:
    (1) Mastopexy
    (2) Nephropexy

(3) Gastropexy

(4) Hysteropexy

42. A procedure to examine a part of the esophagus is called an:
    (1) Esophagoscopy
    (2) Esophagectomy
    (3) Esophagalgia
    (4) Esophagitis

43. An opening between two hollow viscera or vessels established via a surgical procedure is called:
    (1) Ankylosis
    (2) Anthracosis
    (3) Anastomosis
    (4) Anisocytosis

44. The surgical incision of the abdomen that permits exploration of the abdominal cavity is called:
    (1) Lithotomy
    (2) Laparotomy
    (3) Laryngotomy
    (4) Lymphadenotomy

45. The creation of a surgical opening into the stomach for the purpose of tube feedings is known as a:
    (1) Gastromegaly
    (2) Gastroplegia
    (3) Gastrostomy
    (4) Gastroscopy

46. Splenectomy denotes:
    (1) Splenic pain
    (2) Tumor of the spleen
    (3) Removal of the spleen
    (4) Enlargement of the spleen

47. A cystolithectomy refers to the:
    (1) Surgical repair of a cystocele
    (2) Excision of a stone from the bladder
    (3) Removal of the kidney and its ureter
    (4) Reimplantation of a ureter into the bladder

48. The word "prostatectomy" denotes:
    (1) Pain in the prostate gland
    (2) Flow from the prostate gland
    (3) Removal of the prostate gland
    (4) Inflammation of the prostate gland

49. The medical word element "glosso" stands for:
    (1) Tooth
    (2) Tonsil
    (3) Tongue
    (4) Trachea

RATIONALES

1.
   (1) Phlebtomy is incorrect. Phleb/o/tomy is the correct use of the combining vowel "o" in this medical term. A combining vowel is used to link a root word to a suffix that begins with a consonant.
   * (2) The root word "erythr" and the suffix "cyte" are correctly linked with the combining vowel "o". This makes the word easier to pronounce.
   (3) Gastroectomy is incorrect. Gastr/ectomy is the correct linkage of the root word "gastr" and the suffix "ectomy." A combining vowel is not used before a suffix that begins with a vowel.
   (4) Gastrenteritis is incorrect. Gastr/o/enter/itis is the correct linkage. It uses the combining vowel "o" to link the root words "gastr" and "enter." The combining vowel is usually retained between two roots even if the second root begins with a vowel.

2.
   (1) "Leuk" is a root word.
   (2) "O" is a combining vowel.
   (3) "Cyt" is a root word.
   * (4) "Penia," a suffix, is added to the end of a medical term to modify its meaning; "-penia" means decreased, deficiency, or lack of.

3.
   * (1) "-Centesis" means surgical puncture and is considered a suffix denoting a surgical perforation.
   (2) "-Plasty" means surgical repair and denotes reconstructive surgery.
   (3) "-Plegia" means paralysis or stroke.
   (4) "-Lysis" means to destroy, breakdown, or separate.

4.
   * (1) "-Algia" means pain and is a symptomatic suffix.
   (2) "-Desis" means binding, stabilization, or fusion and denotes reconstructive surgery.
   (3) "-Tripsy" means crush and is a surgical suffix used to denote a crushing action.
   (4) "-Ectomy" means excision or removal and denotes a surgical excision.

5.
   * (1) "-Pexy" means fixation or suspension and denotes reconstructive surgery.
   (2) "-Tome" means instrument to cut and is classified as a surgical suffix or can be used as a noun meaning knife.
   (3) "-Emia" means a condition of the blood and is classified as a diagnostic and symptomatic suffix.
   (4) "-Ology" means the study of and is classified as a diagnostic and symptomatic suffix; "o" is a combining vowel.

6.
   (1) "-Plasia" means formation, development, or growth.
   * (2) "-Ptosis" means dropping, prolapse, or falling.
   (3) "-Phasia" means speech.
   (4) "-Poiesis" means formation or production.

7.
   (1) Dilation is indicated by the suffix "-ectasis."
   * (2) Digestion is indicated by the suffix "-pepsia."
   (3) Discharge is indicated by the suffix "-rrhea."
   (4) Difficulty is indicated by the prefix "dys-."

8.   (1) "-Phasia" means speech.
        (2) "-Phagia" means swallow or eat.
      * (3) "-Plasia" means formation or growth.
        (4) "-Pathy" means disease.

9.   (1) "-Rrhexis" means rupture.
        (2) "-Rrhophy" means suture.
        (3) "-Rrhagia" means bursting forth.
      * (4) "-Rrhea" means discharge or flow.

10.   (1) These are prefixes, not suffixes. Suffixes are added to the end of a root word or combining form to alter the meaning.
      * (2) "Hypo," "intra," and "supra" are all prefixes. A prefix is placed before a word or word root to make a new word to change its meaning.
        (3) A root word is the foundation of a word and may or may not be a complete word. Some medical terms contain more than one root word. A root word usually denotes a body part or fluid.
        (4) A combining form consists of a root word and a vowel. The vowel makes a term easier to pronounce when added to a suffix or another root word that begins with a consonant.

11.   (1) Bronchi is the correct plural form of the word bronchus.
        (2) Thoraces is the correct plural form of the word thorax.
        (3) Pleurae is the correct plural form of the word pleura.
      * (4) Lumina is the correct pleural form of the word lumen.

12.   (1) An immunologist is a specialist who is associated with the study of immunity.
      * (2) A hematologist is a specialist who is associated with the study of blood. "Hemat" denotes blood, "logist" is a suffix that denotes one who studies, and "o" is the combining vowel.
        (3) A pathologist is a specialist who is associated with the study of diseases.
        (4) An internist is a physician who specializes in internal medicine.

13.   (1) A discharge of fluid, cells, or other substances is called exudate.
        (2) An escape of blood or serum into the tissues is called extravasation.
      * (3) An exacerbation is an increase in the seriousness of a disease or disorder that is identified by an escalation in the intensity of the signs or symptoms exhibited by the patient.
        (4) Although a progressive deterioration of health can happen with chronic illnesses, this does not describe an exacerbation.

14.   * (1) "Orchid" refers to testes and "-ic" refers to pertaining to.
        (2) This is testicular pain.
        (3) Same as answer number two.
        (4) Same as as answer number two.

15.   (1) The suffix that stands for destroy is "-lysis."
        (2) The suffix that stands for dilation is "-ectasis."
      * (3) This is correct. When "-penia" is connected with a root word the medical term indicates a (specified) deficiency. For example leukopenia refers to deficiency in leukocytes.
        (4) The suffix that stands for development is "-plasia."

16.
    (1) The medical word element for bile is "chol/e."
    (2) The medical word element for bile duct is "choledoch/o."
  * (3) "Cholangi/o" is the medical word element that stands for bile vessel. This word element is used in the medical term "cholangiogram," which is an x-ray of the biliary ducts once a radiopaque material is intravenously injected or directly instilled into the area.
    (4) The medical word element for biliary system is "bil/i."

17.
  * (1) A "-tome" is a combining form that denotes cutting instrument. A "dermomyotome" is a cutting instrument used to cut skin or muscle. "Derm/o" is the medical word element for skin, "my/o" is the medical word element for muscle, and "-tome" indicates cutting instrument.
    (2) A "-scope" is an instrument used to view or examine.
    (3) A "-graph" is an instrument used to record.
    (4) A "-meter" is an instrument used to measure.

18.
    (1) The medical word element "lob/o" stands for lobe.
    (2) The medical word element "lumb/o" stands for loins.
  * (3) The medical word element "hepat/o" stands for liver.
    (4) The medical word element "lymph/o" stands for lymph.

19.
    (1) "Cervic/o" is the medical word element for neck.
  * (2) "Rhin/o" means pertaining to the nose or to a noselike structure. "Pathy" is a combining form meaning disease. The word "rhinopathy" indicates a disease or malformation of the nose.
    (3) "Neur/o" is the medical word element for nerve.
    (4) "Thel/o" is the medical word element for nipple.

20.
  * (1) "Phylaxis" means protection.
    (2) The medical word element "poiesis" stands for production.
    (3) The medical word element "lympho" stands for lymph tissue.
    (4) The medical word element "globin" stands for "protein."

21.
  * (1) "Desis" means stabilization, binding, or fusion.
    (2) "Plexy" is the medical word element for suspension.
    (3) "Tropin" is the medical word element for stimulate.
    (4) "Ortho" is the medical word element for straight.

22.
    (1) "Oligo" is the medical word element that means scanty.
    (2) "Sialo" is the medical word element that stands for saliva.
  * (3) "Squamo" is a combining form that means scales.
    (4) "Homo" is the medical word element that stands for same.

23.
    (1) "Physis" means to grow.
  * (2) "Philia" is the medical word element that refers to attraction for or love. For example, pedophilia is a psychosexual disorder characterized by an abnormal interest in children.
    (3) "-Clast" is the medical word element that stands for to break.
    (4) "-Crine" is the medical word element that stands for to secrete.

24.
  * (1) "Endo" is the medical word element that stands for within or inward.
    (2) "Hydro" stands for water.

      (3) "Gyneco" stands for woman.
      (4) "Hystero" stands for uterus or womb.

25.   (1) "Hypo" stands for beneath or deficient.
      (2) "Blepharo" stands for eyelid.
  * (3) The medical word element "bucco" refers to cheek.
      (4) "Brady" stands for slow.

26.   (1) "Cervico" stands for neck or cervix.
  * (2) The medical word element "cephalo" means head.
      (3) "Cheilo" stands for lip.
      (4) "Chromo" stands for color.

27.   (1) "Lipo" refers to fat.
      (2) "Lobo" refers to lobe.
  * (3) The medical word element "labio" means lips.
      (4) "Linguo" refers to tongue.

28. * (1) The medical word element "vesico" indicates the bladder or a blister.
      (2) The medical word element "viscero" denotes organ.
      (3) "Vesiculo" denotes seminal vesicle.
      (4) "Ventriculo" denotes ventricle.

29.   (1) "Endo" is a combining form meaning inward or within.
      (2) "Cranio" denotes skull.
      (3) "Cerebro" stands for cerebrum.
  * (4) The medical word element "encephalo" means brain.

30.   (1) The suffix "-plegia" denotes paralysis.
      (2) The suffix "-algesia" denotes pain.
  * (3) The suffix "-kinesia" denotes movement, motion, or activation.
      (4) The suffix "-esthesia" denotes feeling or sensation.

31.   (1) The suffix "-trophy" means nourishment or development.
  * (2) The suffix "-taxia" denotes impaired muscular coordination or impaired physical or mental control.
      (3) The suffix "-paresis" means incomplete paralysis.
      (4) The suffix "-esthesia" means feeling or sensation.

32.   (1) "Ataxia" indicates impaired muscle coordination.
  * (2) "Aphasia" indicates a neurological condition that interferes with the ability to understand and/or transmit a verbal message.
      (3) "Asthenia" denotes weakness or lack of strength.
      (4) "Anesthesia" denotes lack of sensation.

33. * (1) "Craniotomy" refers to incision of the skull bones or cranium.
      (2) "Craniectomy" refers to excision of part of the skull.
      (3) "Cerebrotomy" refers to incision of the cerebrum.
      (4) "Cranioplasty" refers to surgical repair of the skull.

34.   (1) "Encephalopyosis" denotes brain abscess.
  * (2) "Encephalo" is the combining form for brain and the suffix "-pathy" denotes disease.

(3) "Encephalocele" denotes herniation of the brain.

(4) "Encephalogram" denotes radiography of the brain.

35. * (1) "Neuro" indicates nerve or neuron and the suffix "-algia" denotes pain. The combining vowel "o" is dropped when "neuro" is combined with a suffix that begins with a vowel.

(2) "Neuroglial" denotes one of the two main cells comprising the nervous system.

(3) "Neurotripsy" denotes surgical crushing of a nerve.

(4) "Neurorrhaphy" denotes suturing the ends of nerves.

36. * (1) "Myringo" is the combining form that denotes tympanic membrane or eardrum. "Plasty" is the suffix that denotes repair of.

(2) "Myringomycosis" denotes fungal infection of the eardrum.

(3) "Myringotomy" denotes incision into the tympanic membrane.

(4) "Myringomastoiditis" denotes inflammation of the tympanum and mastoid cells.

37. (1) "Vertigo" refers to dizziness.

* (2) "Cerumen" is earwax produced by the vestigial apocrine sweat glands in the external ear canal.

(3) "Smegma" is a secretion of sebaceous glands found under the foreskin of the penis in men and at the base of the labia minora in women.

(4) "Sebum" is the secretion of the sebaceous glands of the skin.

38. * (1) "Oto" denotes the ear. "Pyo" denotes pus. "Rrhea" denotes discharge.

(2) "Otorrhagia" denotes hemorrhage from the ear.

(3) "Otodynia" denotes pain in the ear.

(4) "Otalgia" also denotes pain in the ear.

39. * (1) "Proliferate" denotes reproducing rapidly and repeatedly.

(2) "Metastasis" denotes spreading of tumor cells to a distant part of the body.

(3) "Exacerbation" denotes an increase in intensity.

(4) "Infiltrating" denotes penetration or diffusion into the spaces within tissue.

40. * (1) "Cystotomy" denotes an incision of the bladder. "Cysto-" is the combining form for the word bladder and "-tomy" denotes cut into or incision.

(2) "Colectomy" denotes excision of part of the colon.

(3) "Mastectomy" denotes excision of a breast.

(4) "Phlebotomy" denotes incision of a vein.

41. (1) "Mastopexy" denotes the surgical fixation of a pendulous breast.

(2) "Nephropexy" denotes the surgical fixation of a floating kidney.

(3) "Gastropexy" denotes suture of the stomach wall.

* (4) "Hysteropexy" denotes the surgical fixation of the uterus. "Hyster" refers to the uterus, "o" is the combining vowel, and "-pexy" refers to surgical fixation.

42. * (1) "Esophagoscopy" refers to the use of an endoscope to examine the esophagus.

(2) "Esophagectomy" is an excision of part of the esophagus.

(3) "Esophagalgia" is pain in the esophagus.

(4) "Esophagitis" is an inflammation of the esophagus.

43. (1) "Ankylosis" indicates stiffening of the joints.
  (2) "Anthracosis" indicates lung pathology as a result of inhaled minute particles of coal dust.
* (3) "Anastomosis" is a surgically created communication between two tubular organs.
  (4) "Anisocytosis" indicates a condition in which there is a significant variation in cell size being either macrocytic or microcytic cells.

44. (1) "Lithotomy" is the surgical excision of a calculus, usually from the urinary system.
* (2) "Laparotomy" indicates any surgical incision into the peritoneal cavity, usually to establish a differential diagnosis or to treat the underlying pathological condition.
  (3) "Laryngotomy" is the surgical repair of the larynx.
  (4) "Lymphadenotomy" denotes an incision of a lymph node.

45. (1) "Gastromegaly" indicates enlargement of the stomach.
  (2) "Gastroplegia" refers to paralysis of the stomach.
* (3) "Gastrostomy" is the surgical creation of an artificial opening into the stomach through the abdominal wall.
  (4) "Gastroscopy" is the visual inspection of the interior of the stomach via a flexible fiberoptic scope inserted via the esophagus.

46. (1) "Splenalgia" denotes splenic pain.
  (2) "Splenoma" denotes a tumor of the spleen.
* (3) "Splen" refers to the spleen and "ectomy" refers to surgical removal.
  (4) "Splenomegaly" refers to an abnormal enlargement of the spleen.

47. (1) This is a cystoplasty.
* (2) This is correct. "Cysto" refers to bladder, "lith" refers to stone, and "ectomy" refers to excision.
  (3) This is a nephroureterectomy.
  (4) This is an ureterovesicostomy.

48. (1) This is prostatodynia or prostatalgia, not prostatectomy, which is removal of the prostate.
  (2) This is prostatorrhea.
* (3) "Prostat" refers to prostate and "-ectomy" refers to removal or excision.
  (4) This is prostatitis.

49. (1) The medical word element "dento-" means tooth.
  (2) The medical word element "tonsillo-" means tonsil.
* (3) The combining form "glosso-" means the tongue.
  (4) The medical word element "tracheo-" means trachea.

ANATOMY AND PHYSIOLOGY

This section encompasses questions that test the knowledge of the structure and function of the body. Questions address normal changes that occur throughout the lifespan and normal physiological defensive mechanisms of the body.

QUESTIONS

1. The primary physiological reason why elderly people tend to have higher blood pressures than members of other age groups is because older people have:
   (1) Vessels that are less elastic
   (2) Stressful lifestyle changes
   (3) Blood that is thicker
   (4) Hearts that are aging

2. Which of the following statements is accurate?
   (1) The neck is superior to the head.
   (2) The wrist is proximal to the elbow.
   (3) The sternum is posterior to the vertebrae.
   (4) The visceral membrane lines the abdominal cavity.

3. The glands of the body that secrete oil are the:
   (1) Sweat glands
   (2) Sebaceous glands
   (3) Ceruminous glands
   (4) Sudoriferous glands

4. Groups of cells that perform the same basic function are called a(n):
   (1) Organism
   (2) Tissue
   (3) System
   (4) Organ

5. The plane that divides the body into equal right and left halves is the:
   (1) Coronal plane
   (2) Sagittal plane
   (3) Transverse plane
   (4) Midsagittal plane

6. The cartilaginous structure overhanging the larynx that prevents matter from entering the respiratory tract when swallowing is called the:
   (1) Epidermis
   (2) Epistaxis
   (3) Epiglottis
   (4) Epicarditis

7. The main long portion or shaft of the bone is called the:
   (1) Epiphyses
   (2) Diaphysis
   (3) Periosteum
   (4) Hematopoiesis

8. A large projection of a bone that provides a point of attachment for muscles and ligaments is the:
   (1) Fossa
   (2) Condyle
   (3) Trochanter
   (4) Fontanel

9. A gland that is attached to the hypothalamus in the brain that secretes thyrotropic hormone is the:
   (1) Pineal gland
   (2) Adrenal gland
   (3) Thyroid gland
   (4) Pituitary gland

10. The parathyroid glands are involved in the:
   (1) Production of mineralocorticoids
   (2) Secretion of the antidiuretic hormone
   (3) Secretion of insulin from the beta cells
   (4) Absorption of calcium from foods in the intestines

11. Which statement is a principle of blood pressure physiology?
   (1) A trough pressure occurs during systole.
   (2) The pulse pressure occurs during diastole.
   (3) A peak pressure occurs when the ventricles relax.
   (4) The blood pressure reaches a peak followed by a trough.

12. A patient who drinks small amounts of fluid will:
   (1) Produce urine with a specific gravity of 1.020
   (2) Urinate small amounts at each voiding
   (3) Develop an atonic bladder
   (4) Have dark amber urine

13. When urine output is less than fluid intake, the patient will:
   (1) Gain weight
   (2) Void frequently
   (3) Become jaundiced
   (4) Experience nausea

14. When the amount of calories ingested is not sufficient for the patient's basal metabolic rate, the patient will:
   (1) Become dehydrated
   (2) Develop anorexia
   (3) Lose weight
   (4) Sleep more

15. To maintain **normal** fluid balance, how much fluid should a person receive during 24 hours?
   (1) 500 cc
   (2) 1000 cc
   (3) 2000 cc
   (4) 3000 cc

16. Iron absorption is facilitated by vitamin:
   (1) D
   (2) C
   (3) A
   (4) K

17. To maintain life the most important nutrients are:
    (1) Carbohydrates
    (2) Vitamins
    (3) Proteins
    (4) Fluids

18. Normal breathing is based on which of the following?
    (1) Competence of the phrenic nerve to innervate accessory muscles
    (2) Ability of the intrapleural pressure to become positive
    (3) Capability of the diaphragm to fall during expiration
    (4) Lack of resistance in the airway during inspiration

19. A productive cough means it:
    (1) Precipitates pain
    (2) Results in sputum
    (3) Gets progressively worse
    (4) Interferes with breathing

20. The exchange of respiratory gases is based on the principle of:
    (1) Osmosis
    (2) Invasion
    (3) Diffusion
    (4) Decompression

21. A tough fibrous tissue that makes up the outermost layer of five sixths of the bulb of the eye is the:
    (1) Retina
    (2) Sclera
    (3) Cornea
    (4) Choroid

22. The structure that is attached to the lateral side of the head, is made up of cartilage covered with skin, and funnels sound waves into the ear canal is called an:
    (1) Anacusis
    (2) Aphonia
    (3) Auricle
    (4) Aura

23. Which statement is accurate about the respiratory system?
    (1) On inspiration the diaphragm assumes a dome shape.
    (2) The exchange of gas takes place because of osmosis.
    (3) Respiration is the exchange of oxygen and carbon dioxide.
    (4) Ventilation refers to the exchange of gas between the air and blood.

24. When blood exits the pulmonary veins it enters the:
    (1) Aorta
    (2) Left atrium
    (3) Right ventricle
    (4) Systemic circulation

25. A joint in which the convex surface of one bone fits into the concave surface of another bone is known as a:

(1) Pivot joint
(2) Hinge joint
(3) Condyloid joint
(4) Ball-and-socket joint

26. A structure that is associated with the inner ear is the:
    (1) Vestibule
    (2) Tympanum
    (3) Malleus
    (4) Pinna

27. The General Adaptation Syndrome (GAS) is primarily controlled by the:
    (1) Endocrine system
    (2) Respiratory system
    (3) Integumentary system
    (4) Cardiovascular system

RATIONALES

1. * (1) Vascular changes and the accumulation of sclerotic plaques along the walls of vessels make them more rigid.
      (2) Stressful lifestyle changes is a generalization that may or may not be true depending on the individual; the older adult will have physical, cognitive, and social changes, and how the person perceives them and adapts to them will determine if the lifestyle is stressful.
      (3) High blood pressure in the elderly is generally caused by smoking, obesity, lack of exercise, and stress, not blood that is thicker.
      (4) A decreased contractile strength of the myocardium results in a decreased cardiac output, which the body compensates for by increasing the heart rate, not the blood pressure.

2.   (1) The neck is inferior, not superior, to the head.
      (2) The wrist is distal, not proximal, to the elbow.
      (3) The sternum is anterior, not posterior, to the vertebrae.
    * (4) This is correct. The visceral membrane lines the abdominal cavity.

3.   (1) Sweat glands are also called sudoriferous glands. Sudoriferous glands secrete sweat, not oil.
    * (2) Sebaceous glands secrete oil; this is the correct answer.
      (3) Ceruminous glands secrete wax, not sweat. They line the external auditory canal.
      (4) Same as answer number one.

4.   (1) An organism is a living thing composed of systems.
    * (2) A tissue is a group or layer of similarly specialized cells that together perform specific functions; this is the correct answer.
      (3) A system is a group of organs that work together to perform a function.
      (4) An organ is a group of tissues that work together to perform a specialized function.

5.   (1) The coronal plane divides the body into an anterior and posterior position of the body, not the plane that divides the body into equal right and left halves.

    (2) The sagittal plane divides the body into unequal right and left sides of the body, not equal halves.

    (3) The transverse plane is a horizontal plane, dividing the body or organ into upper and lower portions (inferior and superior), not equal halves.

    * (4) The midsagittal plane is correct. This plane is also known as the median plane.

6.   (1) Epidermis is the outer layer of skin.

    (2) Epistaxis denotes bleeding from the nose.

    * (3) "Epi" means upon and "glottis" refers to the vocal cords and the opening between them. The epiglottis prevents choking by blocking of the passageway to the lungs during swallowing.

    (4) Epicarditis is an inflammation of the outer most layer of the heart, not bleeding from the nose.

7.   (1) Epiphyses is the term used to refer to the two ends of a long bone.

    * (2) Diaphysis is the shaft of a long bone, consisting of a tube of compact bone enclosing the medullary cavity.

    (3) Periosteum is the dense white fibrous membrane that covers the surface of bone.

    (4) Hematopoiesis refers to blood cell formation.

8.   (1) Fossa is a depression in a bone surface.

    (2) Condyle is a rounded process at the end of a bone that forms an articulation.

    * (3) Trochanter is a very large projection that provides a point of attachment for muscles and ligaments. An example would be the greater trochanter of the femur.

    (4) Fontanelle is a soft spot at the junction of sutures in the incompletely ossified skull of an infant.

9.   (1) The pineal gland is attached to the posterior part of the third ventricle of the brain and is believed to secrete melatonin hormone.

    (2) The adrenal glands are located at the top of each kidney. Each gland consists of a medulla and cortex, which have independent functions. The cortex secretes cortisol and androgens and the medulla manufactures epinephrine and norepinephrine.

    (3) The thyroid gland is located in the front of the neck and secretes the hormone thyroxine, triiodothyronine, and calcitonin.

    * (4) The pituitary gland is attached to the hypothalamus in the brain and is divided into the anterior lobe and the posterior lobe. The anterior lobe secretes growth hormone (somatotropin), thyrotropic hormone, adrenocorticotrophic hormone (ACTH), two gonadotrophic hormones, follicle-stimulating hormone (FSH), luteinizing hormone (LH), and prolactin. The posterior lobe stores oxytocin and vasopressin.

10.   (1) The adrenal glands, not the parathyroid glands, are involved in the production and secretion of mineralocorticoids.

    (2) The pituitary gland, not the parathyroid glands, is involved in the production and secretion of antidiuretic hormone.

      (3) The pancreas (islets of Langerhans) contain alpha and beta cells. The beta cells produce insulin, not the parathyroid glands.

* (4) This is correct. Also, the parathyroid hormone causes the kidneys to conserve blood calcium and stimulates osteoblast formation.

11.   (1) Peak pressures occur during systole. Trough pressures occur during diastole.

      (2) Pulse pressure is the difference between the systolic and diastolic pressures.

      (3) Peak pressures occur when the ventricles contract.

* (4) Peak pressures occur when the ventricles contract, and trough pressures occur when the ventricles relax; these occur with each contraction and relaxation of the heart.

12.   (1) Reduced fluid intake will produce a concentrated urine with a specific gravity higher than 1.025.

      (2) This is not true; the bladder will still fill to the patient's normal capacity before there is a perceived need to void.

      (3) An atonic bladder is caused by a neurological problem; it is a loss of the sensation of fullness which leads to distension from overfilling.

* (4) This is the color of urine that one can expect when fluid intake is below 1500 to 2000 ml per day; the urine is concentrated.

13. * (1) Fluid has mass; when fluid is retained, the patient will gain weight. A patient can gain 6 to 8 pounds before edema can be identified through inspection.

      (2) The patient will not void frequently; the opposite is true.

      (3) Jaundice is related to impaired liver and biliary function, not fluid volume excess.

      (4) Nausea is not a common sign of fluid volume excess.

14.   (1) Dehydration occurs when fluid intake is insufficient, not when calories are insufficient.

      (2) Anorexia is a loss of appetite that usually contributes to insufficient intake, not the result of insufficient intake.

* (3) When calories are insufficient to meet metabolic needs, the body catabolizes fat and as a result the patient will lose weight.

      (4) Excessive sleep is not directly related; however, a patient may tire easily if anemic from an inappropriate diet.

15.   (1) 500 cc of fluid is inadequate intake to maintain life.

      (2) 1000 cc of fluid is inadequate to maintain life.

* (3) 2000 cc is an average daily intake necessary to maintain normal fluid balance.

      (4) 3000 cc is more than the body needs for normal fluid balance.

16.   (1) Vitamin D is essential for adequate absorption and utilization of calcium in bone and tooth growth; it does not facilitate the absorption of iron.

* (2) Ascorbic acid (vitamin C) helps to change dietary iron to a form that can be absorbed by the body.

      (3) Vitamin A is essential for growth and maintenance of epithelial tissue, maintenance of night vision, and promotion of resistance to infection, not the absorption of iron.

(4) Vitamin K is essential for the formation of prothrombin, which prevents bleeding not the absorption of iron.

17.
(1) Although important, the body can survive longer without carbohydrates than it can without water.
(2) The body can survive longer without vitamins than it can without water.
(3) The body can survive longer without proteins than it can without water.
* (4) The most basic nutrient need is water; 57% of the body of an average healthy man is water. Women have a smaller percentage than men because they have proportionately more fat. All body processes require an adequate fluid balance in the body.

18.
(1) The phrenic nerve innervates the diaphragm, not the accessory muscles.
(2) For air to flow into the lungs, the intrapleural pressure must become negative, not positive.
(3) On expiration the diaphragm rises, not falls.
* (4) Clear air passages are essential for adequate volumes of air to reach the lungs; airway resistance increases in response to an obstruction of the airway, edema of the lining of the air passages, or a disease of the respiratory passages.

19.
(1) A productive cough may or may not produce pain depending on the patient's underlying condition.
* (2) A productive cough is accompanied by expectorated secretions.
(3) Productive does not indicate progressive.
(4) When a patient raises respiratory secretions and expectorates them, breathing usually improves.

20.
(1) Osmosis is the passage of a solvent through a semipermeable membrane from an area of lesser solute concentration to an area of greater solute concentration.
(2) Invasion refers to metastasis of a tumor by direct extension.
* (3) Diffusion is the movement of gases from an area of greater pressure or concentration to an area of lesser pressure or concentration.
(4) Decompression is the lowering of pressure within a space by removing fluid or gas; for example, a nasogastric tube can be used to remove gastric contents, decompressing the stomach.

21.
(1) The retina is the nervous tissue of the eye that receives and transmits visual impulses via the optic nerve to the brain and is the innermost layer of the eye.
* (2) The sclera provides a protective shield over five sixths of the eye bulb; it is made up of a tough, inelastic, opaque membrane and is attached to muscles that move the eye.
(3) The cornea is a transparent, fibrous structure that covers one sixth of the eye bulb and projects like a dome from the sclera at the anterior portion of the eye.
(4) The choroid is a vascular membrane that provides the blood supply to the eye and is located between the sclera and the retina.

22.　　　　(1) Anacusis refers to deafness.

(2) Aphonia refers to a speech dysfunction, characterized by an inability to produce normal speech sounds.

* (3) Auricle refers to the structure of the external ear; it is also known as the pinna.

(4) Aura refers to the sensation that may occur before a tonic-clonic seizure or migraine episode.

23.　　　　(1) Because the lungs expand on inspiration, the diaphragm assumes a shape that is flat.

(2) Diffusion, not osmosis, occurs when molecules move from an area of greater concentration to an area of lesser concentration. Diffusion is the basic principle underlying internal and external respiration.

* (3) Respiration is the exchange of oxygen and carbon dioxide between the alveoli and the pulmonary capillary blood (external respiration) and between the tissue capillaries and body cells (internal respiration).

(4) Ventilation refers to breathing and includes the process of inhaling and exhaling, not the actual exchange of gases.

24.　　　　(1) Blood from the pulmonary veins must first enter the left atrium and progress through the left ventricle before it exits the heart into the ascending aorta.

* (2) Oxygenated blood returns from the lungs via the pulmonary veins and enters the heart at the left atrium.

(3) Blood that enters the right ventricle must proceed to the lungs via the pulmonary arteries before it returns to the heart via the pulmonary veins.

(4) Blood must first be oxygenated in the lungs; return to the left atrium via the pulmonary veins; and pass through the left ventricle, the aortic valve, and aorta before it reaches the systemic circulation.

25.　　　　(1) In a pivot or trochoid joint a rounded, pointed, or conical surface of one bone articulates within a ring formed partly by bone and partly by a ligament. The primary movement permitted is rotation and it is therefore known as monaxil. An example of a pivotal joint is the joint between the atlas and axis.

* (2) In a hinge or ginglymus joint a convex surface of one bone fits into the concave surface of another bone. Movement is in one plane, such as flexion and extension, and is therefore known as monaxial or uniaxial. An example of a hinge joint is the elbow.

(3) In a condyloid or ellipsoidal joint an oval-shaped condyle of one bone fits into an elliptical cavity of another bone. Because the joint permits side-to-side and back-and-forth movements it is known as biaxial. An example of a condyloid joint is when there is abduction and adduction along with flexion and extension of the wrist.

(4) In a ball-and-socket or spheroid joint a ball-like surface of one bone fits into a cuplike depression of another bone. The joint permits movement in three planes (flexion-extension, abduction-adduction, and rotation) and is know as triaxial. An example of a ball-and-socket joint is the hip joint.

26.   * (1) The vestibule is the chamber that connects the cochlea to the semicircular canals and is located in the inner ear.

        (2) The tympanum is a flat membrane that is situated at the end of the ear canal of the external ear. Sound waves strike against this tympanic membrane or eardrum.

        (3) The malleus is a hammer-shaped bone that, along with the stapes and incus, transmits vibrations between the tympanic membrane and the cochlea. These bones are in the middle ear.

        (4) The pinna is an external structure of the ear designed to collect sound waves.

27.   * (1) The General Adaptation Syndrome (GAS) primarily involves the endocrine system and autonomic nervous system; the antidiuretic hormone (ADH), adrenocorticotropic hormone (ACTH), cortisol, aldosterone, epinephrine, and norepinephrine are all involved with the fight-or-flight response.

        (2) The respiratory system is stimulated by the hormone epinephrine.

        (3) The autonomic nervous system affects the integumentary system.

        (4) The cardiovascular system is stimulated by the hormones epinephrine and norepinephrine.

PATHOPHYSIOLOGY

This section encompasses questions that address the biologic and physical manifestations of common health problems. The questions identify alterations in structure or function associated with common diseases that reflect a cross section of body systems.

QUESTIONS

1. The process of blood destruction is:
   (1) Hemolysis
   (2) Hematology
   (3) Hemoglobin
   (4) Hematopoiesis

2. The process of scab formation over sores or wounds during healing is:
   (1) Necrosis
   (2) Abrasion
   (3) Crustation
   (4) Excoriation

3. Redness of the skin seen in partial thickness burns is known as?
   (1) Eczema
   (2) Erythema
   (3) Ecchymosis
   (4) Erythrocytosis

4. Inflammation of the breast is referred to as:
   (1) Mastoptosis

(2) Mastalgia
(3) Mastitis
(4) Amastia

5. Hives, a pruritic eruption of the skin, also are known as:
   (1) Nevi
   (2) Wheals
   (3) Vesicles
   (4) Urticaria

6. A fatty tumor is also called a(n):
   (1) Lipoma
   (2) Adenoma
   (3) Lipocele
   (4) Adipogenous

7. A decrease in lymphocytes in the blood is known as:
   (1) Lymphocytopenia
   (2) Lymphocytosis
   (3) Lymphopoiesis
   (4) Lymphadenoma

8. An obstruction of the bowel caused by a twisting of the bowel on itself is called:
   (1) Stenosis
   (2) Volvulus
   (3) Enterospasm
   (4) Diverticulum

9. A slow heart rate is known as:
   (1) Angina
   (2) Dyspnea
   (3) Bradycardia
   (4) Tachycardia

10. When air accumulates in the pleural cavity, causing the lung to collapse, it is known as a:
    (1) Pyothorax
    (2) Hemothorax
    (3) Hydrothorax
    (4) Pneumothorax

11. Pathologic changes in the lung caused by inhaling minute particles of coal dust are called:
    (1) Silicosis
    (2) Siderosis
    (3) Chalicosis
    (4) Anthracosis

12. Hematemesis means:
    (1) Vomiting blood
    (2) Enlargement of the liver
    (3) Surgical repair of a hernia
    (4) Weakness on one side of the body

13. A condition characterized by loss of bone density is:
    (1) Rheumatoid arthritis
    (2) Ewing's sarcoma
    (3) Osteoporosis
    (4) Kyphosis

14. A disease of the neuromuscular system that is specifically characterized by muscle weakness of the eyes and face, difficulty swallowing, and problems with chewing and talking is:
    (1) Spina bifida
    (2) Myasthenia gravis
    (3) Muscular dystrophy
    (4) Rheumatoid arthritis

15. A sexually transmitted disease that is characterized by a greenish-yellowish cervical discharge in women and a mucopurulent urethral discharge in men is:
    (1) Syphilis
    (2) Gonorrhea
    (3) Chlamydia
    (4) Herpes simplex

16. The condition resulting in muscle twitches and spasms because of hypocalcemia is:
    (1) Edema
    (2) Tetany
    (3) Diuresis
    (4) Stenosis

17. The endocrine system disease that is characterized by an elevated metabolic rate, weight loss, muscular weakness, excessive perspiration, heat intolerance, palpitations, nervousness, a fine hand tremor, and emotional liability is:
    (1) Cushing's syndrome
    (2) Addison's disease
    (3) Diabetes mellitus
    (4) Grave's disease

18. A diabetic coma that may develop as a result of too little insulin is known as:
    (1) Glycosuria
    (2) Ketoacidosis
    (3) Hypoglycemia
    (4) Hyperkalemia

19. Hypothyroidism in an adult is also called:
    (1) Cretinism
    (2) Dwarfism
    (3) Myxedema
    (4) Giantism

20. When the stool appears black because of upper gastrointestinal (GI) bleeding, the stool is characterized as:
    (1) Tarry
    (2) Necrotic
    (3) Purulent
    (4) Melanin

21. A systemic adaptation to an infection includes:
    (1) Pain
    (2) Edema
    (3) Fever
    (4) Erythema

22. When a patient has a draining pressure ulcer, which of the following losses will be most significant?
    (1) Fluid
    (2) Weight
    (3) Protein
    (4) Leukocytes

23. An infection of a surgical wound usually demonstrates clinical signs:
    (1) Between 3 to 5 days following surgery
    (2) Between day 1 and 2 following surgery
    (3) After 7 to 10 days following surgery
    (4) Within 24 hours following surgery

24. Which of the following patients would be at the highest risk for developing constipation?
    (1) A child who is physically active
    (2) An elderly man who drinks a lot of fluid
    (3) A middle-aged woman who eats whole-grain cereal
    (4) An adolescent who is experiencing problems in school

25. Foods likely to cause constipation are:
    (1) Fruits
    (2) Vegetables
    (3) Whole grains
    (4) Dairy products

26. Which individual would most likely have life-threatening complications when experiencing a respiratory infection?
    (1) Infant
    (2) Adolescent
    (3) Elderly person
    (4) School-aged child

27. A common local adaptation to pressure is specifically referred to as:
    (1) Edema
    (2) Ischemia
    (3) Orthopnea
    (4) Hypovolemia

28. Which patient with a respiratory tract infection would have the highest risk for an airway obstruction?
    (1) 2-year-old toddler
    (2) 16-year-old child
    (3) Middle-aged woman
    (4) Elderly man

29. A fever can result in tachypnea because of the:
    (1) Need to retain carbon dioxide

(2) Increase in the metabolic rate

(3) Decrease in carbon dioxide levels

(4) Attempt to compensate for respiratory alkalosis

30. A serious complication that can develop as a result of prolonged wheelchair use is:
    (1) Respiratory infections
    (2) Urinary tract infections
    (3) Thrombophlebitis of the legs
    (4) Extension contractures of the hips

31. A contracture is most often caused by:
    (1) Excessive pressure
    (2) Joint disease
    (3) Inactivity
    (4) Aging

32. The main cause of decubitus ulcers is:
    (1) Gravity
    (2) Pressure
    (3) Skin breakdown
    (4) Cellular necrosis

33. Multiple sclerosis is a progressive degenerative disease in which there is a:
    (1) Buildup of lipid material in central nervous system cells
    (2) Destruction of the myelin sheath surrounding neurons
    (3) Functional disorder of the seventh cranial nerve
    (4) Decrease in cerebral circulation

34. A progressive neurologic disorder of unknown etiology characterized by memory loss, impaired cognition, and emotional instability is:
    (1) Cerebral palsy
    (2) Alzheimer's disease
    (3) Multiple sclerosis
    (4) Spina bifida

35. A pathologic condition in the infant characterized by abnormal head growth, separation of the sutures, and bulging fontanels because of an abnormal collection of cerebrospinal fluid (CSF) within the cranial vault is known as:
    (1) Hydramnios
    (2) Hydradenitis
    (3) Hydrocephalus
    (4) Hydronephrosis

36. With sclerosis there is:
    (1) Hardening of tissue
    (2) Inflammation of the sclera
    (3) Softening of the eye sclera
    (4) Fibrous degeneration of connective tissue

37. Malignant neoplasms are characterized by:
    (1) Cells that are similar to tissue from which they arise
    (2) Cell division that follows an orderly process

    (3) Cellular proliferation and metastasis
    (4) Cellular containment within a capsule

38. Tumor nomenclature is partially based on the type of tissue from which the tumor arises. This is called:
    (1) Differentiation
    (2) Histogenesis
    (3) Staging
    (4) Grading

39. Leukemia is a malignant disease of:
    (1) Hematopoietic cells
    (2) Epithelial tissue
    (3) Bone tissue
    (4) Nerve cells

RATIONALES

1.   * (1) Hemolysis is the destruction of red blood cells (erythrocytes), which releases hemoglobin into the plasma.
    (2) Hematology is the science concerned with the morphology of blood and blood forming organs.
    (3) Hemoglobin is that part of the red blood cell that carries oxygen to body tissues.
    (4) Hematopoiesis is the maturation of blood cells.

2.   (1) Necrosis denotes dead tissue.
    (2) Abrasion is a scraping away of epidermal tissue.
    * (3) Crustation is a term used to describe the drying of body exudate or secretions that forms a hard covering.
    (4) Excoriation is a superficial loss of tissue.

3.   (1) Eczema refers to a cutaneous inflammation of the skin characterized by papules, vesicles, pustules, scales, or scabs in any combination.
    * (2) Erythema is caused by the congestion of the capillaries in the lower layer of the skin in response to inflammation.
    (3) Ecchymosis refers to an irregularly formed hemorrhagic area of the skin (commonly known as black and blue).
    (4) Erythrocytosis is an abnormal increase in the number of circulating red blood cells.

4.   (1) Mastoptosis refers to drooping of the breast.
    (2) Mastalgia refers to pain in the breast.
    * (3) Mastitis refers to inflammation of the breast. "Mast" denotes breast and "-itis" denotes inflammation.
    (4) Amastia refers to the absence of breast development.

5.   (1) Nevi or moles are common skin tumors.
    (2) Wheals are slightly elevated patches on the skin, not hives.
    (3) Vesicles are blisterlike elevations of the skin, containing serous fluid.
    * (4) This is correct. Urticaria is the medical term for hives.

6.   * (1) Lipoma is a benign fatty tumor usually composed of mature fat cells.
         (2) Adenoma is a benign tumor in which the cells are derived from glandular epithelium.
         (3) Lipocele denotes a hernia containing fat or fatty tissue, not a fatty tumor.
         (4) Adipogenous denotes beginning or formation of fat, not a fatty tumor.

7.   * (1) Lymphocytopenia is a smaller than normal number of lymphocytes in the peripheral circulation. The normal range of lymphocytes is 1000 to 3000 per mm^3.
         (2) Lymphocytosis is an increase in lymphocytes in the blood.
         (3) Lymphopoiesis refers to the production of lymph.
         (4) Lymphadenoma is a tumor of a lymph gland.

8.   (1) Stenosis is a stricture.
     * (2) Volvulus is a torsion of a loop of intestine, causing obstruction of the bowel.
         (3) Enterospasm is painful peristalsis or spasm of the small bowel.
         (4) Diverticulum is an out-pouching in the wall of the bowel.

9.   (1) Angina is chest pain caused by temporary myocardial ischemia.
         (2) Dyspnea is difficulty breathing.
     * (3) Bradycardia is a heart rate of fewer than 60 beats per minute.
         (4) Tachycardia is a heart rate greater than 100 beats per minute.

10.   (1) Pyothorax is the presence of pus in the pleural cavity.
         (2) Hemothorax is the presence of blood in the pleural cavity.
         (3) Hydrothorax is the presence of serum in the pleural cavity.
     * (4) Pneumothorax is the presence of air trapped in the pleural cavity, which increases the intrapleural pressure, collapsing the lung.

11.   (1) Silicosis is caused by inhaling minute particles of sand over a long period of time.
         (2) Siderosis is caused by inhaling minute particles of iron over a long period of time.
         (3) Chalicosis is caused by inhaling minute particles of limestone over a long period of time.
     * (4) Anthracosis, also called black lung, is a chronic lung disease characterized by deposits of coal dust in the lungs and the formation of black nodules on the bronchioles, resulting in focal emphysema.

12.   * (1) "Hemat" means blood and "emesis" pertains to the act of vomiting.
         (2) Hepatomegaly denotes enlargement of the liver.
         (3) Herniorrhaphy refers the surgical repair of a hernia.
         (4) Hemiparesis refers to weakness on one side of the body.

13.   (1) Rheumatoid arthritis is a chronic collagen disease with an autoimmune component characterized by inflammation of the synovium and swelling of the joint.
         (2) Ewing's sarcoma is a swelling on a long bone caused by endothelial myeloma.
     * (3) Osteoporosis is a loss of bone substance and mass that occurs at a greater rate than bone formation, resulting in a decrease in bone density.
         (4) Kyphosis is a term that denotes a hunch or humpback as a result of an

increase in the angulation of the thoracic curve of the vertebral column. Some contributing factors include poor posture, rheumatoid arthritis, rickets, or respiratory problems.

14.
(1) Spina bifida is a genetic disorder that results in a variety of malformations of the spine due to incomplete joining of the vertebrae.

* (2) Myasthenia gravis is caused by a defect in the transmission of impulses from nerve to muscle cells due to loss of available or normal receptors on the postsynaptic membrane of the neuromuscular junction. The cranial nerves are most frequently affected, resulting in the adaptations identified in the stem of the item.

(3) Muscular dystrophy is a genetic disorder that results in progressive muscle weakness and atrophy due to degenerative myopathy of the skeletal and voluntary muscles.

(4) Rheumatoid arthritis is a degenerative disease of the joints and related structures that results in crippling deformities. It is characterized by inflammation of the synovium and joint.

15.
(1) Syphilis is characterized by a chancre, not a discharge, that develops within 90 days after initial contact with an infected individual.

* (2) This is correct. *Neisseria gonorrhoea* affects the mucous membranes of the urinary system and genitalia.

(3) Chlamydia is characterized by the formation of a lesion on the genitalia or perineal area. This lesion can be a minor erosion or a small macule or papule, not a discharge, which is characteristic of gonorrhea.

(4) Herpes simplex is characterized by the formation of painful, red blisterlike sores on the genitalia.

16.
(1) Edema is the accumulation of fluid in the interstitial spaces.

* (2) Tetany is an adaptation to abnormal calcium metabolism associated with vitamin D deficiency, hypoparathyroidism, alkalosis, or the ingestion of alkaline salts.

(3) Diuresis is the increased production and excretion of urine.

(4) Stenosis is the narrowing of an opening or passage way.

17.
(1) Cushing's syndrome is a disease caused by an increased secretion of the adrenal cortex, causing an excessive production of glucocorticoids. It is characterized by a moon-face, a striae-covered pad of fat on the chest and abdomen, fatigue, an elevated blood pressure, edema, hypokalemia, muscle atrophy, and emotional changes.

(2) Addison's disease is a condition caused by partial or complete failure of adrenocortical function. It is believed to be caused by an autoimmune process. Symptoms do not usually appear until 90% of the gland is affected and is characterized by severe dehydration, low blood pressure (hypotension), low serum sodium level (hyponatremia), high serum potassium level (hyperkalemia), an increased pigmentation of the skin and mucous membranes, anorexia, gastrointestinal distress, anxiety, depression, low blood glucose level (hypoglycemia), fatigue, and muscle weakness.

(3) Diabetes mellitus is a complex disease because of a lack of insulin production by the beta cells of the pancreas or an inability of insulin to facilitate the conversion of glucose to glycogen. Diabetes is characterized by exces-

sive blood glucose levels (hyperglycemia), excessive glucose in the urine (glycosuria), excessive urination (polyuria) resulting in dehydration, excessive thirst (polydipsia), and excessive ingestion of food (polyphagia).

* (4) This is correct. Grave's disease, also known as hyperthyroidism, is associated with an excessive production of thyroid hormones.

18.   (1) Glycosuria is glucose in the urine, not diabetic coma.

* (2) This is correct. When glucose is not metabolized, fat cells are catabolized, causing an accumulation of ketones in the blood and resulting in metabolic acidosis.

(3) Hypoglycemia is an elevation of blood glucose levels.

(4) Hyperkalemia is an elevated serum potassium level.

19.   (1) Cretinism is a congenital absence of thyroid gland secretion causing arrested physical and mental development. The child with cretinism has abnormal bone formation, impaired growth, mental retardation, a thick protruding tongue, lack of coordination, a large head, short limbs, and puffy eyes.

(2) An infant who develops cretinism because of hypothyroidism that goes untreated will experience dwarfism. Dwarfism is an underdevelopment of the body characterized by extreme shortness.

* (3) This is correct. Myxedema is a condition caused by advanced hypothyroidism and is characterized by nonpitting edema, swollen lips, a thickened nose, weight gain, and fatigue.

(4) Giantism, characterized by excessive body size and stature, results from hypersecretion of growth hormone from the pituitary.

20.   * (1) Tarry is used to indicate a black-colored stool caused by digested blood within the stool. This is also called melena. It occurs when a person experiences bleeding in the upper gastrointestinal tract.

(2) Necrotic stands for localized tissue death due to injury or disease.

(3) Purulent stands for containing or producing pus.

(4) Melanin stands for black or dark-brown pigment mainly in the skin.

21.   (1) Pain is a local adaptation to the stimulation of nerve endings at the site of infection.

(2) Edema is a local adaptation resulting from local vasodilation and increased vessel permeability.

* (3) The inflammatory response is stimulated by trauma or infection, which increase the basal metabolic rate; with infection fever results from the affect of pyrogens on the temperature regulating center in the hypothalamus.

(4) Erythema is a local adaptation resulting from increased circulation and local vasodilation in the involved area.

22.   (1) Although fluid is lost from a draining pressure ulcer, it is the loss of protein in that fluid that has the most serious implication.

(2) Weight loss is related to inadequate caloric intake, not the presence of a pressure ulcer.

* (3) Protein loss is a serious concern when a patient has a draining pressure ulcer. A patient can lose as much as 50 g of protein daily from a draining pressure ulcer; this is a large percentage of the normal daily requirement

of protein. Patients with draining pressure ulcers should ingest two to four times the normal daily requirements of protein to rebuild epidermal tissue.

    (4) Leukocyte counts increase in response to the threat of infection; if the pressure ulcer is infected the leukocyte count will increase, not decrease. Decreased white blood cell levels are a response to bone marrow depression caused by a stress other than a pressure ulcer.

23.   * (1) Exposure to microorganisms during the perioperative period can precipitate an infection in approximately 3 to 5 days; erythema, pain, edema, chills, fever, and purulent drainage indicate infection.

    (2) Between day 1 and 2 postsurgery is too short a time period for an infectious process to develop from a surgical incision; a contaminated, traumatic wound could precipitate an infection this early.

    (3) An infectious process would manifest itself before 7 to 10 days; wound dehiscence or evisceration may occur during this time frame before collagen formation occurs.

    (4) Within 24 hours postsurgery is too short a time period for an infectious process to develop from a surgical incision.

24.   (1) Physical activity, fluid, and fiber help to prevent constipation.

    (2) Same as answer number one.

    (3) Same as answer number one.

   * (4) Psychological stress decreases intestinal motility, as a response to parasympathetic nervous system stimulation, contributing to constipation.

25.   (1) Fruits provide bulk (undigested residue) in the diet, which facilitates fecal elimination, not constipation.

    (2) Vegetables also provide bulk in the diet.

    (3) Whole grains also provide bulk in the diet.

   * (4) Dairy products are low in roughage and lack bulk. Dairy products produce too little waste to stimulate the defecation reflex; low residue foods move more slowly through the intestinal tract, permitting increased fluid uptake from stool and resulting in hard-formed stools and constipation.

26.   * (1) Infants and toddlers are at serious risk for airway obstruction that can develop as a result of respiratory tract infection; epiglottitis, bronchiolitis, and laryngospasm are acute conditions with a sudden onset that have serious implications if not immediately treated.

    (2) The healthy adolescent usually does not encounter any serious event in response to respiratory infections.

    (3) Although the respiratory system undergoes changes during the aging process and there is a decline in respiratory function, complications related to infection are usually not as acute, sudden, or life-threatening as with the infant.

    (4) The healthy school-aged child usually does not encounter any serious event in response to respiratory infections; however, school-aged children generally have respiratory infections more frequently because of the exposure to other children.

27.   (1) Edema is fluid in the interstitial compartment.

   * (2) Pressure constricts blood vessels, which in turn decreases blood supply to a body part (tissue ischemia).

(3) Orthopnea is the ability to breathe only in an upright position such as sitting or standing.

(4) Hypovolemia is a reduction in blood volume.

28. * (1) Because of the small size of the respiratory system and its narrow passages in the toddler, this age group is at risk for obstruction as a result of edema associated with the inflammatory response.

(2) Although all patients with a respiratory tract infection should be monitored for obstruction, this age group is not at as high a risk for an obstruction as a toddler.

(3) Same as answer number two.

(4) Same as answer number two.

29. (1) The body has a need to exhale carbon dioxide.

* (2) Because of the energy required to fight an infection, the basal metabolic rate increases, resulting in an increased respiratory rate.

(3) Tachypnea occurs in the presence of elevated levels of carbon dioxide and carbonic acid.

(4) With infection the patient is more likely to be in metabolic acidosis; tachypnea that progresses to hyperventilation causes respiratory alkalosis.

30. (1) As long as a patient can cough and deep breath, respiratory complications can be minimized even if a patient is confined to a wheelchair.

(2) Urinary tract infection is more of a problem when a patient is immobilized on bed rest rather than in a wheelchair.

* (3) Thrombophlebitis of the legs can develop because decreased muscular contraction and prolonged hip flexion can result in venous stasis and hypercoagulability.

(4) Flexion, not extension, contractures are a concern with prolonged wheelchair use.

31. (1) Excessive pressure causes pressure (decubitus) ulcers.

(2) Joint diseases can contribute to contractures; however, immobility is generally the cause of contractures, not a disease process.

* (3) When a person is inactive, flexion muscles contract and extension muscles relax, causing flexion muscles to shorten and extender muscles to lengthen resulting in a contracture.

(4) Aging does not cause a contracture; inactivity causes contractures.

32. (1) It is pressure, not gravity, that causes reduced oxygenation to local tissue.

* (2) Pressure causes ischemia to local tissue. When cells are deprived of oxygen and nutrients, pathologic changes begin within 1 to 2 hours; if pressure is not relieved, tissue breakdown and cellular death occur.

(3) Pressue causes skin breakdown.

(4) Cellular necrosis is a stage 4 pressure (decubitus) ulcer; it is the death of tissues in response to prolonged pressure and oxygen deprivation.

33. (1) The buildup of lipid material in central nervous system cells is the etiology of Tay-Sachs disease, not multiple sclerosis.

* (2) Multiple sclerosis is characterized by inflammation and consequent demyelination of nerve fibers in areas of the spinal cord and brain. Altered myelin interferes with the transmission of electrical impulses among neurons.

      (3) Bell's palsy is a facial paralysis subsequent to a disorder of the seventh cranial nerve.

      (4) A cerebral vascular accident (stroke) results from an impairment of cerebral circulation caused by cerebral hemorrhage or vessel occlusion.

34.   (1) Cerebral palsy (CP) is a motor function disorder caused by a permanent, nonprogressive brain lesion present at birth or shortly thereafter.

   * (2) Alzheimer's disease is a presenile dementia beginning in later middle life, characterized by the pathologic traits of very small plaques in the cortex and degeneration within pyramidal ganglion cells.

      (3) Although multiple sclerosis (MS) is a progressive neurological disorder it is characterized by remissions and exacerbations. Although a patient with MS may experience emotional liability it is mainly characterized by tremors, weakness of muscles, paresthesias, and visual disturbances.

      (4) Spina bifida is a congenital neural tube defect causing several types of malformations of the spine at the posterior vertebral arch, most frequently in the lumbosacral area. In its least severe form no herniation of intraspinal contents occurs. In its severe form spinal contents protrude into a saclike structure that contains meninges and cerebrospinal fluid.

35.   (1) Hydramnios is excessive amniotic fluid and is an abnormal condition of pregnancy.

      (2) Hydradenitis is an inflammation or infection of the sweat glands.

   * (3) Hydrocephalus may be caused by an increased production of CSF, obstruction within the ventricular system, or interference with reabsorption of CSF; these alterations can result from infection, trauma, cranial tumors, or developmental aberrations.

      (4) Hydronephrosis is a backup of urine into the pelvis and calyces of a kidney because of an obstruction in a ureter; this results in distention of the kidney.

36.   * (1) Sclerosis means an abnormal hardening of tissue; it can be caused by inflammation, deposits of mineral salts, and infiltration of connective tissue fibers.

      (2) Scleritis is an inflammation of the sclera.

      (3) Scleromalacia is a softening and sloughing of the sclera of the eye and is a complication of rheumatoid arthritis.

      (4) Scleroderma is an autoimmune disease characterized by fibrous degeneration of the connective tissue of the skin and internal organs, particularly the esophagus, kidneys, and lungs.

37.   (1) Malignant cells usually do not resemble the tissue from which they arise; this is more likely to occur with benign tumors rather than cancerous tumors.

      (2) Malignant cells do not follow an orderly process. They lack specialization in structure and function and replicate at an uncontrolled rate.

   * (3) Proliferation and metastasis refer to the characteristic rapid spreading of malignant cells by direct extension or by malignant cells being carried to remote parts of the body by lymph or blood.

      (4) Malignant neoplasms are nonencapsulated and are characterized by projections that infiltrate surrounding structures; benign tumors are more likely to be encapsulated than cancerous tumors.

38.   (1) Differentiation denotes the ability of a cell to achieve a specific form, characteristic, function, or chemical property; neoplastic cells are undifferentiated rather than differentiated.

    * (2) Histogenesis refers to the type of tissue from which a neoplasm originates.

    (3) Staging defines the magnitude of involvement and includes the size of the tumor, degree of nodal involvement, and extent of metastasis.

    (4) Grading seeks to define the origin of the tumor tissue and the degree to which these cells retain the functional and histologic characteristics of the tissue of origin. The more undifferentiated the cells the less the tissue resembles the tissue of origin and the more serious the prognosis.

39.   * (1) Leukemias are associated with blood forming organs and include the spleen, bone marrow, and the lymphatic system. "Hemato" refers to blood, "poiet" refers to formation or production, and "ic" refers to pertaining to.

    (2) Epithelial tissue is divided into two types: epithelial tissue forms the outer covering of external body surfaces and some internal organs, and glandular epithelium constitutes the secreting portion of glands. A malignancy that arises from the external skin is known as squamous cell carcinoma and a malignancy that arises from glandular tissues is known as adenocarcinoma.

    (3) A malignancy that arises from bone tissue is known as osteosarcoma.

    (4) A malignancy that arises from nerve cells is known as glioma.

THERAPEUTIC INTERVENTION

This section encompasses questions that relate to the treatment of common health problems. Preventative, diagnostic, palliative, rehabilitative, and curative therapeutic measures commonly used in the medical profession are included.

QUESTIONS

1. An arthrocentesis is performed to:
   (1) Inject a radiopaque material into a joint
   (2) Permit direct visualization of a joint
   (3) Remove synovial fluid from a joint
   (4) Immobilize a joint

2. A patient is in continuous pain from cancer that has metastasized to the bone. Pain medication provides little relief and the patient refuses to move. Caregivers should plan to:
   (1) Let the patient perform self-care
   (2) Complete care as quickly as possible
   (3) Touch the patient gently when assisting with required care
   (4) Reassure the patient that staff members will not cause pain

3. Cold is effective in reducing the discomfort associated with a local inflammatory response because it:
   (1) Anesthetizes nerve endings

(2) Lowers tissue metabolism
(3) Decreases venous return
(4) Causes vasodilation

4. Heat effectively reduces discomfort at a local inflammatory site because it:
   (1) Limits capillary permeability
   (2) Decreases tissue metabolism
   (3) Promotes muscle relaxation
   (4) Provides local anesthesia

5. While walking in the hospital corridor, a patient with a history of heart disease holds one hand over the mid-sternum and complains of a severe upset stomach. The first action should be to:
   (1) Sit the patient in a chair
   (2) Walk the patient back to bed
   (3) Inform the nurse immediately
   (4) Listen to the patient's complaints

6. An essential vitamin for a patient with anemia would be:
   (1) Ascorbic acid
   (2) Riboflavin
   (3) Folic acid
   (4) Thiamin

7. Leg exercises following surgery are encouraged primarily to:
   (1) Promote venous return
   (2) Prevent muscle atrophy
   (3) Increase muscle strength
   (4) Limit joint contractures

8. Pressure dressings following surgery are used to:
   (1) Limit infection
   (2) Prevent drainage
   (3) Promote hemostasis
   (4) Facilitate healing

9. While eating, a person clutches the upper chest with the hands, appears unable to breathe, and has a frightened facial expression. The most appropriate initial action would be to:
   (1) Perform the abdominal thrust maneuver
   (2) Slap the person on the back three times
   (3) Ask the person to try to speak
   (4) Start artificial respirations

10. Which of the following actions is correct technique when implementing tracheal suctioning in an adult?
    (1) Use wall suction with a pressure setting below 80 mm Hg
    (2) Apply intermittent suction during removal of the catheter
    (3) Employ a rotating motion during insertion of the catheter
    (4) Apply suction to the nasotracheal area after the oropharyngeal area

11. When teaching the use of an incentive spirometer the patient would demonstrate an understanding of its use when stating, "I should:

(1) inhale with a rapid, low-volume breath."
(2) snap the ball to the top of the chamber."
(3) get the ball to raise and lower smoothly."
(4) inhale slowly and keep the ball floating."

12. Which of the following should prevent atelectasis following surgery?
    (1) Oxygen via nasal cannula
    (2) Diaphragmatic breathing
    (3) Progressive activity
    (4) Postural drainage

13. Passive range-of-motion exercises primarily prevent which of the following complications?
    (1) Joint contractures
    (2) Pressure ulcers
    (3) Muscle atrophy
    (4) Muscle spasms

14. Following surgery the most common reason patients will have a nasogastric tube in place is for the purpose of:
    (1) Decompression
    (2) Instillation
    (3) Lavage
    (4) Gavage

15. To prevent pulmonary complications postoperatively the patient should be instructed to perform:
    (1) Incisional splinting
    (2) Progressive ambulation
    (3) Diaphragmatic breathing
    (4) Range-of-motion exercises

16. A patient has dependent edema of the ankles and feet and is obese. For this patient, the physician will probably order a diet that is:
    (1) Low in salt and high in fat
    (2) Low in salt and low in calories
    (3) High in salt and high in protein
    (4) High in salt and low in carbohydrates

17. To provide support for the patient who complains of nausea, the caregiver should:
    (1) Offer a small sip of water
    (2) Place the patient in the supine position
    (3) Position an emesis basin in easy reach
    (4) Explain that the nausea will lessen with time

18. A patient complains that the oxygen mask is too tight against the face. The caregiver should:
    (1) Explain that it must always stay firmly in place
    (2) Replace the face mask with a nasal cannula
    (3) Pad the straps with gauze
    (4) Adjust the elastic strap

19. The physician orders a 2 g sodium diet. Which group of nutrients would be most appropriate for this diet?
    (1) Fruit, vegetables, and bread
    (2) Hamburger, onions, and ketchup
    (3) Hot dogs, mustard, and pickles
    (4) Luncheon meats, rolls, and vegetables

RATIONALES

1.   (1) Injecting a radiopaque material into a joint is arthrography, not arthrocentesis.
        (2) Direct visualization of a joint is arthroscopy, not arthrocentesis.
    * (3) This is correct. "Arthro" refers to joint and "centesis" refers to surgical puncture of a body cavity or membrane.
        (4) Immobilizing a joint is arthrodesis, not arthrocentesis.

2.   (1) The patient refuses to move now and will probably avoid any self-care that requires movement.
        (2) Completing care quickly can intensify pain; also it can tire the patient, which may intensify pain.
    * (3) Touching the patient gently conveys an understanding that the patient needs to move slowly, gently, and carefully; avoiding quick and firm movements will contribute to the patient's comfort.
        (4) Stating that staff members will not cause pain is false reassurance; this is something that cannot be promised.

3.   * (1) Cold is a form of cutaneous stimulation that slows the nervous conduction of impulses, which relaxes muscle tension and relieves pain.
        (2) Although cold does lower tissue metabolism, this is not the physiologic response that reduces pain.
        (3) Although a decreased venous return would occur with vasoconstriction, it is not the reason for pain relief.
        (4) Application of cold causes vasoconstriction, not vasodilation.

4.   (1) Heat increases capillary vasodilation and permeability.
        (2) Heat increases, not decreases, tissue metabolism; heat causes vasodilatation, facilitating the exchange of nutrients and waste products, increasing cellular metabolism.
    * (3) Heat is known to relax muscle spasms and the discomfort associated with muscle spasms; the mechanism is unknown.
        (4) Cold applications cause local anesthesia, not the application of heat.

5.   * (1) If the problem is cardiac rather than gastric, this action would interrupt the patient's activity thereby limiting the demand for oxygen and decreasing the workload of the heart.
        (2) Walking the patient back to bed is unsafe; if the problem is cardiac, rather than gastric, walking will increase the demands on the heart.
        (3) The nurse should be informed after the patient's activity is interrupted.

    (4) Although listening to the patient's complaints would be done, it is most important that the patient's activity be interrupted.

6.
    (1) Vitamin C mainly functions to promote collagen formation, enhance iron absorption, and maintain capillary wall integrity.

    (2) Vitamin B_2 functions as a coenzyme in the metabolism of carbohydrates, fats, amino acids, and alcohol.

    * (3) Vitamin B_9 promotes the maturation of red blood cells.

    (4) Vitamin B_1 performs as a coenzyme in the metabolism of carbohydrates, fats, amino acids, and alcohol.

7.
    * (1) Circulatory stasis occurs with immobility; leg exercises promote venous return and prevent the formation of thrombi and thrombophlebitis.

    (2) Although this is a benefit, it is not the reason for performing leg exercises postoperatively.

    (3) Same as answer number two.

    (4) Range-of-motion exercises are performed to prevent joint contractures; this is not the purpose of postoperative leg exercises.

8.
    (1) Surgical asepsis limits infection.

    (2) Dressings absorb drainage; they do not prevent drainage.

    * (3) Pressure causes constriction of peripheral blood vessels, which prevents bleeding; it also eliminates dead space in underlying tissue so that healing can progress.

    (4) All dressings provide an environment conducive to healing; however, the specific purpose of a pressure dressing is to prevent bleeding.

9.
    (1) Performing the abdominal thrust maneuver is done once it is determined that the patient cannot speak.

    (2) Slapping the person on the back could cause the aspirated object to lodge deeper in the respiratory passages.

    * (3) If the person can speak the airway is not totally obstructed; it is safer to allow the person time to attempt to clear the airway by coughing.

    (4) The person is not in respiratory arrest; food is lodged in the respiratory passages. The initial intervention is different for each of these situations.

10.
    (1) For wall suctioning to be effective when suctioning an adult, it should be maintained at 80 to 150 mm Hg.

    * (2) Intermittent suction is exerted on withdrawal of the suction catheter; this prevents trauma to any one section of the respiratory mucosa because of prolonged suction pressure.

    (3) The catheter is rotated on removal, not insertion, of the catheter; rotating the catheter removes secretions from all surfaces of the respiratory mucosa as the catheter is withdrawn.

    (4) The opposite is acceptable technique; the nasotracheal area is considered sterile and is suctioned before the oropharyngeal area, which is considered clean; this minimizes contamination of the sterile area.

11.
    (1) The patient should inhale with a high-volume breath to bring enough air into the lungs to inflate the alveoli.

    (2) Brisk, low-volume breaths tend to snap the ball to the top and should be avoided; the ball should rise slowly and remain at the top for as long as

possible to maintain increased airway pressure at the height of inhalation (maximum sustained inhalation).

(3) The ball will drop abruptly as soon as the patient exhales. The purpose of incentive spirometry is to inhale and inflate the alveoli; the focus is on inhalation, not exhalation.

* (4) A slow, deep inhalation that is sustained at the height of inspiration ensures adequate ventilation of the alveoli.

12.   (1) Exogenous oxygen increases the partial pressure of oxygen; it does not prevent atelectasis.

* (2) Deep breathing expands the alveoli and precipitates coughing, which prevent the accumulation and stagnation of secretions.

(3) Activity is not specific to preventing just atelectasis; activity will promote cardiopulmonary and circulatory functioning in general.

(4) Postural drainage is not done routinely.

13.   * (1) Range of motion (ROM) can minimize or prevent the formation of joint contractures by preventing the permanent shortening of muscles, ligaments, and tendons from disuse.

(2) Decubitus ulcers are caused by pressure not lack of ROM.

(3) Muscle atrophy is caused by immobility; ROM does not prevent decreased muscle mass.

(4) ROM is not done to prevent muscle spasms. Various active exercises can strengthen muscles, which may prevent muscle spasm; however, passive ROM is not one of these exercises.

14.   * (1) Negative pressure exerted through a tube inserted in the stomach removes secretions and gaseous substances from the stomach, preventing abdominal distention.

(2) Instillation is not the most common purpose of a nasogastric tube following surgery; instillations in a nasogastric tube following surgery are done to promote patency.

(3) Lavage is not the most common purpose of a nasogastric tube following surgery; lavage following surgery is usually done to promote hemostasis in the presence of gastric bleeding.

(4) Gavage would be contraindicated following surgery until peristalsis returns.

15.   (1) Splinting limits incisional pain and prevents dehiscence.

(2) Although ambulation increases the respiratory rate, its primary purpose is to prevent circulatory complications such as thrombosis.

* (3) Diaphragmatic breathing helps promote alveolar expansion and facilitate oxygen-carbon dioxide exchange.

(4) Range-of-motion exercises prevent contractures and circulatory complications.

16.   (1) Although a low-salt diet wold be appropriate to limit edema, a diet high in fat should be avoided by an obese individual because fats are high in calories.

* (2) Salt promotes fluid retention and increased calories add to body weight; therefore, both should be avoided by this patient.

(3) Salt promotes fluid retention and should be avoided by this patient; protein is unrelated to this patient's problem.

(4) Although carbohydrates may be restricted in an obese individual to facilitate weight loss, a high-salt diet would promote fluid retention and should be avoided.

17.
(1) A sip of water may potentiate the nausea and precipitate vomiting.

(2) The supine position is unsafe; if vomiting occurs the patient could aspirate.

* (3) An emesis basin provides for physical and emotional comfort; the emesis basin collects vomitus and reduces the patient's concern regarding soiling.

(4) This is false reassurance; no one can predict when nausea will subside.

18.
(1) Straps and a mask that are firm against the skin can cause tissue trauma; the elastic straps can be adjusted for comfort, while keeping the edges of the mask gently against the skin.

(2) A nasal cannula requires a physician's order.

(3) Although padding the straps may be done it does not address the tightness of the mask against the skin of the face.

* (4) Loosening the elastic straps will reduce the excessive pressure of the mask against the face.

19.
* (1) Fruits, vegetables, and bread contain the least amount of sodium as compared with the other options.

(2) Ketchup is high in sodium and should be avoided.

(3) Hot dogs, mustard, and pickles all contain a high level of sodium and should be avoided.

(4) Luncheon meats are processed foods that contain a high level of sodium and should be avoided.

Practice Tests

Instructions for Practice Tests A and B

Practice Tests A and B have been included to provide you with an opportunity to practice test-taking techniques. Each test consists of 30 items that reflect information common to the various healthcare disciplines. One or more of the test-taking techniques presented in Chapter 5 can be applied to each item. Although you can read this chapter and use this information in any sequence you find helpful, the following suggested approach should challenge your ability to apply test-taking techniques and reinforce the theory presented in this textbook.

Before taking Practice Test A, obtain a piece of blank paper for use as a template. As you read each question, expose only the question and test-taking tip, keeping the template over the rationales and question analysis information related to the question. Read the question and select the number that you believe is the correct answer. Now, read the test-taking tip and reexamine the question to decide if you should keep your first choice or choose another option. Once you settle on your final choice, slide the template down and read the rationale for your selected option. An asterisk will appear after the rationale for the correct answer.

If you have chosen the correct answer, read each of the other options and its related rationale. This will reinforce theory and principles associated with the content presented in the question. If you did not choose the correct answer, re-cover the rationales with the template, reread the question, and select another option. Repeat these steps until you select the correct answer.

After reading all of the rationales, review the question analysis to determine the test-taking technique(s) and/or critical thinking strategy that facilitated success in answering the question. Finally, critique your ability to apply the test-taking technique(s) included in the question analysis.

Analyze the reasons you may have selected a distractor instead of the correct answer. Ask yourself questions such as, "Was I careless?" "Did I quickly jump to the wrong conclusion?" "Did I miss an important word in the stem?" "Did I lack knowledge about the content?" "Did I read into the question and make it more complicated?" or "Did I misunderstand what the question was asking?" It is important to determine why you answered an item incorrectly so that you can identify patterns of errors in test-taking and implement corrective action to improve your performance. As you review each item, make notes referring to the content in questions that you answered incorrectly. This will direct your future study to these areas of concern.

Practice tests are learning experiences because they permit the application of test-taking strategies, reinforce information you understand, identify content areas that need to be emphasized in future study, and contribute to a positive mental attitude. Taking practice tests is an excellent way to improve the effectiveness of your test-taking techniques and to feel empowered and in control. Have fun!

PRACTICE TEST A

Question 1

When considering definitions about health, one concept basic to most definitions is that health is:
(1) Absence of disease
(2) A progressive state
(3) A right of all human beings
(4) Relative to one's value system

Test-Taking Tip—Question 1

Look for the specific determiners in the options. A specific determiner is a word or statement that conveys a thought that has no exceptions. Generally options with specific determiners are distractors and can be eliminated from consideration.

Rationales—Question 1

(1) The World Health Organization's definition of health is, "A state of complete physical, mental, and social well being, and not merely the absence of disease or infirmity." Some people who have a chronic illness consider themselves healthy because they are able to function independently.

(2) Health is on a continuum rather than progressive; movement can occur up or down the continuum, not only in one direction.

(3) Everyone should have a right to obtain health care, but health is not a right and cannot be guaranteed.

*(4) A definition of health is highly individualized; it is based on each person's own experiences, values, and perceptions. Health can mean different things to each individual; people tend to define health based on the presence or absence of symptoms, perceptions of how they feel, and the capacity to function on a daily basis.

Analysis—Question 1

The word "absence" in option one and the word "all" in option three are both absolute terms that have no exceptions and are therefore specific determiners. These options are distractors and can be eliminated from consideration. Option four is the correct answer.

Question 2

Of the following human needs identified by Maslow, which is the **most** basic?
(1) Physiological needs
(2) Belonging needs
(3) Security needs
(4) Safety needs

Test-Taking Tip—Question 2

Identify the key word in the stem that sets a priority. A word that sets a priority modifies another important word or concept that relates to what is being asked. Identify equally plausible options; these are options that are similar or comparable. Because it is difficult to choose one over the other, they are probably distractors and both can be eliminated from consideration.

Rationales—Question 2

*(1) According to Maslow's Hierarchy of Needs, physiological needs are the most basic: oxygen, food, fluid, rest, sleep, and elimination are basic for life.
 (2) According to Maslow's Hierarchy of Needs, love and belonging needs are ranked third.
 (3) According to Maslow's Hierarchy of Needs, security needs are ranked second.
 (4) According to Maslow's Hierarchy of Needs, safety needs are ranked second.

Analysis—Question 2

The word "most" modifies the word "basic" and sets a priority. All of the options include components of Maslow's Hierarchy of Needs, but **most basic** are the physiological. Safety and security needs identified in options three and four both address the need to be protected from harm. They are comparable and therefore equally plausible distractors and both can be eliminated from consideration. Option one is the correct answer.

Question 3

A woman's husand died 1 week ago. When talking about him she begins to cry. The best response would be to:
(1) Leave her alone to provide privacy

Test-Taking Tip—Question 3

Identify the option that denies the patient's feelings by providing false reassurance. Eliminate this option from consideration.

(2) Encourage her to get grief counseling
(3) Say, "Things will get better as time passes."
(4) State, "This must be a very difficult time for you."

Rationales—Question 3

(1) Leaving the woman alone abandons her at a time when emotional support would be beneficial.
(2) Encouraging grief counseling may eventually be done, but the woman needs immediate support.
(3) This statement is false reassurance.
*(4) This statement identifies feelings, focuses on the woman, and provides an opportunity to share feelings.

Analysis—Question 3

Option three provides false reassurance. It ignores the patient's present concerns and optimistically predicts that everything will be all right. This option can be deleted from consideration. Option four is the correct answer.

Question 4

When assessing a patient in acute pain, which of the following signs should be expected?
(1) Decreased respiratory rate
(2) Constricted pupils
(3) Flushed skin
(4) Pallor

Test-Taking Tip—Question 4

Identify the two options that are opposites. They must be given serious consideration. One of them will be the correct answer, or they both can be eliminated.

Rationales—Question 4

(1) With acute pain the patient will have an increased respiratory rate.
(2) In the General Adaptation Syndrome the pupils dilate to increase visual acuity.
(3) Flushed skin would not occur as part of the sympathetic nervous system response to pain.
*(4) Pallor is expected; peripheral vasoconstriction occurs in an effort to shift the blood supply from the periphery to the skeletal muscles, viscera, and brain.

Analysis—Question 4

Options three and four are opposites. If you correctly evaluate opposite options, you can increase your chances of selecting the correct answer to 50% because you have reduced the potentially correct answers to two. In this question one of these two options (option four) is the correct answer.

Question 5

When an assessment reveals a change in a patient's blood pressure the person performing the assessment should first:
(1) Report the change to other caregivers
(2) Document the monitored change
(3) Obtain the other vital signs
(4) Notify the physician

Test-Taking Tip—Question 5

Identify the options that are equally plausible. When options are parallel, they are usually distractors and both can be deleted from consideration.

Rationales—Question 5

(1) Reporting the change to other caregivers may be done after the other vital signs are obtained.
(2) Documenting the observed change may be done after the other vital signs are obtained.
*(3) Because of the interrelationships among the circulatory system, respiratory system, and the basal metabolic rate, all the vital signs should be obtained for a significant assessment.
(4) Notifying the physician may be done after the other vital signs are obtained.

Analysis—Question 5

Options one and four are comparable because the physician is also a caregiver. These options are distractors and can be eliminated from consideration. Option three is the correct answer.

Question 6

Which statement regarding blood pressure (BP) is true:
(1) A BP differs 5 to 10 mm Hg between arms.
(2) The second sound is more intense than the first.
(3) The arm must be kept below the apex of the heart to obtain an accurate BP.
(4) The arm must be kept above the apex of the heart to obtain an accurate reading.

Test-Taking Tip—Question 6

Identify opposites among the options. Give these options serious consideration because one of them will be the correct answer or they are both distractors and can be eliminated.

Rationales—Question 6

*(1) Because of variations in structure and distance, there might be 5 to 10 mm Hg difference between arms; the arm with the higher blood pressure should be used for subsequent assessments.

(2) The first sound is more intense than the second.
(3) Keeping the arm below the apex of the heart would result in an abnormally higher blood pressure.
(4) Keeping the arm above the apex of the heart would result in an abnormally lower blood pressure.

Analysis—Question 6

Options three and four are opposites. Assess these options carefully because one is the correct answer or they are both distractors. In this question they are both distractors and therefore can be deleted from consideration. Option one is the correct answer.

Question 7

Which clinical signs are indicative of internal hemorrhage?
(1) Decreased blood pressure and decreased heart rate
(2) Decreased blood pressure and increased heart rate
(3) Increased blood pressure and decreased heart rate
(4) Increased blood pressure and increased heart rate

Test-Taking Tip—Question 7

Identify the duplicate facts in the options. If you recognize one fact as being wrong you can eliminate two options from consideration. Identify the options that are opposites. One of these options will be the correct answer or they both can be eliminated.

Rationales—Question 7

(1) Only half of the statement is accurate.
*(2) Both parts of this option are accurate. The blood pressure decreases when there is a reduction in circulating blood volume and the heart rate increases in an effort to oxygenate all body cells in the presence of hypovolemia.
(3) Only half of this statement is accurate.
(4) The blood pressure and the heart rate do not increase in response to hemorrhage.

Analysis—Question 7

This question is testing two patient responses to hemorrhage: blood pressure and heart rate. If you know that a decreased blood pressure (hypotension) occurs with hemorrhage you can eliminate options three and four. If you know that an increased heart rate occurs with hemorrhage you can delete options one and three. In either case you raise your chances of selecting the correct answer to 50%. Review options two and three carefully because they are opposites. Option two is the correct answer.

Question 8

The *best* source of information about a newly admitted alert patient with a fractured leg is the:
(1) Emergency room nurse
(2) Patient's family
(3) Physician
(4) Patient

Test-Taking Tip—Question 8

Identify the key word in the stem that sets a priority. Stems that set a priority are asking you to select the option that has the highest significance in relation to the question.

Rationales—Question 8

(1) The emergency room nurse is a secondary source.
(2) The patient's family is a secondary source.
(3) The physician is a secondary source.
*(4) The patient is the center of the health team and is the primary source for current objective and subjective data.

Analysis—Question 8

The key word in this question is **best** source of information. All of the options are sources of information but only one is the best source. Progressively eliminate one option that is least important until you are left with one option. The patient is the most important member of the health team and is therefore the best source. Option four is the correct answer.

Question 9

When auscultation of the lungs is performed, the caregiver should recognize that wheezes are unrelated to:
(1) Fluid in the alveoli
(2) Narrowed air passages
(3) Constriction of the bronchi
(4) Inflammation in the bronchioles

Test-Taking Tip—Question 9

Identify the key word in the stem that indicates negative polarity. Questions with negative polarity are concerned with what is false.

Rationales—Question 9

*(1) Fluid in the alveoli is related to crackles (rales), not wheezes.
(2) Wheezes are related to narrowed air passages.
(3) Wheezes are related to constriction of the bronchi.
(4) Inflammation of the bronchioles decreases the lumen of the airways, which can produce wheezes.

Analysis—Question 9

The word "unrelated" indicates that the stem has negative polarity. The question is asking what is **not related** to wheezes. Options two, three, and four are related to wheezes and option one is not related to wheezes. If at first several options look correct, reread the stem looking for a word indicating negative polarity. Option one is the correct answer.

Question 10

Bacteria multiply rapidly in environments that are:
(1) Hot
(2) Warm
(3) Cool
(4) Cold

Test-Taking Tip—Question 10

Identify opposites in the stem. Usually one of the opposites is the correct answer or they are both distractors. Look at these options carefully in relation to the other options.

Rationales—Question 10

(1) Hot temperatures are used to destroy bacteria (e.g., sterilization).
*(2) Bacteria grow most rapidly in dark, warm, and moist environments.
(3) Bacteria do not grow well in cool environments.
(4) Bacteria do not grow well in cold environments.

Analysis—Question 10

All of the options are on a continuum concerning temperature. Options one and four are on opposite ends of the continuum. They are extremes of temperature. In this question they are both distractors and each can be deleted from consideration. Option two is the correct answer.

Question 11

What is the abbreviation for the word "immediately?"
(1) s.o.s.
(2) stat.
(3) p.r.n.
(4) a.c.

Test-Taking Tip—Question 11

Identify the option that is unique. One option is different from the others. Consider this option carefully. More often than not a unique option is the correct answer.

Rationales—Question 11

(1) The abbreviation s.o.s. (*si opus sit*) means "if necessary."
*(2) The abbreviation stat. (*statim*) means "immediately."
(3) The abbreviation p.r.n. (*pro re nata*) means "when required."
(4) The abbreviation a.c. (*ante cibum*) means "before meals."

Analysis—Question 11

Option two is different from the other options. Options one, three, and four have periods after each letter and option two does not. Option two is unique and is the correct answer.

Question 12

What do the initials CBC represent?
(1) Red blood cells
(2) Complete bed rest
(3) White blood cells
(4) Complete blood count

Identify clues in the stem. A clue is information in the stem that leads you to the correct answer.

Rationales—Question 12

(1) The abbreviation for red blood cells is RBC.
(2) Complete bed rest is represented by the initials CBR.
(3) The abbreviation for white blood cells is WBC.
*(4) A complete blood count (CBC) involves obtaining a venous blood sample and testing for hemoglobin (Hgb) and hematocrit (Hct) measurements, erythrocyte (RBC) count, leukocyte (WBC) count, and a differential RBC and WBC count.

Analysis—Question 12

Many abbreviations use the first letter of each word in the phrase being represented. Option four is the only option where each word begins with the letters included in the abbreviation—Complete Blood Count and is the correct answer.

Question 13

An unexpected response to chest physiotherapy is:
(1) The tracheobronchial mucosa is altered
(2) The air passages are clear
(3) Secretions are mobilized
(4) Coughing is induced

Test-Taking Tip—Question 13

Identify the word in the stem that indicates negative polarity. Questions with negative polarity are concerned with exceptions to the content being discussed.

Rationales—Question 13

(1) Chest physiotherapy will not alter the tracheobronchial mucosa; it mobilizes secretions within the respiratory tract and promotes a patent airway.
(2) Chest physiotherapy will promote patency of the airways, which is an expected outcome of chest physiotherapy.
(3) Chest percussion (cupping, clapping) and vibration mechanically dislodge tenacious secretions from the walls of the respiratory passages, while postural drainage drains secretions from various lung segments via gravity. Collectively these actions are called "chest physiotherapy" and they will mobilize secretions.
*(4) Chest physiotherapy will induce coughing, which is an expected response.

Analysis—Question 13

The words "unexpected response" in the stem indicates negative polarity. The question is asking what is **not** related to chest physiotherapy. When reviewing the options, if many of them seem to be correct then you probably missed the word or words indicating negative polarity. Reread the stem. Option one is the only option unrelated to chest physiology and is therefore the correct answer.

Question 14

The major difference between acute and chronic pain is that chronic pain is usually:
(1) Intense
(2) Relentless
(3) Predictable
(4) Excruciating

Test-Taking Tip—Question 14

Identify the two options that are very similar. Equally plausible options are usually distractors and can be eliminated from consideration.

Rationales—Question 14

(1) Both acute and chronic pain can be intense.
*(2) Chronic pain lasts over a prolonged period of time; acute pain usually has a short duration.
(3) Both acute and chronic pain can be predictable.
(4) Both acute and chronic pain can be excruciating.

Analysis—Question 14

In option one the word "intense" means extreme in degree. In option four the word "excruciating" means extremely painful. It would be difficult to choose between these two options because they are similar and equally plausible. By eliminating options one and four, you have raised your chances of choosing the correct answer to 50%. Option two is the correct answer.

Question 15

Women have a higher incidence of urinary tract infections than men have because:
(1) Urine always flows toward the rectum via gravity when voiding
(2) Women must sit rather than stand when toileting
(3) Women use bedpans, which harbor microorganisms
(4) The rectum is closer to the urinary meatus

Test-Taking Tip—Question 15

Identify the specific determiner in an option. A specific determiner is a word that modifies another word in such a way that there are no exceptions. An option with a specific determiner is usually incorrect and can be eliminated.

Rationales—Question 15

(1) Urine that flows toward the rectum rarely causes urinary tract infections.

(2) Sitting rather than standing should not increase the incidence of infection.

(3) If properly cleaned after use, bedpans are not a source of infection.

*(4) Stool wiped toward the urinary meatus can cause urinary tract infections; *Escherichia coli*, a common bacteria in stool, causes urinary tract infections.

Analysis—Question 15

Option one contains the specific determiner "always." Urine does not always flow toward the rectum when a woman voids because the direction it flows depends on the woman's position when voiding. Urine usually flows toward the rectum when a woman is in a semi-recumbent position because the rectum is dependent to the urinary meatus. Option four is the correct answer.

Question 16

Obese patients often have serious difficulty breathing when positioned in the:

(1) Supine position
(2) Contour position
(3) Orthopneic position
(4) Semi-Fowler's position

Test-Taking Tip—Question 16

Identify the unique option. One of these options is not like the others. This is probably the correct answer because the other three options are equally plausible.

Rationales—Question 16

*(1) The weight of the chest and pressure of the abdominal organs against the diaphragm limit thoracic excursion, causing dyspnea.

(2) With the head elevated the abdominal organs drop via gravity, allowing the diaphragm to effectively contract and promoting full expansion of the lungs.

(3) With the head elevated the abdominal organs drop via gravity, allowing the diaphragm to effectively contract and promoting full expansion of the lungs.

(4) With the head elevated the abdominal organs drop via gravity, allowing the diaphragm to effectively contract and promoting full expansion of the lungs.

Analysis—Question 16

Picture a patient assuming each of these positions and identify how one of them is different from the others. When a person is in the supine position (option one) the person is horizontal, flat, or level.

When a person is in the contour, orthopneic, or semi-Fowler's positions the head will be elevated. Option one is different from the others and is the correct answer.

Question 17

During a procedure, the patient states that the procedure is very upsetting. The caregiver's best response would be to:
(1) Explore the patient's concern.
(2) Complete the procedure as quickly as possible.
(3) Inform the physician of the patient's feelings.
(4) Explain that the procedure is necessary for recovery.

Test-Taking Tip—Question 17

Identify the option that is patient centered. To be patient centered, an option should support a patient's feelings or concerns.

Rationales—Question 17

*(1) Exploring the patient's concern provides an opportunity for the patient to verbalize further; it focuses on the patient and the patient's feelings.
 (2) Completing the procedure quickly ignores and denies the patient's feelings and concerns.
 (3) Informing the physician does not address the patient's immediate concern; the physician can be informed later.
 (4) Explaining that the procedure is necessary denies the patient's feelings and concerns.

Analysis—Queston 17

Option two totally ignores the patient's distress. Option three does not immediately address the distress of the patient. Although option four attempts to provide information as a form of encouragement, it still denies the patient's feelings and concerns. Option one is the only option that focuses on the patient's immediate feelings. If you are able to identify that options two, three, and four do not immediately address the distress of the patient then you can eliminate these options from consideration and choose option one as the correct answer.

Question 18

The most significant contributing factor to the formation of a decubitus ulcer is:
(1) Pressure
(2) Cachexia
(3) Incontinence
(4) Malnutrition

Test-Taking Tip—Question 18

Determine which options are interrelated and therefore equally plausible. Eliminate these options. Identify the word in the stem that is setting a priority.

Rationales—Question 18

*(1) Prolonged pressure over a bony prominence results in hypoxia to tissues and is the main contributing factor in the formation of decubitus ulcers, which are also known as pressure ulcers.

(2) Cachexia denotes a state of general ill health and extreme weight loss. The patient who is cachectic is at risk for developing a pressure ulcer; however, pressure is the most significant contributing factor.

(3) Patients who are incontinent are at a higher risk for developing pressure ulcers than patients who are continent; however, pressure is the most significant contributing factor.

(4) Patients who are malnourished are at a higher risk for pressure ulcers than patients who are well nourished; however, pressure is the most significant contributing factor.

Analysis—Question 18

In option two the word "cachexia" means general ill health and malnutrition marked by emaciation. In option four the word "malnutrition" means a condition caused by an insufficient or unbalanced diet or defective digestion, absorption, or utilization of nutrients. These words are interrelated and comparable, although the relationship between them is less obvious. One option is no better or worse than the other option in relation to the statement in the stem. Both of these distractors can be deleted. The word "most" indicates that more than one of the options may cause a pressure ulcer. You must select the one that is **most** significant. Option one is the correct answer.

Question 19

Systemic adaptations to an infection include:
(1) Tachycardia and increased temperature
(2) Increased temperature and edema
(3) Pain and tachycardia
(4) Edema and pain

Test-Taking Tip—Question 19

Identify duplicate facts in the options. When a fact is correct you must seriously consider the options that contain this fact. When a fact is incorrect you can eliminate the options that contain this fact.

Rationales—Question 19

*(1) Tachycardia is a systemic adaptation associated with an infection because of the increase in the basal metabolic rate. Fever, a systemic response, is associated with an infection because of pyrogens affecting the temperature regulating center in the hypothalamus.

(2) Although an increased temperature is a systemic adaptation related to an infection, edema is a localized, not systemic response.

(3) Although tachycardia is a systemic adaptation associated with an infection, pain is a localized, not a systemic, adaptation.

(4) Edema, in response to an increase in vascular permeability caused by chemical mediators, and pain are both local, not systemic, responses to infection.

Analysis—Question 19

Take each fact and determine if it is correct in relation to the question being asked. If you know that pain is a local, rather than a systemic, response then delete options three and four. If you know that edema is a local, rather than a systemic, response then delete options two and four. If you know only one of the facts you increase your chances of getting the answer correct to 50%. If an increased temperature is the only fact you know that is related to the question being asked then choose between options one and two. If tachycardia is the only fact you know that is related to the question being asked then choose between options one and three. Obviously, the more facts you know the better able you will be to reduce the options you are left with from which to make your final selection. Option one is the correct answer.

Question 20

A medical word that means "creation of a surgical passage through the abdominal wall into the ileum" is?

(1) Idiopathic
(2) Ileostomy
(3) Ischemia
(4) Icterus

Test-Taking Tip—Question 20

Identify the clue in the stem. A clue is a word that is similar to a word in the correct answer.

Rationales—Question 20

(1) "Idiopathic" means **occurring without cause**.
*(2) "Ile/o" refers to the third part of the small intestine, the **ileum**; "-stomy" means **forming a new opening**. Ileostomy means forming a new opening into the ileum.
(3) "Ischemia" means **a deficiency in blood to a part**.
(4) "Icterus" means **jaundice**, which is a yellow coloration of the skin because of excessive bilirubin.

Analysis—Question 20

The clue in the stem is **ileum** "Ile/o" is the word element for ileum. Option two is the only option that somewhat resembles the word "ileum" and is therefore the correct answer.

Question 21

Which medical term contains a prefix that reflects the direction **within** a structure?
(1) Paranasal
(2) Periosteum
(3) Preoperative
(4) Intramuscular

Test-Taking Tip—Question 21

Identify the key word in the stem. A key word is identical or similar to a word in the correct answer. Identify the option that is unique. Which one of the options is not like the others?

Rationales—Question 21

(1) The prefix "para-" means **near** or **beside**, "nas" means **nose**, and "al" is an adjective ending.
(2) The prefix "peri-" means **around**, "oste" means **bone**, and "um" is a noun ending.
(3) The prefix "pre-" means **before**, "operative" means **operation**.
*(4) The prefix "intra-" means **within**, "muscul" means **muscle**, and "ar" is an adjective ending.

Analysis—Question 21

The word that is a clue in the stem is **within**. The word element **in** apears in the words **within** and **intramuscular**. There is a similarity between these words and you should, therefore, closely examine option four. Options one, two, and three all have prefixes that start with a "p." Option four is different and unique. By eliminating distractors using test-taking techniques you can select the correct answer without knowing the meaning of any of the four options in this question. Option four is the correct answer.

Question 22

The medical word element "dorso" stands for:
(1) After
(2) Before
(3) Above
(4) Back

Test-Taking Tip—Question 22

Identify the options that are opposite to each other. Consider these options carefully. One is the correct answer or they are both distractors.

Rationales—Question 22

(1) The medical word element for "after" is **post-**.
(2) The medical word elements for "before" are **ante-**, **antero-**, **pre-**, or **pro-**.
(3) The medical word elements for "above" are **hyper-**, **super-**, or **supra-**.
*(4) This is correct. "Dorso" is a combining form meaning **pertaining to a dorsum or to the back**.

Analysis—Question 22

Options one and two are opposites. "Before" and "after" reflect opposite periods of time in relation to an event. In this question they are both distractors. Option four is the correct answer.

Question 23

Which word contains a prefix that reflects the middle of the structure indicated in the root?
(1) Intercostal
(2) Midsternum
(3) Hypodermic
(4) Postnatal

Test-Taking Tip—Question 23

Look for the clue in the stem. A clue is a word or phrase that is similar to a word or phrase used in the option.

Rationales—Question 23

(1) The prefix "inter-" means **between**, "cost" means **ribs**, and "al" is an adjective ending.
*(2) The prefix "mid-" means **middle**, "stern" means **chest**, and "um" is a noun ending.
(3) The prefix "hypo-" means **under**, "derm" means **skin**, and "ic" is an adjective ending.
(4) The prefix "post-" means **after**, "nat" means **birth**, and "al" is an adjective ending.

Analysis—Question 23

The word **middle** is a clue contained in the stem. Option two includes the word **midsterum**. The prefix "**mid-**" means **middle**. The similarity between **mid** and **middle** should clue you to seriously consider option two. Option two is the correct answer.

Question 24

Which of the following is *not* a prefix?
(1) Plegia
(2) Hyper
(3) Supra
(4) Peri

Test-Taking Tip—Question 24

Carefully examine the stem for a word that indicates negative polarity. Questions with negative polarity are concerned with exceptions.

Rationales—Question 24

*(1) "Plegia" is a suffix that means **paralysis**. A suffix is added to the end of a word root to alter its meaning.
(2) "Hyper" is a prefix that means **abnormally increased or excessive**. A prefix is added to the beginning of a word root to alter its meaning or to create a new word.

(3) "Supra" is a prefix that means **above**. A prefix is added to the beginning of a word root to alter its meaning or to create a new word.

(4) "Peri" is a prefix that means **around**. A prefix is added to the beginning of a word root to alter its meaning or to create a new word.

Analysis—Question 24

The key word in the stem is "**not**." The stem is asking you to select the option that is **not** a prefix. If you misread the question and look for a prefix then there will be more than one correct answer. When there appears to be more than one answer, reread the stem for a key negative word that you may have missed. Option one is the correct answer.

Question 25

Which rule guides the building of medical terms?
(1) A compound word never uses more than one root word.
(2) A combining vowel is always used before a suffix that begins with a vowel.
(3) Suffixes, when added to root words, indicate the part of speech of the medical term.
(4) A combining vowel is generally not used to link a root word to a suffix that begins with a consonant.

Test-Taking Tip—Question 25

Look for the specific determiner in the options. A specific determiner is a word or statement that conveys a thought or concept that has no exceptions.

Rationales—Question 25

(1) Many medical terms use more than one root word. For example, "leuk/o/cyt/o/penia," **leuk** and **cyt** are both root words.
(2) A combining vowel is unnecessary before a suffix that begins with a vowel. For example, when combining **cyst** (a root word) with **itis** (a suffix) to form the word "cystitis" there is no need to use a combined vowel. A combining vowel is used between a root word and a suffix that begins with a consonant.
*(3) This is true. For example, **ic** is an adjective ending in the word "gastric" and **ia** is the noun ending in the word "gastria."
(4) A combining vowel is used to link a root word to a suffix that begins with a consonant. This reduces the awkwardness of pronunciation. For example, "lith/o/tripsy" is easier to pronounce than "lith/tripsy," which is incorrect. The **o** is the combining vowel.

Analysis—Question 25

Options one and two contain specific determiners. The words **never** and **always** are absolute and are easy to identify. Because there are few absolutes in this world, options that contain specific determiners are usually incorrect and can be eliminated. By eliminating options one and two you have increased your chances of selecting the correct answer to 50%. Option three is the correct answer.

Question 26

Which of the following diagnostic or symptomatic suffixes means tumor?
(1) -oma
(2) -itis
(3) -iasis
(4) -stasis

Test-Taking Tip—Question 26

Examine the options for the one that is unique or different from the others. Look for an obscure clue in the stem that may lead you to the correct answer. A clue in the stem may be a word that is identical or similar to a word used in the correct answer.

Rationales—Question 26

*(1) "-oma" means **tumor**.
 (2) "-itis" means **inflammation**.
 (3) "-iasis" means **formation of, presence of, or condition**.
 (4) "-stasis" means **standing still**.

Analysis—Question 26

Options two, three, and four are similar and equally plausible because they all end in "is." Option one is different and unique because it is the only option that ends in "a." The clue in the stem is the spelling of the word "tumor." Of the options offered, option one is the only option that uses the same letters "m" and "o." By applying the test-taking skills of "equally plausible and unique options" and "identify clues in the stem" you could select the correct answer without knowing the meaning of the medical word elements in the options. Option one is the correct answer.

Question 27

Which of the following is **not** an example of a root word?
(1) Tomy
(2) Mast
(3) Oste
(4) Cephal

Test-Taking Tip—Question 27

Carefully examine the stem for a word that indicates negative polarity. Questions with negative polarity are concerned with exceptions.

Rationales—Question 27

*(1) "-tomy," which refers to an incision, is an example of a suffix that begins with a consonant.

(2) "Mast," which refers to breast, is a root word.
(3) "Oste," which refers to bone, is a root word.
(4) "Cephal," which refers to head, is a root word.

Analysis—Question 27

The key word in the stem is **not**. The stem is asking you to select the option that is **not a root word**. If you misread the question and look for word elements that are root words then there will be more than one correct answer. When there appears to be more than one correct answer, reread the stem for a key negative word that you may have missed. Option one is the correct answer.

Question 28

The combining vowel used most often is the letter:
(1) A
(2) E
(3) I
(4) O

Test-Taking Tip—Question 28

Identify the key word in the stem that sets a priority. A word that sets a priority modifies another important word or concept that relates to what is being asked.

Rationales—Question 28

(1) Although this vowel is used occasionally as a combining vowel, it is not the vowel that is used most often.
(2) Although this vowel is used occasionally as a combining vowel, it is not the vowel that is used most often.
(3) Although this vowel is used occasionally as a combining vowel, it is not the vowel that is used most often.
*(4) The "o" vowel is the most frequently used combining vowel of all the vowels.

Analysis—Question 28

The word "most" modifies the words **often used** and sets a priority. All of the options include vowels that are used to combine word elements but only one is **used most often**. Progressively eliminate one option that is least important until you are left with one remaining option. The "o" vowel facilitates the pronunciation of a word. Option four is the correct answer.

Question 29

Which individual would have the most dramatic increase in the need for oxygen?
(1) A pregnant woman
(2) A man with a fever
(3) A person exercising
(4) A patient under anesthesia

Test-Taking Tip—Question 29

Identify the key word in the stem that sets a priority. A word that sets a priority modifies another important word or concept that relates to what is being asked.

Rationales—Question 29

(1) A pregnant woman's metabolic rate is increased; however, pregnancy does not place as high a demand on the body's need for oxygen as the correct answer.

(2) A fever causes an increase in a person's metabolic rate; however, a fever does not place as high a demand on the body's need for oxygen as the correct answer.

*(3) All types of exercise dramatically increase the metabolic rate, which in turn increases the body's demand for oxygen.

(4) General anesthesia relaxes the muscles of the body; when muscles are relaxed, the metabolic rate decreases and the demand for oxygen also decreases.

Analysis—Question 29

The key word "most" modifies the concept **dramatic increase in the need for oxygen** and sets a priority. Stems that set a priority are asking you to select the option that has the highest significance in relation to the question. All of the options identify individuals who have an increased need for oxygen but only one would have the most dramatic increase in the need for oxygen. Option three is the correct answer.

Question 30

When administering a subcutaneous injection with a 5/8-inch needle it should be inserted at an angle of:
(1) 30 degrees
(2) 45 degrees
(3) 90 degrees
(4) 180 degrees

Test-Taking Tip—Question 30

Identify the two options that are opposites among the choices offered. They must be given serious consideration. One of them will be the correct answer, or they both can be eliminated.

Rationales—Question 30

(1) This is too shallow an angle.

*(2) This injects the solution into the loose connective tissue under the dermis when using a 5/8-inch needle. A subcutaneous injection with a 1/2-inch needle should be inserted at a 90-degree angle.

(3) This angle is too great. This angle is acceptable when administering insulin or heparin with a 1/2-inch needle or when administering an intramuscular injection with a 1 1/2-inch needle.

(4) This is impossible; various injection methods use angles from 5 degrees to 90 degrees, not 180 degrees.

Analysis—Question 30

All of the options are on a continuum concerning angles related to the insertion of a needle for the administration of parenteral medication. Options one and four are opposites. If you correctly evaluate opposite options, you can increase your chances of selecting the correct answer to 50% because you have reduced the potentially correct answers to the two remaining options. In this question options one and four are the extremes and can be eliminated as distractors. Of the two remaining options, two and three, option two is the correct answer.

PRACTICE TEST B

Question 1

A healthcare provider makes work assignments for subordinates. An acceptable expectation of the healthcare provider is that the subordinates will:
(1) Complete everything that has been assigned
(2) Be friendly with other health team members
(3) Perform within the limits of their role
(4) Work with minimal supervision

Test-Taking Tip—Question 1

Look for the specific determiner in an option. A specific determiner is a word or statement that conveys a thought that has no exceptions. Generally an option with a specific determiner is a distractor and can be eliminated from consideration.

Rationales—Question 1

(1) Subordinates can refuse to perform tasks that are outside the parameters of their role and job responsibilities.
(2) Health team members must have a professional relationship with mutual respect; they do not have to be friends.
*(3) The responsibilities and job description of health team members must be clear to other members of the health team; individuals should perform only those tasks that are within their role and have been learned.
(4) Although subordinates can be self-directed within their roles, they must work under the direction of a supervisor.

Analysis—Question 1

The word "everything" in option one is an absolute term that has no exception and is therefore a specific determiner. This option is a distractor and can be eliminated from consideration. Option three is the correct answer.

Question 2

According to Maslow's Hierarchy of Needs, which of the needs listed below takes precedence over the others?
(1) Security
(2) Belonging

Test-Taking Tip—Question 2

Identify the key word in the stem that indicates a priority. A word or phrase that sets a priority modifies another important word or concept that relates to what is being asked.

(3) Self-esteem
(4) Self-actualization

Rationales—Question 2

*(1) Safety and security needs, second-level needs according to Maslow, occur after basic physiological needs and before the need for love and belonging; people need to feel physically and emotionally safe.

(2) This third-level need according to Maslow occurs after safety and security needs; a bond of affection is necessary for well-being.

(3) This fourth-level need according to Maslow occurs after love and belonging needs; people need to feel competent and respected.

(4) This is the fifth and final level according to Maslow; maximizing abilities and feeling content within the self are necessary for self-satisfaction.

Analysis—Question 2

The phrase "takes precedence" is the key phrase in the stem. This phrase asks you to rank the options in order of priority and to choose the option that is ranked first. All of the options include components of Maslow's Hierarchy of Needs, but security needs are ranked first among the options offered and option one is, therefore, the correct answer.

Question 3

A patient, with a left-sided hemiplegia as the result of a cerebral vascular accident, states in a disgusted tone of voice, "I feel like a 2-year-old child. I can't even get dressed by myself." The BEST response would be:

(1) "It must be hard to feel dependent on others."

(2) "Most people who have had a stroke feel this way."

(3) "It must be difficult not being able to move your arm."

(4) "You are feeling down today, but things will get better."

Test-Taking Tip—Question 3

Identify the option that denies the patient's feelings by providing false reassurance. Eliminate this option from consideration.

Rationales—Question 3

*(1) This statement identifies the patient's feelings and provides an opportunity for further discussion.

(2) This statement is a generalization that may not be true; it also cuts off communication.

(3) This statement focuses on the inability to move, rather than feelings of helplessness, dependence, and regression.

(4) This statement is false reassurance because no one knows if things will really get better.

Analysis—Question 3

Option four initially identifies the patient's emotional status but then offers false reassurance, which cuts off communication. Delete this option from consideration. Option one is the correct answer.

Question 4

Which patient assessment would be expected in a patient who has lost 2 units of blood?
(1) Rapid, shallow breathing
(2) Increased urinary output
(3) Hypertension
(4) Bradypnea

Test-Taking Tip—Question 4

Identify the two options that are opposites. They must be given serious consideration. One of them will be the correct answer, or they both can be eliminated.

Rationales—Question 4

*(1) With a decrease in circulating red blood cells, the respiratory rate will increase to meet oxygen needs.

 (2) With a reduction in blood volume, there will be less blood circulating through the kidneys, resulting in a decreased, not increased, urinary output.

 (3) With a reduction in blood volume, the blood pressure will be decreased, not elevated.

 (4) Bradypnea is not associated with blood loss.

Analysis—Question 4

Options one and four are opposites. If you correctly evaluate opposite options, you can increase your chances of selecting the correct answer to 50% because you have reduced the potentially correct answers to two. In this question one of these options, option one, is the correct answer.

Question 5

When opening the pressure valve of a sphygmomanometer the manometer reading drops quickly. The first action should be to:
(1) Remove the cuff and send the sphygmomanometer for repair.
(2) Squeeze the air out of the cuff and try again.

Test-Taking Tip—Question 5

Identify the options that are equally plausible. When options are similar, they are usually distractors and both can be eliminated from consideration.

(3) Wait 2 minutes before pumping up the cuff a second time.

(4) Check the tubing and cuff for air leaks.

Rationales—Question 5

(1) There are insufficient data to come to this conclusion.

(2) This is unsafe; pumping the cuff too soon traps excess blood in the extremity resulting in an inaccurate reading and possible discomfort.

*(3) This allows for venous return and prevents falsely elevated results.

(4) The sphygomomanometer should have been checked for proper functioning prior to use.

Analysis—Question 5

Options one and four both focus on the fact that the sphygmomanometer is broken. It is difficult to choose between them because they are comparable. Equally plausible options are usually distractors and can be deleted from consideration. Option three is the correct answer.

Question 6

A concern that is common to the collection of specimens, regardless of their source, for culture and sensitivity tests is:

(1) The specimen should be collected in the morning.

(2) The specimen should be obtained at night.

(3) Surgical asepsis must be maintained.

(4) Two specimens should be obtained.

Test-Taking Tip—Question 6

Identify opposites in the options. Give these options serious consideration because one of them will be the correct answer or they are both distractors and can be deleted from consideration.

Rationales—Question 6

(1) It is not necessary to collect most specimens for culture and sensitivity in the morning.

(2) It is not necessary to collect specimens for culture and sensitivity at night.

*(3) The results of a culture and sensitivity are faulty and erroneous if the collection container is not kept sterile; a contaminated specimen container introduces extraneous microorganisms that falsify and misrepresent results. Surgical asepsis (sterile technique) must be maintained.

(4) Generally if a specimen is collected using proper technique, one specimen is sufficient for testing for culture and sensitivity.

Analysis—Question 6

Options one and two are opposites. Thoughtfully review these options because they are both distractors or one of them is the correct answer. In this question they are both distractors and therefore are incorrect answers. Option three is the correct answer.

Question 7

Which are examples of objective data?
(1) Nausea, bradycardia, pain
(2) Pain, bradycardia, fatigue
(3) Fatigue, tachycardia, nausea
(4) Fever, tachycardia, hypotension

Test-Taking Tip—Question 7

Identify the duplicate facts in the options. If you recognize one fact as being wrong you can usually eliminate two options from consideration. Look for the unique option that is different from the others. Often times the unique option is the correct answer.

Rationales—Question 7

(1) Nausea and pain are subjective data.
(2) Pain and fatigue are subjective data.
(3) Fatigue and nausea are subjective data.
*(4) These are objective data because they can be measured; subjective data are a patient's perceptions, feelings, sensations, or ideas.

Analysis—Question 7

This question is testing your knowledge of objective data in relation to patient adaptations. Because most of the data presented appear in at least two options, if you know that one of them is subjective then two options can be eliminated from consideration: nausea—eliminate options one and three; pain—eliminate options one and two; fatigue—eliminate options two and three. Option four is unique because only one of the three facts appears in another option. Two of the three facts in the distractors (options one, two, and three) appear in another option. Option four is the correct answer.

Question 8

The <u>most</u> subjective characteristic of pain is its:
(1) Intensity
(2) Duration
(3) Location
(4) Quality

Test-Taking Tip—Question 8

Identify the key phrase in the stem that sets a priority. All of the options are probably related to the question being asked but you are being asked to identify the one that is most related to subjectivity.

Rationales—Question 8

*(1) Intensity is the most subjective characteristic of pain; a patient's perception of pain influences the descriptive report about the severity of pain.
(2) The description of the duration of pain is based on determining the onset, periodicity, frequency, and length of the pain; it is

based on time frames that can be objectively measured by the patient.

(3) This description is based on anatomical landmarks in the patient's attempt to localize the pain; it is more objective than the correct answer.

(4) Although somewhat subjective, the quality of pain is more objective than the correct answer. There is consistency in the language used to describe types of pain; surgical pain is generally described as "sharp" and pain related to a heart attack is described as "crushing."

Analysis—Question 8

The key phrase in this stem is "most subjective characteristic." All of the options are characteristics of pain. First eliminate those options that are least subjective and most objective such as options two and three, then consider the two remaining options to select the correct answer. You have increased your chances of selecting the correct answer to 50%. Option one is the correct answer.

Question 9

When assessing the vital signs of a patient with hypovolemia, an unexpected patient adaptation would be:
(1) Tachycardia
(2) Hypertension
(3) Thready pulse
(4) Increased temperature

Test-Taking Tip—Question 9

Identify the key word in the stem that indicates negative polarity. Questions with negative polarity are asking you to identify the exception among the options presented.

Rationales—Question 9

(1) The heart rate would increase with hypovolemia in an attempt to increase the cardiac output.

*(2) Hypotension, not hypertension, would occur with hypovolemia because of the decreased circulating blood volume.

(3) A thready pulse would occur with hypovolemia because of the decreased circulating blood volume.

(4) Hypovolemia can activate the sympathetic nervous system, increasing the body's basal metabolic rate and temperature.

Analysis—Question 9

The word "unexpected" indicates that the stem has negative polarity. The question is asking what is **not an adaptation** to hypovolemia. Options one, three, and four are associated with hypovolemia and option 2 is not related to hypovolemia. If at first several options look correct, reread the stem because you may have missed a word that reflects negative polarity. Option two is the correct answer.

Question 10

When an agitated patient on bed rest is attempting to pull out the intravenous catheter the physician orders wrist restraints. Wrist restraints should be tied to the:
(1) Side rails
(2) Footboard
(3) Headboard
(4) Bed frame

Test-Taking Tip—Question 10

Identify opposites in the stem. Seriously consider these options. Look for the equally plausible options. One is no better than the other in relation to the statement presented in the stem.

Rationales—Question 10

(1) Wrist restraints attached to side rails do not provide a stable base of support; injury can occur when the rails are inadvertently lowered before the straps are removed.
(2) Wrist restraints attached to the footboard would require an excessively long strap in which the patient's legs could get entangled.
(3) Wrist restraints attached to the headboard could result in an uncomfortable line of pull with the arm above the head.
*(4) Wrist restraints should be attached to the bed frame because it is a stable base of support and is beyond the patient's reach.

Analysis—Question 10

Options two and three are opposite ends of a bed. Carefully consider these options because they are both distractors or one of them is the correct answer. Options two and three are also equally plausible. They are comparable and it is difficult to differentiate between the two. Options two and three are distractors and can be eliminated from consideration. By eliminating options two and three, you have raised your chances of selecting the correct answer to 50%. Option four is the correct answer.

Question 11

A commonly used symbol is $<$. What does this symbol represent?
(1) Decreased
(2) Less than
(3) Greater than
(4) Not equal to

Test-Taking Tip—Question 11

Identify the opposites among the options. One of these options may be the correct answer; or they will both be distractors. Evaluate these options carefully.

Rationales—Question 11

(1) "Decreased" is represented by the symbol $\downarrow$.
*(2) "Less than" is represented by the symbol $<$. This symbol can be modified for additional meanings such as $\nless$ "not less than" or $\leq$ "equal to or less than."

(3) "Greater than" is represented by the symbol >.

(4) "Not equal to" is represented by the symbol ≠.

Analysis—Question 11

Options two and three are opposites. They convey converse messages. In this question, option two is the correct answer.

Question 12

The initials COPD represent:

(1) Central venous pressure

(2) Partial pressure of carbon dioxide

(3) Chronic obstructive pulmonary disease

(4) Centers for Disease Control and Prevention

Test-Taking Tip—Question 12

Identify clues in the stem. A clue is information in the stem that leads you to the correct answer.

Rationales—Question 12

(1) Central venous pressure is represented by the initials CVP.

(2) The partial pressure of carbon dioxide is represented by the symbol P_{CO_2}.

*(3) COPD is an abbreviation for chronic obstructive pulmonary disease. These diseases include asthma, emphysema, chronic bronchitis, and chronic bronchiectasis.

(4) Centers for Disease Control and Prevention is represented by the abbreviation CDC.

Analysis—Question 12

More often than not abbreviations are composed of the first letter of each word in the phrase being represented. Option three is the only option where each word begins with the letter in the abbreviation—Chronic Obstructive Pulmonary Disease.

Question 13

Which of the following is **not** associated with diaphragmatic breathing?

(1) Feeling the abdomen flatten on inspiration

(2) Raising the shoulders and chest when inhaling

(3) Holding the breath for 3 seconds on inspiration

(4) Placing the palms of the hand against the abdomen on inhalation

Test-Taking Tip—Question 13

Pick out the word in the stem that indicates negative polarity. A negative word can be opposite to a positive word or it can be a word that modifies a positive word.

Rationales—Question 13

(1) The abdomen rises on inspiration.

(2) These accessory muscles should not consciously be involved with diaphragmatic breathing.

*(3) Diaphragmatic breathing involves a pattern of a slow deep inhalation followed by a slow exhalation with a tightening of the abdominal muscles to aid exhalation; the patient should not hold the breath at any time during the cycle when performing diaphragmatic breathing.

(4) This encourages the patient to feel and concentrate on the abdomen rising during inhalation and falling and contracting on exhalation.

Analysis—Question 13

The word **not** in the stem indicates negative polarity. It is modifying the word "associated." When one thing is not associated with a list of other things, it is an exception. Option three is the correct answer.

Question 14

Which local adaptation would indicate that the patient has entered the second phase of the inflammatory response?

(1) Pain

(2) A fever

(3) An exudate

(4) Hyperthermia

Test-Taking Tip—Question 14

Identify the two options that are very similar. Equally plausible options are usually distractors and can be eliminated from consideration.

Rationales—Question 14

(1) Pain occurs during the first phase of the inflammatory response. When histamine is released at the injury site, it promotes vessel permeability, which increases edema and causes pressure on nerve endings.

(2) Fever, an increase in body temperature, is a systemic adaptation that occurs when the set point regulated by the hypothalamus is readjusted to a higher level.

*(3) Phase two of the inflammatory response is characterized by the formation of an exudate; it consists of a combination of cells and fluids produced at the injury site.

(4) Hyperthemia, an increase in body temperature, is a systemic adaptation that occurs when the set point regulated by the hypothalamus is readjusted to a higher level.

Analysis—Question 14

In option two the word "fever" means an abnormal elevation in temperature. In option four the word "hyperthermia" means a higher than normal body temperature. It would be difficult to choose between these two options because they are similar and equally plausible. By eliminating options two and four you have raised your chances of choosing the correct answer to 50%. Option three is the correct answer.

Question 15

When a patient has atherosclerosis it is sometimes difficult to reduce cholesterol levels because:
(1) Cholesterol is synthesized in the body.
(2) All foods contain a small amount of cholesterol.
(3) Vitamin D maximizes the deposition of cholesterol.
(4) Excess cholesterol is totally absorbed rather than excreted.

Test-Taking Tip—Question 15

Identify the specific determiners in the options. A specific determiner is a word that modifies another word or statement in such a way that there are no exceptions.

Rationales—Question 15

*(1) The body manufactures about 1000 g of cholesterol a day, mainly in the liver.
(2) Cholesterol is not present in foods of plant origin.
(3) Cholesterol acts as the precursor for the synthesis of vitamin D at the surface of the skin.
(4) The liver filters out excess cholesterol and helps to eliminate it from the body.

Analysis—Question 15

Option two contains the word "all" and option four includes the word "totally." These words are specific determiners. "All" and "totally" are inclusive and can be eliminated. You have just increased your chances of answering this question to 50%. Option one is the correct answer.

Question 16

The patient at the highest risk for developing a pressure ulcer would be a patient with:
(1) Paraplegia
(2) Hypotension
(3) Heart failure
(4) Angina pectoris

Test-Taking Tip—Question 16

Identify the unique option. Three options are very similar or related and one is not. The option that is different from the three that are similar is probably the correct answer.

Rationales—Question 16

*(1) Paralysis of the lower extremities results in reduced mobility; maintaining one position causes pressure and tissue hypoxia, which can result in pressure ulcers.

(2) A patient with hypotension is at risk for falls because postural hypotension can cause dizziness.

(3) A patient with heart failure is at risk for developing a dysrhythmia.

(4) A patient with angina pectoris is at risk for developing a myocardial infarction (heart attack).

Analysis—Question 16

If you know the definition of these four terms you understand that hypotension, angina pectoris, and heart failure all relate to the cardiovascular system. Options two, three, and four are interrelated. Option one is different or unique because it relates to the neuromuscular system and is the correct answer.

Question 17

While a caregiver is providing care to a patient, the patient says, "As soon as no one is looking I'm going to take all my sleeping pills at one time." The best initial response would be:

(1) "It sounds like you feel overwhelmed."

(2) "I'm going to have to tell your wife about your plan."

(3) "Suicide is not the answer to your problems. Let's talk about this."

(4) "I just can't let that happen. Please give me your sleeping pills."

Test-Taking Tip—Question 17

Identify options that are patient centered. To be patient centered an option should support a patient's feelings or concerns.

Rationales—Question 17

*(1) The use of reflective technique opens the channels of communication by identifying feelings; it provides immediate support by encouraging the patient to discuss the issue further in a nonjudgmental environment.

(2) This statement infantizes the patient, ignores the patient's feelings, and cuts off communication.

(3) Although the second part of the statement invites the patient to talk about the problem, the first part of this response is judgmental and may set up a barrier to communication.

(4) This focuses on the role of the caregiver, infantizes the patient, and cuts off communication. Although the sleeping pills may be taken away to protect the patient, it is not the best initial action by the caregiver.

Analysis—Question 17

Options two and four focus on a person other than the patient and ignores the patient's feelings and concerns. Although option three eventually invites the patient to talk about the problem the first part of the option is judgmental and may cut off communication. Option one is the only option that focuses on the feelings of the patient and is open-ended, inviting the patient to explore feelings more fully. If you are able to identify that options two, three, and four do not address the distress of the patient in a nonjudgmental environment then you can eliminate these options from consideration and choose option one as the correct answer.

Question 18

The position that would contribute to the development of a pressure ulcer in the sacral area is the:
(1) Prone position
(2) Lateral position
(3) Side-lying position
(4) High-Fowler's position

Test-Taking Tip—Question 18

Identify equally plausible options. When options are comparable, similar, alike, or parallel they are usually distractors and can be deleted.

Rationales—Question 18

(1) The prone position avoids pressure on the sacral area; prone is lying on the abdomen.
(2) In the lateral position, pressure is off the sacral area. In the lateral position, body weight is on the dependent hip and shoulder.
(3) The side-lying position avoids pressure on the sacral area. In the side-lying position, body weight is on the dependent hip and shoulder.
*(4) In the high-Fowler's position, most of the weight is placed on the sacral area, the posterior position of the pelvis; this causes sacral pressure.

Analysis—Question 18

The terms "lateral position" and "side-lying position" are used interchangeably. Because they are the same, neither can be the correct answer. Eliminate options two and three because they are equally plausible distractors. Option four is the correct answer.

Question 19

Localized responses to an infection include:
(1) Pain and erythema
(2) Leukocytosis and pain
(3) Erythema and bradycardia
(4) Bradycardia and leukocytosis

Test-Taking Tip—Question 19

Identify duplicate facts in the options. When a fact is correct you must seriously consider the options that contain this fact. When a fact is incorrect you can eliminate the options that contain this fact.

Rationales—Question 19

*(1) Pain and erythema are both responses to a local infection. Pain is the result of edema of inflamed tissue increasing pressure on local nerve endings. Erythema, or local redness, is caused by increased local blood flow in response to chemical mediators that increase the permeability of small blood vessels.

(2) Although pain is a response to a local infection, leukocytosis, or an increase in the systemic white blood cell count, is a response to a systemic, not local, infection.

(3) Although erythema, or local redness, is caused by increased local blood flow in response to chemical mediators that increase the permeability of small blood vessels, bradycardia (a heart rate below 60 beats per minute) is unrelated to either a local or systemic infection.

(4) Bradycardia, a heart rate below 60 beats per minute, is unrelated to either a local or systemic infection. Leukocytosis, an increase in the systemic white blood cell count, is related to a systemic, not a local, infection.

Analysis—Question 19

Take each fact and determine if it is correct in relation to the question being asked. If you know that leukocytosis is a systemic, rather than a local, response then delete options two and four. If you know that bradycardia is unrelated to either local or systemic infections you can delete options three and four. If you know only one of the facts you increase your chances of getting the answer correct by 50%. If pain is the only fact you know that is related to the question being asked then choose between options one and two. If erythema is the only fact you know that is related to the question being asked then choose between options one and three. Obviously, the more facts you know the better able you will be to reduce the options you are left with from which to make your final selection. Option one is the correct answer.

Question 20

The method of exactly locating an area in the brain or breast using three-dimensional measurement is called:
(1) Strabismus
(2) Stereotaxis
(3) Steatorrhea
(4) Stomatoplasty

Test-Taking Tip—Question 20

Identify the clue in the stem that leads you to the correct answer. This clue is somewhat covert and draws on your general knowledge rather than your knowledge of medical terminology.

Rationales—Question 20

(1) Strabismus is an abnormal ocular condition in which the eyes are crossed.

*(2) Stereotaxis is an imaging procedure to precisely pinpoint the location of a tumor, usually in the breast or brain.

(3) Steatorrhea denotes feces that contain excessive amounts of fat.

(4) Stomatoplasty denotes reconstruction of the mouth via surgery.

Analysis—Question 20

The clue in the stem is "three-dimensional measurement." In the English language the word "stereo" means *three dimensional*. A stereophonic system provides sound from more than one dimension. Familiarity with the word "stereo" provides a clue to the correct answer, option two.

Question 21

Which medical word reflects a blisterlike elevation of the skin that contains pus?
(1) Vesicle
(2) Pustule
(3) Papule
(4) Wheal

Test-Taking Tip—Question 21

Identify the clue in the stem. A clue is a word that is similar to a word in the correct answer.

Rationales—Question 21

(1) A vesicle is a blisterlike elevation of the skin that contains serous fluid, not pus.

*(2) A pustule is a small, circumscribed elevation of the skin that contains fluid, which is usually purulent.

(3) A papule is a small, solid raised skin lesion.

(4) A wheal is a pruritic, circumscribed, edematous, usually transitory skin lesion associated with hypersensitivity.

Analysis—Question 21

The clue in the stem is "pus." Option two is the only option that is similar to pus. **Pus**tules and **pus** are related.

Question 22

A suffix that means "surgical repair" is
(1) plasty
(2) peri
(3) post
(4) pre

Test-Taking Tip—Question 22

Look for opposites in the options. They can reflect extremes on a continuum and convey converse messages. When opposites appear in the options one of them will be correct or they both can be eliminated from consideration.

Rationales—Question 22

*(1) "-plasty" is a suffix that means surgical repair.

(2) "Peri-" is a prefix that means around.

(3) "Post-" is a prefix that means after or behind.

(4) "Pre-" is a prefix that means before.

Analysis—Question 22

Options three and four are opposites and must be given careful consideration. In this question they are distractors attempting to divert your attention from the correct answer. The prefixes "*pre-*" and "*post-*" are commonly used in the English language to describe a time line of before and after. Because "before" and "after" are unrelated to surgical repair, options three and four can be eliminated from consideration. If you correctly evaluate opposite options you can increase your chances of selecting the correct answer by 50% because you have reduced the plausible options to two, options one and two. Option one is the correct answer.

Question 23

Which word contains a prefix that reflects the color purple?
(1) Purpura
(2) Melanoma
(3) Cyanosis
(4) Cirrhosis

Test-Taking Tip—Question 23

Identify the word that is a clue in the stem. A clue is a word or phrase that is identical or similar to a word or phrase in an option.

Rationales—Question 23

*(1) "Purpur" means purple, and "a" is a noun ending.
 (2) "Melan" means black, and "oma" means tumor.
 (3) "Cyan" means blue, and "osis" means an increase in.
 (4) "Cirrh" means yellow, and "osis" means an increase in.

Analysis—Question 23

The key word in the stem is "purple." Option one, **purpura** is the only choice that is similar to the word "purple." Carefully assess option one because it is the correct answer.

Question 24

Which word element is unrelated to the musculoskeletal system?
(1) Coccyx
(2) Ostealgia
(3) Periosteum
(4) Cardiomegaly

Test-Taking Tip—Question 24

Carefully examine the stem for a word that indicates negative polarity. Questions with negative polarity are concerned with exceptions.

Rationales—Question 24

 (1) The coccyx is a beaklike structure made of bone joined to the sacrum at the base of the vertebral column and is a part of the musculoskeletal system.
 (2) "*Oste*" is the word element that refers to bone and "*algia*" refers to pain or painful condition. "Ostealgia" means bone pain and is related to the musculoskeletal system.

(3) "*Peri*" means around, "*oste*" means bone, and "*um*" is a noun ending. "Periosteum" is a fibrous vascular membrane surrounding the bones except at points of articulation and is a structure associated with the musculoskeletal system.

*(4) "*Cardio*" is the combining form that means heart, and "*megaly*" means enlargement. "Cardiomegaly" refers to a condition of the cardiovascular system, not the musculoskeletal system.

Analysis—Question 24

The key word in the stem is "unrelated." The stem is asking you to select the option that is a word that is **not** associated with the musculoskeletal system. If you misread the question and look for words that are related to the musculoskeletal system then there would be more than one correct answer. When there appears to be more than one correct answer, reread the stem for a key negative word that you may have missed. Option four is the correct answer.

Question 25

Which rule guides the building of medical terms?
(1) When building words with more than one root, the combining vowel is never retained when the second word root begins with a consonant.
(2) The combining vowel is always retained between two root words even if the second root begins with a vowel.
(3) The combining vowel is usually dropped before a suffix that begins with a vowel.
(4) Prefixes, when added to root words, indicate the part of speech of the medical term.

Test-Taking Tip—Question 25

Look for specific determiners in the options. A specific determiner is a word or statement that conveys a thought or concept that has no exceptions. Usually these options can be eliminated from consideration.

Rationales—Question 25

(1) When building words with more than one root word the combining vowel is retained, rather than never retained, when the second root word begins with a consonant.
(2) The combining vowel is usually, not always, retained between two root words even if the second root word begins with a vowel.
*(3) This statement is correct. In most instances a combining vowel is not necessary when building a medical term with a suffix that begins with a vowel. For example, "*mast*" is a root word that means breast and "*ectomy*" is a suffix that begins with a vowel that means excision. When "*mast*" and "*ectomy*" are combined to form the word mastectomy (excision of the breast) a combining vowel is not used.

(4) Suffixes, not prefixes, when added to root words, indicate the part of speech of the medical term.

Analysis—Question 25

Options one and two contain specific determiners. The words "never" and "always" are absolute and are easy to identify. Because there are few absolutes in this world, options that contain specific determiners are usually incorrect and can be eliminated. By eliminating options one and two you have increased your chances of selecting the correct answer by 50%. Option three is the correct answer.

Question 26

Which suffix means "stone" or "calculus"?
(1) -lith
(2) -lysis
(3) -stenosis
(4) -sclerosis

Test-Taking Tip—Question 26

Look carefully at all the options and try to select the one that appears unique or different. Which one is not like the others?

Rationales—Question 26

(1) "-lith*" means stone or calculus.
(2) "*-lysis*" means separate, destroy, or breakdown.
(3) "*-stenosis*" means constriction or narrowing.
(4) "*-sclerosis*" means abnormal hardening of a tissue.

Analysis—Question 26

The correct answer to a test item can sometimes be identified by using the concept of similarities and differences. Which one of the options is not the same? Which one is unique? Options two, three, and four all end in "sis." Option one is different, it ends in "ith." Option one is the correct answer.

Question 27

All of the following suffixes indicate the meaning "pertaining to" EXCEPT:
(1) -al
(2) -ar
(3) -er
(4) -ic

Test-Taking Tip—Question 27

Carefully examine the stem for a word that indicates negative polarity. Questions with negative polarity are concerned with exceptions.

Rationales—Question 27

(1) "*-al*" means pertaining to.
(2) "*-ar*" means pertaining to.
(3) "-er*" means one who, not pertaining to.
(4) "*-ic*" means pertaining to.

Analysis—Question 27

The key word in the stem is "EXCEPT." The stem is asking you to select the option that is **not** the suffix that means "pertaining to." If you misread the question and look for a suffix that means "pertaining to" then there will be more than one correct answer. When there appears to be more than one answer, reread the stem for a key negative word that you may have missed. Option three is the correct answer.

Question 28

Which of the following word elements is used only as a prefix?
(1) Mature
(2) Hyper
(3) Super
(4) Pre

Test-Taking Tip—Question 28

Identify the key word in the stem that sets a priority. A word that sets a priority modifies another important word or concept that relates to what is being asked.

Rationales—Question 28

  (1) "Mature" is both a word and a suffix.
  (2) "Hyper" is both a slang word and a prefix.
  (3) "Super" is both a slang word and a prefix.
*(4) "Pre-" is used only as a prefix and means before or prior to.

Analysis—Question 28

The word "only" modifies the words "used as a prefix" and sets a priority. The word "only" when used to set a priority is more obscure than words such as "first" or "most." Of the options offered one option is **used only as a prefix**. Progressively eliminate one option at a time that is least likely the answer until you are left with one remaining option. Option four is the correct answer.

Question 29

Which technique is most effective for maintaining a patent airway?
(1) Active coughing
(2) Abdominal breathing
(3) Incentive spirometry
(4) Nebulizer treatment

Test-Taking Tip—Question 29

Identify the key word in the stem that sets a priority. A key word that sets a priority modifies another important word or concept that relates to what is being asked.

Rationales—Question 29

*(1) A cough forcefully expels air from the lungs and is an effective self-protective reflex to clear the trachea and bronchi of secretions.
  (2) Abdominal breathing does not clear the air passages. It helps to decrease air trapping and reduce the work of breathing; it is

used postoperatively, during labor, and with pulmonary diseases to promote relaxation and pain control.

(3) This is used to encourage voluntary deep breathing, not to clear an airway; it is used to prevent or treat atelectasis.

(4) This does not clear an airway; it adds moisture or medication to inspired air to alter the tracheobronchial mucosa.

Analysis—Question 29

The key word "most" modifies the concept "effective for maintaining a patent airway." Stems that set a priority are asking you to select the option that has the highest significance in relation to what is being asked. Options two, three, and four are interventions related to respiratory care but when implemented without coughing will not clear an airway. They are often implemented prior to coughing to help facilitate the effectiveness of coughing to clear an airway. Option one is the correct answer.

Question 30

When aspirating the plunger of a syringe when administering an intramuscular injection, blood appears at the hub of the needle. The action by the caregiver should be to:

(1) Remove the syringe and attach a new needle.

(2) Discard the syringe and prepare a new injection.

(3) Interrupt the procedure and notify the physician.

(4) Withdraw the needle slightly and inject the solution.

Test-Taking Tip—Question 30

Identify the two options that are opposites. They must be given serious consideration. One of them will be the correct answer or they both can be eliminated.

Rationales—Question 30

(1) Removing the syringe and attaching a new needle is unsafe. The fluid in the syringe would be contaminated.

*(2) The equipment should be discarded because the fluid and needle are contaminated, and a new sterile syringe should be prepared.

(3) It is unnecessary to notify the physician.

(4) Withdrawing the needle slightly and injecting the solution is unsafe. The fluid in the syringe would be contaminated.

Analysis—Question 30

Options two and four are actions that are basically opposite to each other. Option two basically states, the caregiver must start over again from the beginning using all new equipment. Option four basically states, modify the procedure slightly but give the medication without using new equipment. While more obscure than other examples of opposites in this text, options two and four are still opposites and must be given careful consideration. In this question option two is the only safe action when blood is aspirated during an intramuscular injection and is therefore the correct answer.

Index